on track ...

Jefferson Airplane

every album, every song

Richard Butterworth

sonicbondpublishing.com

Sonicbond Publishing Limited
www.sonicbondpublishing.co.uk
Email: info@sonicbondpublishing.co.uk

First Published in the United Kingdom 2021
First Published in the United States 2021

British Library Cataloguing in Publication Data:
A Catalogue record for this book is available from the British Library

Copyright Richard Butterworth 2021

ISBN 978-1-78952-143-6

Typeset in ITC Garamond & ITC Avant Garde
Printed and bound in England

Graphic design and typesetting: Full Moon Media

on track ...

Jefferson Airplane

every album, every song

Richard Butterworth

sonicbondpublishing.com

Acknowledgments

My sincere thanks to the world's two foremost Airplaneologists: Craig Fenton, whose magisterial Airplane chronicle, *Take Me to a Circus Tent*, proved an invaluable resource and whose prompt, friendly responses to my badgering emails demystified minutiae obscured by half-a-century; and Jeff Tamarkin, whose superb *Got a Revolution!* is, and will remain, the definitive biographical work on Jefferson Airplane.

More than anyone, my eternal thanks and fond love to my wonderful partner Sue, who over the past 18 months has stoically weathered more authorly blockages and moods than I had any right to expect.

A word to my publisher, Stephen Lambe, and his editing team: kudos and respect for affording me the opportunity.

And finally, thanks to Grace, Marty, Paul, Jorma, Jack and Spencer. You don't know it – and sadly some will never know it – but you've fed my head with a lifetime of more pleasure than should be legal.

on track ...

Jefferson Airplane

Contents

Author's Note

Except where stated, opinions, appraisals and critical analyses are the author's own. Information sources are varied, all as reliable as direct quotes, memoirs and Google search results can be. Even the most authoritative voices don't always tally, and some details might not correspond with readers' own theories, particularly with respect to dates and concert venues.

Sadly the author's sketchy grasp of formal musical structure precludes talk of such wonders as flatted fifths and Mixolydian scales. Instead, I've sought the heart of each song by describing in lay terms what I hear, discussing its background and what I believe the writer was trying to say. Convoluted lyricism based, typically, on allegory and metaphor, chemically/herbally-inspired or not, can defy objective analysis; sometimes, the shapes and worlds evoked by the words are enough. The views and reminiscences of those who were there don't always accord with what they might have asserted 20 or more years later; indeed, surviving Airplane family members have since conceded that some lyrics and song titles were never intended to mean anything anyway.

While readers' interpretations might differ wildly, I hope it goes without saying that yours are no less valid than mine. The internet teems with opinion; in some cases, I've found it useful to corral the diverse views of fans and journalists with the songwriters' own recollections where available, then add my own highly subjective and doubtlessly credulous viewpoint. Whether this works, I'll leave to you; if you're already seasoned in the joys of Airplane, I'm sure the reviews will provide fresh food for thought; if you're a newbie, I hope they'll move you to buy the records. 50 years is plenty of time for fact to become speculation or even downright fiction. My conscience is clear: for once, that hoary old cliché 'If you can remember anything about the sixties, you weren't really there' is entirely apt: among those with a strong claim to its invention was one Paul Kantner.

Foreword

Like many kids aged fourteen in 1968, I belonged to a youth club. 'Satan's Rejects' was a provocation that somehow got past the Anglican clerics in whose church hall – if not name – the club was run. Other than the occasional teenage bedroom séance we had no occult inclinations, and posing as San Francisco motorcycle outlaws was plain daft, given none of us was allowed any two-wheeler bigger than a racing pushbike. But we were a mild bunch of suburban adolescents with parental lockdowns on live rock concerts; other than John Peel's essential radio show *Top Gear,* Satan's Rejects was the only setting in which we could congregate in adoration of the devil's music.

Every evening was a voyage of discovery, a chance for young tastebuds, hitherto blighted by a canonical Radio One diet of Leapy Lee and Engelbert Humperdinck, to savour the Luciferian joys of Muddy Waters, Canned Heat and John Mayall: the 'underground' music that Tony Blackburn somehow forgot to play. One night an older boy brought along a 45rpm single on the black R.C.A.-Victor label. I was a lover of anything aeronautical, so I liked it immediately; even though, despite the great name and the eye-catching album sleeves I'd browsed in Alex Strickland's, I knew little of this mysterious group called Jefferson Airplane.

I was already a fan of 'serious' rock music: Cream's heavy jazz-blues workouts, Jimi Hendrix's searing guitar callisthenics, the Nice's tortuous commingling of Bach, Gershwin and Keith Emerson. But this was something else altogether, a pop song from another dimension. The A-side was a remote, chilly, sexy female lead vocal over a solemn, bass-driven rhythm: a Spanish bolero, I later learned. On the flipside, an echoey march with howling lead guitar and a story about 'lady-chrome-covered clothes', 'trapezoid thermometers' and other mysteries. On nothing more psychedelic than Old Holborn rollups I was through the looking glass, out of the draughty church hall and into a parallel universe of altered soundscapes and weird visions. And even if for a while 'White Rabbit' and 'Plastic Fantastic Lover' were as likely to evoke ping-pong and parquet flooring as the synaptic esoterica promised by Grace Slick and Marty Balin, I was sold.

I was also about two years too young to have appreciated how huge this single had been in America. I'd missed out on what I'd come to understand was the Summer of Love. But at least I'd guessed something was up in San Francisco. Scott McKenzie and the Flower Pot Men made sure of it. Only later did I realise that, while the rest of the world drifted to hell on a cloud of napalm, the City by the Bay was a locus of heavenly optimism, where a potent, countercultural cocktail of emergent youth, flower power and lysergic exploration had bred a sublimely unusual strain of rock music. And leading The Grateful Dead, Quicksilver Messenger Service, Country Joe & the Fish and Big Brother & The Holding Company were Jefferson Airplane: custodians of the doctrine, flagbearers for rock'n'roll's new world order.

In their pomp, Airplane comprised Marty Balin (lead vocal, guitar), Grace Slick (lead vocal, piano), Paul Kantner (lead vocal, rhythm guitar), Jorma Kaukonen (lead guitar, vocal), Jack Casady (bass) and Spencer Dryden (drums): the highest of high priests of West Coast cool, at whose altar worshipped every British psychedelic guitarslinger, every crystal-voiced hippie maid, creating in Airplane's image bands like Fairport Convention, Trees and Eclection. In autumn 1968, English prayers were answered when Airplane landed for the maiden Isle of Wight Festival and a weekend of concerts with The Doors at London's Chalk Farm Roundhouse. Feverishly *Melody Maker* ran a centre spread on respective 'lifelines', boosting ticket sales with an overexcited report of rioting crowds in the U.S. whenever the two bands shared the same bill.

Airplane took on the big American outdoor pop festivals: Monterey in June 1967, Woodstock in August 1969, Altamont that same black December. But after the latter debacle it all went sour for everyone. Airplane eventually transitioned to a Starship, adrift in a parallel universe of well-played, competently-written yet ultimately dull A.O.R. Gone was the untidy, scattergun inspiration of the classic formation: six musicians, quipped Spencer Dryden, permanently in search of an arrangement. But unpredictable or not, that lineup delivered five peerless albums that captured perfectly the pulsating, saturated, lava-lamp intensity of the psychedelic decade.

This book revisits those great Airplane records, the earlier and later releases and the ethos (or lack of same) that fostered them: heartbreakingly gorgeous love songs, lengthily searching instrumental jams, sophisticated musicianship, inventive arrangements – planned or not – and anthemic, hypnagogic, intellectually rigorous experimentalism that symbolised an epoch. All underpinned by one of the finest rhythm sections in rock, topped off by searing lead guitar and the voluptuous West Coast honey of those bewitching stacked-harmony vocal choruses. The passage might have been brief, but it was the best ride any Satan's Reject could desire.

Introduction

This book is concerned solely with Jefferson Airplane. I've covered the eight principal albums released under that name during the band's existence, plus associated singles and tracks discarded from original releases before dissolution, beginning with *Jefferson Airplane Takes Off* (1966) and concluding with *Long John Silver* (1972). The live set *Bless Its Pointed Little Head* (1969) is discussed as a regular album release, while a later section deals with some of the more noteworthy (or avoidable) concert issues and bootlegs of recent years, as well as the posthumous live ninth record *Thirty Seconds Over Winterland* (1973). I've also included 1989's reunion album, *Jefferson Airplane,* and a concise digest of archive material and the many Airplane 'Best Of' collections.

Why stop at the original band? Wikipedia's Jefferson Airplane page says it all: 'Not to be confused with Jefferson Starship'. Past anthologies and accounts, from music compilations to written histories, have treated the expedition from Airplane to Starship and beyond as an ongoing saga, as if the decay of 1972 had concerned only the band's name and the eventual induction of younger musicians. Yet other than the crowd-pleasing concert inclusions of a few enduring songs, along with the ins and outs of a small cadre of original members – mainly Paul Kantner, and to a lesser extent Grace Slick and Marty Balin – Jefferson Airplane and Jefferson Starship had little in common. After the final removal of the Jefferson prefix, to speak of Starship's MTV-centric grandiloquence in the same breath as the undisciplined but far more daring and imaginative music of Jefferson Airplane became merely reductionist. Not that there's anything wrong with hard-rock populism *per se;* given the mood, a gurning slab of metallic, four-to-the-floor crunch is fine. And a polished product needn't be a sterile one; sometimes, it's nice to have the abrasive edges sanded off. But, with or without the presidential credentials, Starship simply ain't Jefferson Airplane.

The other crucial element to this story is the fertile West Coast that nurtured Jefferson Airplane in the first place. Was it accidental that Airplane's fortunes, for those few cherishable years after 1965, were so closely synched to those of their hometown? Airplane and their happily chaotic offering were the living avatar of San Francisco's (or at any rate Haight-Ashbury's) own happy chaos in the flower-power era. Messy, joyous, doomed ultimately to collapse under their own structural deficiencies, inbuilt obsolescence a given – you could be talking about band and background equally. For even at their best Jefferson Airplane, their personnel and the music they made seemed to teeter on the brink of anarchy. After the decline of San Francisco as a creative hub around 1970 and the beadier, more business-oriented Los Angeles took over as the U.S. West Coast's proving ground for popular music, Airplane seemed similarly to contract, the two symbiotic organisms assured of their mutual deterioration. If the Haight-Ashbury had had its day, so had the band which, more than any other, captured and encoded its free-spiritedness.

The liberalism that spawned Airplane and its fellow 1960s acid travellers is in San Francisco's D.N.A. From early on, the Bay Area was epitomised by a will to succeed, doused in a fiercely questioning independence. Beat poets, Hell's Angels, Diggers, Pranksters and Black Panthers were birthed here. Technological nous forged in student bedrooms created computing leviathans. This young, instant, boil-in-the-bag boomtown, its infancy the 1849 Gold Rush, had a resumé that simply screamed 'nonconformist'.

Some parts of the city escaped the devastation of the infamous 1906 earthquake. Among these was the neighbourhood now known as Haight-Ashbury, whose stately, late-Victorian townhouses would attract a well-heeled middle class. The area's fortunes ebbed and flowed with broader national economic conditions, with property values – and, crucially, rental costs – plummeting in the 1950s. To the north-east of Haight-Ashbury, the Fillmore district experienced similar rags-to-riches-to-rags-again upheavals. After 1906, the arrival of Japanese, Chinese, Mexican, Jewish and other immigrant and minority groups saw cultivated in Fillmore Street and its surrounds one of the most diverse urban communities in the U.S. African-American families, escaping racist Jim Crow laws in the deep south, brought a flourishing jazz scene, as the potent melange of multiethnicity gave voice to creative forces from every branch of the arts. But the social tensions which the influential city fathers perceived as racially inflamed would dissuade long-term inward investment. By the early 1960s the Fillmore, like the Haight, was looking decidedly rough around the edges.

To a youth disaffected by repressive race laws, the nuclear arms race, the Cold War and its hottest-yet manifestation in Vietnam, these districts felt giddily appealing, purpose-built for a nascent underground's basecamp. The neighbourhoods combined shabby-chic, spacious, cheap-to-rent houses – as they were refurbished, the properties became known as 'painted ladies' – with an arty, multicultural crucible in which could happily germinate a youthful rebellion to shake the world from its post-WWII torpor. From their early habitat of North Beach arrived the Beats, whose jazz-performance poetry sessions were gradually supplanted by the exploratory electric music, dance and drugs culture of the hippies.

Given the anti-war, freedom-loving, nonprofit mulch from which the Haight-Ashbury scene sprang, the huge amounts of money propagated feel hypocritical. But the paradox is no greater than in the cases of the Californian computing giants. Microsoft, Apple, Google, Amazon – every one was the startup dream of a cool, disrupting dude who happened to be both a smart techie and a savvy proto-capitalist. If San Francisco was kickstarted by ruthless entrepreneurialism, the exponential growth of Big Tech through the 1980s and 90s emerged from the same fertile San Franciscan earth as the panhandlers of 1849 – and any hippie from the Haight in 1965.

A year since we've been together - Jefferson Airplane Takes Off (1966)

Marty Balin: vocals
Signe Toly Anderson: vocals
Paul Kantner: rhythm guitar, vocals
Jorma Kaukonen: lead guitar
Jack Casady: bass
Alex 'Skip' Spence: drums
Produced at R.C.A. Victor, Hollywood by Matthew Katz and Tommy Oliver
Released: August 1966
Highest chart placing: U.S. *Billboard* 200: 128

In 1964, the activist/writer Ken Kesey ushered his Merry Pranksters aboard a gaily-painted ex-school bus and embarked on a tour from San Francisco to New York. Kesey, whose first novel *One Flew Over the Cuckoo's Nest* fictionalised his 1959 stint as a voluntary, C.I.A.-sponsored drug guinea pig on a psychiatric ward, officially intended the trek to publicise his new book, *Sometimes a Great Notion.* Unofficially, as recounted by Tom Wolfe in *The Electric Kool-Aid Acid Test,* the expedition hinted at how polite society might cope if an unruly gaggle of writers, musicians, actors, painters, photographers, potheads and runaways quaffed skipfuls of dope and roamed at large among middle America. On his return, Kesey, the charismatic human bridge between the Beat Generation and the hippies, opened his La Honda farm to all comers. Later Ken established the farm as ground zero for the acid tests, where DayGlo-daubed kids would dance till dawn to the best local rock groups and everyone would have their personal doors of perception blown off by a revolutionary new wonder drug.

Not that there was anything especially new about L.S.D. It was meant to be a headache remedy. In 1938, Swiss chemist Albert Hofmann stumbled upon Lysergic acid diethylamide, synthesised from the consciousness-altering natural compounds psilocybin and mescaline. Seeking a mind-control drug, in the 1950s the C.I.A. tested L.S.D. on humans as part of the Agency's notorious MKUltra project. Within ten years, L.S.D.'s hallucinogenic properties had been documented by the novelist Aldous Huxley, the psychologist R. D. Laing and a maverick Harvard academic, Dr Timothy Leary, the latter particularly eager to evangelise the lysergic experience to a growing and receptive counterculture. By 1965, L.S.D. legal until October the following year, the drug was an article of faith, a sacramental portal to psychic and spiritual rebirth for a generation disillusioned by war, racial unrest and the straitjackets of parental society.

One such supplicant, Marty Balin, was busy forming a band. Like every American youngster he'd taken his lead from The Beatles, adding to the mix Bob Dylan, The Byrds and Simon & Garfunkel and, crucially, their respective investigations into folk-rock. This was a high-risk strategy: to purist folkies wedded to 'This Land Is Your Land' and 'Tom Dooley', amplification was as welcome as a south-bound freight train running late. Even Marty's own early vocal group, The Town Criers, resisted his pleas to buy electric guitars and a drumkit. But by 1965, Paul Butterfield's Blues Band, a tough Chicago outfit who'd crinkled the beards by plugging in with Dylan at the Newport Folk Festival, was already a major influence on San Francisco musicians. The scene was set; the kids were into dancing and taking drugs, not sitting around pontificating over a few espressos. Seasoned by marijuana and still-legal L.S.D., the electricity was coursing alluringly through the air – and it was unstoppable.

Marty decided to form a group that would amalgamate, amp up and distort folk, pop, blues and jazz. Playing solo spots at the Drinking Gourd, a popular folk club on Union Street, he began his recruitment drive with a guileless optimism typical of the time, the place and himself: he invited the participation of a local troubadour who happened to look the part, even though they'd never met. In Paul Kantner, already a seasoned, acid-test veteran and an unconventional singer-songwriter galvanised by the possibilities of electric folk-rock, Marty had his crewmate. Seeking a rhythm section, the pair hired 30-year-old double-bass player Bob Harvey and a former Marine drummer, Jerry Peloquin. They also wanted a female lead voice, Paul citing Greenwich Village folk group The Weavers as an early influence. Following a failed audition with a 'brash, wild and weird' blues belter named Joanie Simms, enter Pacific north-westerner Signe Toly Anderson, an equally throaty shouter who performed regularly at Drinking Gourd hootenannies.

As he wrangled his new bandmates, Marty set about creating a venue of his own, where his group and others could perform before youthful, broadminded audiences unphased by electric guitars and readily receptive to the devil's music. He convinced Elliot Sazer, Ted Saunders and Paul Sedlewicz, fellow habitués of the Drinking Gourd, to put up $12,000 to finance his new venture: a nightclub which the partners opened on the site of a failed Fillmore Street pizza restaurant called the Syndicate and a short-lived dive, the Honeybucket. Marty constructed a stage big enough to accommodate a six-piece electric group, ornamented the walls with Egyptian hieroglyphs and hung from the ceiling a large, anticipatory model biplane. He also cast around for a manager; following a chance meeting, Peloquin suggested Matthew Katz, who'd once vainly courted The Town Criers and who knew as much about rock'n'roll as any other wealthy coffee-packaging entrepreneur. Despite doubts, Katz was hired. The Matrix was open for business.

On Paul's recommendation, Airplane Mk1 was completed by Jorma Kaukonen, a prodigiously talented fingerstyle guitarist from Washington D.C. who, like Paul, had been gigging around Bay Area coffee bars since 1962. At heart a blues-roots classicist, Jorma was uncertain at first about the new band's direction. He was won over as the sextet put together a repertoire of amplified originals and folk-blues standards. He was also instrumental in naming the band; a friend at Berkeley, Richmond Talbott, had tagged the guitarist 'Blind

Thomas Jefferson Airplane' after Jorma's main influences, the bluesmen Reverend Gary Davis and Blind Lemon Jefferson. Half the name stuck.

Kesey would publicly disavow the experimental use of psychoactives, allegedly as a ploy to avoid jail. But Jefferson Airplane quickly proved themselves less researchers than devoted experts. Wrapped in a flag of convenience called 'psychedelia' (concocted in the 1950s by a British psychiatrist, Humphry Osmond, after the Greek for 'mind-manifesting'), the drug's effects began to inform their music, lyrics and very reason for being. And at the Matrix, they were being noticed. Besides backing J. C. Burris and the famously picky Lightnin' Hopkins, they also played their own dates, seeding edgy original material into the blues standards and Byrds/Dylan covers. Meanwhile Katz was badgering local influencers, from media types to promoters to record company A&Rs. A Kantner-concocted strapline, 'Jefferson Airplane Loves You', was appended to posters, badges and bumper stickers produced by Marty Balin's lithographer father. Within a month of Airplane's first Matrix gig on 13 August 1965, the suits were circling, sizing up the group for a potential contract.

In September, Harvey and Peloquin became Airplane's first casualties. Neither's musical ambitions matched those of the principals, while both were left in the dust by the virtuosic Kaukonen. For a replacement drummer, Marty rallied the same Tolkienesque instincts that had drawn him to Paul; holding his nose and thinking of Bilbo Baggins, he liberated Alex 'Skip' Spence from The Other Side, an early edition of Quicksilver Messenger Service. It mattered little that Skippy was, first and foremost, a guitarist, with scant drumming experience; the charismatic Balin simply tossed him a pair of sticks and told him to get on with it.

Airplane took a more businesslike route to the new bass player. Jack Casady had worked with fellow Washingtonian Kaukonen back in D.C. By the time Jorma's summons arrived, Jack was still in the east, teaching guitar and bass. Marinated in soul, jazz and blues and recently converted to guitar, Jack nonetheless boasted a bassist's resumé ranging from Little Anthony & The Imperials to James Brown's band. Also wary at first, Jack found himself caught up in Jorma's enthusiasm and he signed on. Once the ink had dried on Airplane's unprecedented $25,000 advance record deal with the archly-conservative R.C.A.-Victor (brokered with Katz by the singer-poet Rod McKuen, a soon-to-be labelmate who hoped – in vain – that Airplane would cover his songs) the band were ready to record the first album.

Airplane's manifesto was set out beautifully, if carefully, in *Jefferson Airplane Takes Off.* Exactly as Marty had planned, the album showed how smoothly the bridgehead could be crossed from the acoustic folk of the overpolite Town Criers to the moodier, less-restrictive amplified progression currently proposed by The Beatles, Bob Dylan and The Byrds. For production and engineering duties, R.C.A. put in two staffers, Tommy Oliver and Dave Hassinger, the latter requested by Airplane for the audial quality the engineer achieved on The

16

Rolling Stones' hit, 'Satisfaction'. Now Hassinger was tasked with recreating, virtually live on the three-track desk, Airplane's concert set, if not its gathering intensity and excitement. For the band's confidence onstage was formidable, the freedom of performance in front of an enthusiastic Matrix or Fillmore crowd rapidly outstripping what Airplane might modestly manage cloistered away in a formal recording facility.

Released in August 1966, *Takes Off* obeys many conventions of contemporary pop music: crisp, short songs and love ballads, dramatically echoey studio reverb, the Byrds-y jangling of Paul's rhythm guitar, the optimism and growing social awareness of the lyrics. Little pre-empts the advances and controversies to come. Yet the band is clearly edging towards something more, driven by Jack's tumbling basslines, Jorma's crisp, plangent blues inflections and the first soundings on record of what would become an Airplane signifier: the rich harmony work of the Mk1 band's vocal trio of Marty, Paul and, her notice handed in just as the album was released, Signe Anderson.

JATO's music is relatively safe, unlike some of its lyrics. R.C.A. agonised over three tracks, two of which were grudgingly edited, the third excised altogether. The fifteen thousand early pressings of the release that escaped the belated cuts are now highly collectable. Although Airplane were relatively agreeable, this was the start of career-long bickering with the businessmen over profanities and dope references. Years later, the label was still being baited by a band which, though the volatility kept the beancounters permanently on Vicodin, was making them enough money to allay the occasional migraine.

The album comprises eleven tracks, of which eight are originals. At this stage, the songwriters are principally Marty and Paul, with Skip Spence's two co-writes (with Marty) showing the early promise that would be only partially fulfilled with his post-Airplane band, Moby Grape. Indeed, one Spence collaboration, 'Don't Slip Away', is among the prototype Airplane's most memorable songs. Like many maiden albums, *JATO* has its share of covers, chosen wisely to reflect the rich folk/blues heritage the band was remodelling in its image.

The musicians photographed for the album's sleeve are as fresh-faced as the music. The sextet is superimposed over a stock image of a vintage aircraft, archaic retouching unconvincingly draping Paul's voluminous scarf around the plane's propeller. The others line up in varying degrees of boredom. They're well-fed, these youngsters, a speccie Jack, in particular, evidencing the puppy fat that would be burned off by subsequent years of dope and the road. As wholesome as they look, the band wear unsmiling expressions which convey the utter tedium of having a manager pose them doing anything other than playing music. Which is precisely what they're about on the rear sleeve, on stage at the Matrix, studiously sincere folkies all, Jack sporting the little moustache that prompted Marty to call him 'Joe Okie'. Splashed across the back, headlining a reprint of a piece from the *San Francisco Chronicle,* is critic Ralph J Gleason's concise summation of the Airplane's music: A JET AGE SOUND. It wasn't yet, not really; two masterpieces released at around the same time, The Beach Boys' *Pet Sounds* and The Beatles' *Revolver* (which included John Lennon's astonishing religious-codex-as-acid-primer 'Tomorrow Never Knows') were the most advanced and innovative pop records yet made. But watch this space: if only the record-buying public – and America – knew what was coming.

Jefferson Airplane Takes Off spent eleven weeks from 17 September 1966 on the *Billboard* Top 200, peaking at #128.

Singles from *Jefferson Airplane Takes Off*:
'It's No Secret'/'Runnin' Around This World'; (7-inch 45; did not chart)
'Come Up the Years'/'Blues From an Airplane'; (7-inch 45; did not chart)
'Bringing Me Down'/'Let Me In' (7-inch 45; did not chart)

'Blues From an Airplane' 2.13 (Balin, Spence)
The album's opening statement showcases two Airplane signifiers: the comely choral threesome and Jack's huge bass underpinning. 'Blues From an Airplane' demonstrates how adeptly the band were distancing themselves from the standard folk-rock model. Jorma's two-note intro is immediately reinforced by Casady, before Spencer's insistent bass drum, hi-hat and gentle swooshes of cymbal bring in the singers:

Do you know how sad it is to be a man alone
I feel so solitary being in my home without you
I don't know what to do and I don't know where you are.

From a personality as optimistic as Balin, the lyrics are surprisingly downbeat. His introspection is a world away from moon-june banality, closer in spirit to the personal and socio-political questioning of folk-rock's showrunners of the era. The words find the ideal home within an unusual time signature and chord structure. And there's a deceptive dynamism about 'Blues From an Airplane'; at the beginning, the arrangement is relatively sedate, but after the bridge, things become frenetic. As Spencer thrashes at his cymbals, at one point he sounds like he's kicking his drums downstairs behind the thick close harmonies of the singers.

'Let Me In' 2.59 (Balin, Kantner)
Only the second track and Kantner's already engineering a fit of the vapours in R.C.A.'s boardroom. On hearing Paul's original lines, 'I gotta get in, you know where' and 'don't tell me you want money', the company immediately discerned implicit sexual frustration – the very thought! – along with the grave intelligence that one of its innocent pop stars might have dallied with ladies of ill-repute. The delinquents were promptly sent back to the studio to right the offences, the suits only signing off on the anodyne, meaningless replacements 'you shut your door now it ain't fair' and 'don't tell me it's so funny'.

Nonetheless 'Let Me In' rocks like a bitch, worried along from the start by Spencer's urgent rimshots and Paul's peeling Rickenbacker. His pleas to be let in become more pressing, as he swears that he '...didn't know that you could be that unkind'. He relaxes for a few bars to admit Jorma's excellent first official recorded Airplane solo against a backdrop of rhythmic mayhem in the engine room, Jack's mighty bass runs plummeting like a Huey in a 'Nam dropzone. Back comes Paul, his frustrations building as the playing intensifies:

Oh, let me in, you know I want only you
I don't want to be told by you what to do
Without a care for me, without a love for me
Who's gonna talk for me, who's gonna speak for me
You walked away for something richer and new.

Like several songs on *JATO*, 'Let Me In' is accredited to Balin/Kantner, although who did what is debatable. According to Jeff Tamarkin, Paul probably wrote most of the words, especially on the three songs that caused R.C.A. such palpitations. The idea is given traction by the song's lyrical acidity; this wasn't a trait of Marty Balin – although he had his moments – but such abrasiveness would soon float to the top of songs by Paul Kantner. On the occasions they wrote co-operatively, it could be argued that Marty was Paul McCartney (upbeat, boyish, emollient) to Paul's John Lennon (dry, acerbic, rebellious). At the end of 'Let Me In', there's a Lennonish pungency in the way that Kantner, finally cleaned out of persuasive entreaties to his unyielding friend, spits a testy dismissal: 'Thanks for nothing!' It might just be a defining moment.

'Bringing Me Down' 2.24 (Balin, Kantner)
Given the apparent mission of R.C.A.'s moral gatekeepers to cleanse Airplane records of drug- and sex-related innuendo, it's surprising that the line 'But I had you last evening/no, it wasn't the same' escaped unscathed. This is Marty issuing a warning to his partner: enough now with this extra-curricular mischief; 'You better get wise now, or things gonna change'. A straightforward arrangement has Marty singing the verses and the Airplane's front line the chorus. Over a tapped hi-hat and restrained walking bass, with Jorma's bee-stinging guitar punctuations and proficient, if slightly hesitant soloing, 'Bringing Me Down' deals with themes of games-playing infidelity that are far from unknown in pop music. Nonetheless, the song delivers the story in a pleasing and entirely adult fashion.

'It's No Secret' 2.40 (Balin)
It was no secret that Marty Balin's admiration for Otis Redding knew no bounds. Having followed the great soulman's career since the earliest days with Stax Records, in 1967 Marty would recommend Otis's peerless 'These Arms of Mine' to Bill Graham as a foretaste of the excitement promised

should the promoter hire Redding for Monterey. Otis duly delivered an unforgettable performance.

Given his esteem, it was only logical that Marty should compose something specifically with Otis in mind. It happened to be his first song for Jefferson Airplane. In 2018 he told *Shindig* magazine: 'I just wanted to write [Otis] a song that had this kind of groove thing.' A Redding-MGs-Memphis Horns take on 'It's No Secret' would surely have been a floor-filler. However, a bout of uncharacteristic shyness kept Marty from approaching his idol. The song remained an Airplane favourite; even as its parent album was released, 'It's No Secret' was metamorphosing onstage from the studio's sweet soul ballad to an unrestrained, nitrate-fuelled rocker.

On *Live in San Francisco 1966*, a bootleg recorded just three months after *JATO's* release (see Live Albums chapter), the band take a set-opening 'It's No Secret' at 100mph and rising, suggesting even at that relatively early date clear blue water was rising between the studio band and the ferocious animal Airplane was becoming onstage. This mightily disproves any assumption that the first album was a faithful facsimile of the Airplane's current live performance. Things were already moving on.

'Tobacco Road' 3.31 (John D Loudermilk)

In 1960, singer-songwriter Loudermilk penned this fable of an impoverished son of toil. He dreams of returning to the boondocks, newly enriched, armed with dynamite and a crane and intent on urban renewal. 'Tobacco Road' was much covered, often differing in length, pace and style. After the Nashville Teens' jaunty transatlantic pop hit in 1964, Bronx psych-punks the Blues Magoos' 1966 version was similarly sprightly; but sexed-up with a 'freak out' middle eight, it showed how 'Tobacco Road' was travelling far beyond its bluesy folk roots; a piece originally as spare and as economical as Elvis' 'Heartbreak Hotel'.

Reverentially, Airplane redress the balance. Following Paul's ringing Rickenbacker intro and abetted by Signe, Marty's full-blooded lead vocal shows how adroitly the singer could inhabit the songs of others and make them his own. 'Tobacco Road' became a frequent flier on Airplane's setlist; like so many others, the song would really come alive in concert, often slower than on the album, permitting Balin to wring from it every last drop of impassioned, sometimes angry emotion.

'Come Up the Years' 2.33 (Balin, Kantner)

Marty's natural conservatism invests this gentle ballad with a moral core inimical to some freedom-loving corners of the 1960s/70s underground. While many a strutting rock star of that era, lasciviously careless of consequence, wore the attentions of predatory fourteen-year-old groupies as a badge of dishonour, here Marty nobly resists underaged sex. But it's a bit of a stretch:

20

I ought to get going
I shouldn't stay here and love you
More than I do
Cause you're so much younger than I am
Come up the years, come up the years
And love me, love me love me.

Since his friend is unlikely suddenly to make eighteen in defiance of biology, Marty has two options: hang around for some action after a year or two, or walk away now. Following recent high-profile scandals, a singer's hesitation to do the latter probably wouldn't get past a modern record company anxious to be seen to be doing the right thing. In 1966, however, the sentiments of the song were thought anodyne (if they were considered at all) and undoubtedly more digestible than the content on this album that *did* cause ears to prick up at R.C.A. Though he finishes the song indecisive, gut feeling tells us that we can trust Marty to have behaved like a gentleman. But given the morés of the time, and the distance we've all travelled since, can we forgive him if he didn't?

'Run Around' 2.40 (Balin, Kantner)

After a guitar intro that twinkles like sunrise on a waterfall, locked down by heavy bass guitar, Paul leads the three-up chorale on this mid-paced, superficially conventional folk-rocker. 'Run Around' is the second song on the album to get the Mother Grundy treatment from R.C.A., which insisted '...flowers that sway as you lay under me be' replaced with '...flowers that sway as you stay here by me'. Gormless editing aside, the song's sentiments could be a sequel to 'Let Me In': having finally been allowed through the door, the singer becomes still more frustrated to discover the object of his desire to be flighty and fidgety, clearly uninterested in his appeal for a measure of permanence in the relationship.

Steadily the singer's frustration becomes more acute, as the lyrics to the track which Marty told Ralph Gleason was about 'making love in outer space' take a psychedelic twist. Notwithstanding R.C.A.'s censoriousness, the conventions of 1966 are forgotten in a lysergic haze:

So couldn't we forget about today, start again from where we were
We use to dance out to space without a care
And our laughter come ringing and singing we rolled round the music,
Blinded by colors come crashing from flowers...

Crunching into the brief instrumental break, Jack's bass seems to become still more bellicose, echoing the increasingly passionate vocal delivery. The lead trio intone the words beautifully throughout, Signe's part looking ahead to the subtle harmonies which, drenched in studio reverb and with Grace Slick on the case, would attain sublime heights on the next album. It's a lovely track that gets better and better with every airing.

21

'Let's Get Together' 3.36 (Chet Powers)

The mercurial Dino Valente, aka Valenti, aka Chet Powers, was a singer-songwriter veteran of the early-60s coffee bars who spent the later S.F. scene toggling between Quicksilver Messenger Service and jail. In 'Let's Get Together' (sometimes just 'Get Together') Valente wrote a memorable ode to love and peace which, though passed over by the earnest jammers of Quicksilver, would become a Top 40 hit for The Youngbloods and was recorded by The Kingston Trio, David Crosby, H. P. Lovecraft, Johnny Cash and numerous others. Despite the covers and their commercial success – in 1970, keen to slip teenybop moorings, The Dave Clark Five hooked up with soul diva Madeline Bell to take a hearty rendition to #8 in the U.K. charts – no money from his creation was made by the songwriter. A habitual stoner, whose relationship with California's correctional system led to a need for bail money, Valente sold the song's rights to The Kingston Trio's manager.

While Marty and Paul were clearly aware of Valente's place among the North Beach folk set, Kantner's attention would surely have been caught by the duo Dino formed with Paul's hero, Fred Neil. A tip of the hat to that partnership alone would have made 'Let's Get Together' a virtual cert for any early Airplane record; but of all the tracks on *Jefferson Airplane Takes Off,* it is this stately, resonant torch song which best captures the spirit of 1966 and what the band was really all about – or at least for now.

'Don't Slip Away' 2.34 (Balin, Spence)

Another delicious love song, with Marty leading as the vocal troika delivers lyrics which this time are very much conventional. My feeling is that Skip Spence wrote the words and Marty the music; even at this early stage in Airplane's development, Balin, like Kantner, was introducing a newly poetic licence to his songwriting, doubtless fuelled by whatever secret blend of herbs and spices he happened upon in the studio kitchen. For Skippy, this was all to come, and tragically so; for the time being, his approach to the romantic business of expressing undying love was studiedly traditional, while still happily falling short of banality. Musically, however, 'Don't Slip Away' is a gem, with a chiming, rollercoaster guitar figure from Jorma and driven, as ever, by Jack's bass.

'Chauffeur Blues' 2.28 (Lester Melrose)

Signe's signature workout was first recorded in 1941 by the Louisiana blues singer Lizzie 'Memphis Minnie' Douglas (who also wrote 'When The Levee Breaks', later misappropriated by Led Zeppelin). However, the provenance is mostly unclear. Although Airplane affixed credit to noted blues record producer Melrose, according to Minnie's original 78rpm edition on Okeh Records, 'Chauffeur Blues' was written by one 'Lawlar', who might have been Minnie's husband, Ernest 'Little Son Joe' Lawlars, or indeed Minnie herself.

As with many old blues pieces, the lyrics whistle up a well-trodden metaphor to evoke liberally distributed sexual favours and their potentially rocky aftermath. The singer's lover is clearly a serial libertine, who '...drives so easy, can't turn my chauffeur down'. Equally typically, if less figuratively, Signe swears that if he doesn't mend his ways, 'she'll steal me a pistol, shoot my chauffeur down'; a reminder of the perils of freewheeling infidelity way down yonder in New Orleans in the 1940s.

Jorma gives himself a fine, bluesy solo for bringing the song to the band from *Woman Blue*, a 1965 album by Judy Roderick (although, again, accounts differ; according to Jeff Tamarkin, Signe found the song for herself on an album by the South African jazz singer Miriam Makeba). While this was Signe's showcase, Airplane rarely performed 'Chauffeur Blues' onstage; appropriately, its final airing was Anderson's exit gig in October 1966. From the following night, Grace Slick would not be reproducing Signe's powerful, if mannered, vibrato on this song.

'And I Like It' 3.20 (Balin, Kaukonen)
Occasionally, and wrongly, entitled 'This Is My Life', the album's final track sees Marty's yearnometer drift into the red. A slow, pained blues that Airplane would sometimes extend onstage to seven or eight minutes, to these ears 'And I Like It' is the least distinguished song on the album. Working in a musical format which, given the guitarist's leanings, is probably all Jorma's, Marty pours his heart and soul into delivering a solemn decree: he's independent, he craves self-determination, and best stand aside if you've a problem with that:

This is my life
I'm satisfied
So watch it
Don't try to keep me tied
So why not
Let me be satisfied
This is my life
This is my way
This is my time
This is my dream
You know I like it.

He elaborates no further. Though onstage the song could, like so many, be dramatically transformed, in the context of the album it feels laboured, and too obviously, perhaps, a set finale.

Associated Tracks
'Runnin' 'Round This World' 2.26 (Balin, Kantner)
'Runnin' 'Round This World' starts as the type of inoffensive folk-pop ephemera that even arch-romantic Marty Balin was hoping to put behind him as the band

fledged. It's harmless and pleasant enough, but there's little clue here of the pandemonium to come. That's until around 55 seconds in, when he drops a big banana-skin right in front of the R.C.A. suits:

The nights I've spent with you
Have been fantastic trips.

Sex *and* drugs! With 10,000 copies of the new record pressed and ready to roll, R.C.A.'s obscenity detector blew a valve. Although 'Runnin' 'Round This World' had been in the public domain since February as the B-side of Airplane's maiden single 'It's No Secret', R.C.A.'s ashen-faced gerontocracy clamoured for the song's immediate amputation from the new album. But just as Steve Marriott and Ronnie Lane knew exactly what they were about when they wrote 'he's always there when I need some speed' for the Small Faces' near-contemporaneous hit 'Here Come The Nice' – and got away with it – it's possible that, with this liberating, if somewhat clunky lyric, Marty was impishly poking Middle America in the sensitivities to see what might squeal.

A little disingenuously, Balin suggested that 'trips' was merely an all-purpose slang term (presumably like 'japes' or 'larks') and that R.C.A. were just boring old fuddy-duddies. Unfortunately, by the time the first album reached final preparation, the A&R men must have checked their freaks' crib-sheet and memorised the fashionable street argot for anything vaguely drug-related. Reluctantly Airplane tried to block out the offending T-word with some strategically-patched arpeggiated guitar, but unhappily 'Runnin' 'Round This World' wouldn't be runnin' 'round anything until the release of *Early Flight,* an archive compilation, in 1974.

'High Flyin' Bird' 2.36 (Billy Wheeler)

'High Flyin' Bird' is a minor-key contemplation of the freedom to fly, mournfully regretful that man's metaphysical lot is to remain 'rooted like a tree'. For the soul to take wing, the body must die, suggested Billy Edd Wheeler, whose folk standard was first covered in 1963 by the Wisconsin singer Judy Henske. Several more versions followed, by artists as diverse as the Au Go Go Singers (featuring a 19-year-old Stephen Stills), the New Christie Minstrels, Richie Havens and the Chicago psychedelic band H. P. Lovecraft.

Wheeler's original had three verses, which Airplane observed in live performance but cut to two in this studio version. A frequent inclusion in the band's early shows, 'High Flyin' Bird' would be memorably captured in D. A. Pennebaker's *Monterey Pop,* wherein the band's principal vocalists got to sing a verse each and evidence was confirmed of the onstage chemistry between Marty Balin and Grace Slick.

A year earlier, with a different singer and one verse deleted, it's here left to Marty and Signe Anderson to pick up the respective solos. In Henske's version, the singer's voice sharpened distinctly as she related the fate of her man, working in a mine and sadly grounded, doomed to perish for the crime of merely wanting to fly. For Airplane, Signe takes her cue from Judy with some gusto, but immediately overcooks it, slamming into overdrive that pronounced vibrato and mannered diction and milking the lachrymose lyric almost parodically. It's a great song, with dramatic reverb and a lovely mid-60s jangle, but Airplane would better this performance by some miles.

Trivia note: the drummer with Henske's band was Earl Palmer, who would mentor and influence a young, pre-Airplane Spencer Dryden.

'It's Alright' 2.17 (Kantner, Spence)
The title sums it up. This ordinary song is about putting distance into a relationship that the singer would prefer to be more casual than it is. In his relaxed, diffident manner, Paul's effectively saying 'don't fence me in', once more asserting his freedom after having been away to taste whatever other delights life has to offer. Criticise as she may, his companion must understand that, although he's back from his roaming, to stand free he no longer needs her. Yup, never mind the counterculture, treat 'em mean, keep 'em keen was still the mantra. To be fair, the melody grows with repeated listening and Jorma takes a pretty good solo.

'Go to Her' 4.09 (Kantner, Irving Estes)
An early demo of a song that was yet some way off refinement. Airplane would tape more demos of 'Go to Her' during sessions for the second album, by which time Signe was gone and Grace Slick was making her presence felt in no uncertain terms. See *Surrealistic Pillow* chapter for a digest of the later, much better version.

'Let Me In' 3.31 (original uncensored version) (Balin, Kantner)
Besides including the lyrics that gave R.C.A. such grief, the original version of 'Let Me In' added 18 seconds to the instrumental break, with the balance accounted for at the end. Length and a revised vocal track aside, there's not an Esmerelda paper between the two versions.

'Run Around' 2.35 (original uncensored version) (Balin, Kantner)
Again, virtually identical to the version first released. The original poetry of the lyric is happily unaltered.

'Chauffeur Blues' 2.50 (alternate version) (Lester Melrose)
With Signe's confident lead vocal and a longer instrumental intro better showcasing Jorma's blues chops, this is punchier, brighter and more interesting than the version that made the final cut. It's also an imperfect mix; the odd all-too-human stumble might explain the decision.

'And I Like It' 8.16 (alternate version) (Balin, Kaukonen)
The album's closing track slowed down still more.

'Blues From an Airplane' 2.10 (hidden track on 2003 reissue CD)
(Balin, Spence)
Play out the reissue CD's lengthy final cut and this kicks in at 8.26; the music only (minus vocals) from the album proper's first track. Interesting as a showcase for Jack Casady and a reminder of Airplane's ability to reinvigorate folk-rock with a massive bassline and an unusual time signature.

Remember what the dormouse said - Surrealistic Pillow (1967)

Marty Balin: guitar, vocals
Grace Slick: piano, organ, recorder, vocals
Paul Kantner: rhythm guitar, vocals
Jorma Kaukonen: lead & rhythm guitar, vocals
Jack Casady: bass, rhythm guitar
Spencer Dryden: drums
Produced at R.C.A. Victor, Hollywood by Rick Jarrard
Released: February 1967
Highest chart place: U.S. *Billboard* 200: 3

January 1966 saw the San Francisco hippie scene's first key event. Unavoidably detained out of town, Jefferson Airplane missed the three-day Trips Festival, which featured instead The Grateful Dead and a pre-Janis Joplin Big Brother & The Holding Company. Promoter Bill Graham was assisted by Augustus Owsley Stanley III, aka the Bear, a colourful sound engineer and acid chemist whose self-styled psychoactives 'factory' would soon be the Bay Area's go-to source for gold-standard product. The festival took place at the Longshoreman's Hall, a little-used union meetinghouse destined, under freaks' collective the Family Dog, to become a proving ground for the mushrooming acid rock scene. Supported by The Great Society, Airplane had played the same venue three months before at a gig that was doubly notable: for catching the ears of the *San Francisco Chronicle's* influential jazz critic Ralph J Gleason, and for Airplane's first experience of the force of nature fronting The Great Society, Grace Slick.

Gleason quickly became a fan. Thanks partially to his patronage, on 3 September 1966 Airplane became the first rock group to play the Monterey Jazz Festival. This was an outrage too far for Gleason's conservative colleague, Leonard Feather. 'All the delicacy and finesse of a mule team knocking down a picket fence,' Feather thundered, only to see his rage fall on stony ground as an amused Airplane co-opted his words for an album advertisement. On 15 October, Signe Anderson sang with Airplane for the last time. 'I want you all to wear smiles and daisies and box balloons,' Signe gushed to the Fillmore audience, as Marty Balin presented the family-loving vocalist with flowers and effusive thanks for services rendered. 'I love you all. Thank you and goodbye.' On which note, Signe returned to her husband, her three-month-old baby Lilith, and rock'n'roll obscurity.

The next evening, at the same venue, Grace Slick sang with Jefferson Airplane for the first time.

Back in the spring, Skip Spence had exhibited an early capriciousness that would tragically escalate. Cueing inevitable comparisons with Syd Barrett, Skippy's natural talents would be blurred by an inability to cope with an operatic drug consumption. For now, the troubled musician returned from an unannounced Mexican holiday to find his paycheque cancelled and himself out of the band. Following a recommendation from Earl Palmer, Spencer Dryden was drafted in from the strip joints of L.A., bringing an approach to percussion that was subtle and jazz-inflected, with an instinctive sense of timing and of what felt right for Airplane's blossoming adventurism. He and Jack Casady would knit perfectly, maturing into one of the most innovative drum-bass sections in all of rock'n'roll.

Signe had been unhappy for months. Airplane felt the same about her husband, then on the payroll as lighting director. Unlike his wife, Jerry Anderson was a committed stoner, his appetite for booze and hard drugs reinforcing an already overbearing manner. Signe cared still less for Airplane's flamboyant, cape-clad manager, Matthew Katz, a showbizzy schemer who wanted Airplane to back topless dancers and had to be talked out of forming a troupe of uniformed female cheerleaders. Unsurprisingly Signe wasn't about to sign any long-term contract. She didn't mince words: 'He's a crook.' She quit in July 1966, shortly before the release of *Jefferson Airplane Takes Off,* keen to concentrate on bringing up Lilith rather than exposing the family to life on the road or any more nonsense from Katz. With Airplane about to lose a key part of their sound, Bill Graham, the dynamic promoter who would soon usurp Katz, offered Anderson a payrise sweetener to stay until the autumn. How Marty's old high school chum, roommate and long-term Airplane factotum Bill Thompson felt about Signe's retention, however, is uncertain. Thompson had tired of the singer's neediness; as sex, drugs and rock'n'roll raged through the Haight, Airplane's road manager and all-round Mr Fixit too often found himself seconded by Signe to babysitting and fetching Lilith's nappies.

Signe soldiered on through a season of October shows at Graham's Winterland Ballroom. The band courted Sherry Snow, whom Paul knew from his L.A. folkie days and who sang in a duo with guitarist Jeff Blackburn, but Sherry preferred to stay with her partner. Briefly Janis Joplin was considered; but good as she was, Janis's style was too closely wedded to raw blues, lacking a certain property which, for now, remained indefinable.

That *je ne sais quoi* wasn't far away. Exactly one year before her introductory Airplane gig, Grace Slick made her first appearance with The Great Society, a new group inspired by Marty's activities (as well, inevitably, as those of The Beatles). At its core were her husband, Jerry Slick, and his brother Darby, alongside friends David Miner, Peter van Gelder and Bard DuPont. With The Great Society frequently playing Balin's Matrix and another Graham venue, the Fillmore Auditorium, Grace soon became well known to Airplane, cutting an exotic, almost untouchable swathe through the Bay Area scene. Already feted in song by Joe McDonald (his 'Grace' would appear on Country Joe & The Fish's first album, *Electric Music for the Mind and Body),* the former model from Illinois was a hot ticket; Kantner later enthused about Grace's 'early punk attitude', her striking beauty, charisma and stagecraft complementing her extensive, as yet untapped talents as a musician and songwriter. Right under the noses of her brother-in-law and (now estranged) husband, Airplane lost no time in a poaching expedition. For Grace, bored with her role as The Great Society's lone lead voice, was increasingly drawn to Airplane's more sophisticated close-harmony vocal experiments. Through the agency of an admiring Jack Casady (although Jorma remembers it was he who made the advance) the deal unsurprisingly went down badly with Darby and co, Thompson's $750 buyout fee scarce recompense for a band losing its biggest asset just as things were looking up. The Great Society soon split, fated to join Signe Anderson in the rock'n'roll backwaters.

At the end of October 1966, *Jefferson Airplane Takes Off* on the shelves for only two months and Grace a full member for just a fortnight, Airplane entered R.C.A. Victor's L.A. studios to begin the sophomore album. If the first was these psychedelic politicians' election manifesto, *Surrealistic Pillow* was the policy enacted, a promise made real. The album would confirm that a new American force had joined The Doors, The Lovin' Spoonful, The Byrds and The Beach Boys in marshalling its creativity to appeal to the underground and the mainstream alike. It would also include some of Airplane's most enduringly beautiful melodies, written mainly by Marty Balin, poignant indications of the founder's true songwriting instincts. Here was forged a point of conflict that would have seismic consequences for Airplane's long-term cohesion: between Marty the eternal romantic, and others in the band, notably Jorma and Jack, whose musical inclinations were more abstruse and exploratory.

Assisted by returning engineer Dave Hassinger, Rick Jarrard came in as producer. Jarrard was another company man, laying down the law in schoolmasterly fashion whenever he spotted the band spliffing up or otherwise misbehaving in the studio. Once again the production team was liberal with the studio reverb (too much so for some band members), while Marty's typically bittersweet odes to love lost, found and regained preserved a clear continuity with *Takes Off.* Yet while Marty's inclination for a lovelorn lyric was unmistakable, so too was the sharp, vinegary edge now etched, with ever more facility, through Airplane's music. Lifted by growing confidence onstage and off, the band sounded harder and freshly urgent, with more testimony to a desire to break out of the folk-rock mould.

This was a period of great productivity, with six tracks in the can in just four evenings between 31 October and 3 November. For later sessions, a redeemed Skip Spence was drafted in to play guitar alongside The Grateful Dead's Jerry Garcia. Lyrics evinced a new social awareness and were occasionally obscure in meaning; chemical-herbal inspiration was clearly at work. (In her 1998 autobiography, Grace conceded that Airplane's lyrical approach had been 'drug-fueled' and 'anomalous'). Garcia's reaction on first hearing the tapes was a famously gnomic (and long misquoted) accolade which supplied the record's name: 'That's as surrealistic as a pillow is soft'. The Dead's leader and Airplane's close friend, now widely respected as San Francisco's resident karmic 'Captain Trips', had been hanging around the studio since the second night, mainly to keep the abstemious Jarrard from turning the new album into an anaemic pop fest. Garcia is understood to have produced and played on several tracks, despite denials by Jarrard and receiving no sleeve credit other than the hip-but-vague 'musical and spiritual adviser'. Memories play tricks: in his memoir, Jorma Kaukonen asserted that production credits belonged solely to Jarrard. According to Grace, however, the real producer was Dave Hassinger: 'Rick Jarrard was always drunk.'

Once again, the lion's share of composer plaudits went to Marty and Paul, the latter enjoying his first solo credit for his exquisite 'D.C.B.A.-25'. A cute 'My Best Friend', the album's first single, gave composers' royalties to the departed Spence, and at the last minute, a surprised Jorma was persuaded by Jarrard to include his two-minute masterclass in acoustic blues fingerpicking, 'Embryonic Journey'.

But two songs in particular accredited to 'Slick', both imported by Grace from The Great Society, lifted *Surrealistic Pillow* from 'difficult second album' to 'zeitgeist nailed'. The commercial implications were clear: released as singles, reaching #5 on the *Billboard* chart in April and #8 in June 1967 respectively, Darby's 'Somebody To Love' and Grace's own 'White Rabbit' boosted Airplane's fortunes massively. For the first time, the band polled enthusiasm from beyond the Bay Area, as Airplane became an American pop institution to rival The Doors, The Beach Boys, The Byrds, The Lovin' Spoonful and The Mamas & The Papas.

Naturally keen to derive financial nourishment from its gravy train, R.C.A. mobilised a nationwide promotional tour, starting with a lavish industry party in Greenwich Village. For the first time, on the band bus to Cleveland, Grace and Spencer became romantically entwined, a liason that alarmed those parts of the music biz still languishing in prim, pre-Haight-Ashbury rectitude. Asked by a stuffed but incredibly envious R.C.A. suit if the couple were married, Grace replied: 'Sure. Just not to each other.'

In 2003 and 2012, *Rolling Stone's* '500 Greatest Albums of All Time' ranked *Surrealistic Pillow*, which was made within 13 days, cost just $8,000 and sold more than a million copies, at #146. The Recording Industry Association of America certified 'Somebody To Love' as platinum in January 2017, with 'White Rabbit' declared gold.

Jefferson Airplane Takes Off had been import-only in the U.K. and remained so for several years, the self-righteous paragons of the British recording industry petrified that a 'psychedelic' record might be a gateway drug; today 'Tobacco Road', tomorrow a terminal smack habit, went the reasoning. Once *Surrealistic Pillow* was finally green-lit, its first U.K. release was a typical domestic fudge, omitting 'She Has Funny Cars', 'Plastic Fantastic Lover' and – R.C.A. presumably hoping for knock-on sales of the separate 45 – 'White Rabbit', replacing them with the still-unreleased first album's 'Don't Slip Away', 'Come Up The Years' and 'Chauffeur Blues'. Although R.C.A. adjusted the tracklist printed on the British sleeve to tally with the revised content, the company clearly couldn't be bothered to do the same with the band's adjusted personnel. This meant that many U.K. fans, your servant among them, believed for ages that Signe Anderson, whose quivering, R'n'B-soaked vocal drove 'Chauffeur Blues', was really Grace Slick after a heavy night on the Lucky Strikes.

For the cover art, the tireless Marty Balin originally designed the title banner and tint overlay in a soothing baby blue, not the synthetic candyfloss pink imposed by R.C.A. The monochrome image by Herb Greene is a group pic of the band against the Matrix's hieroglyphed wall, all as well-scrubbed as on the first album (if, for some possibly fragrant reason, much happier): Jack's profile could be from a police mugshot, Grace holds a recorder and a melting smile, Marty stands tall with what looks like a soprano sax, Jorma's coolly inscrutable under his Wayfarers, Paul squints through a violin head and Spencer clasps a banjo overprinted with the band's name. The appealing personnel and gently quirky poses aside, it's a mediocre, easily-missed package for one of the finest records of its – or any – era.

Surrealistic Pillow's highest chart position in the U.S. (it failed to chart in the U.K.) was #3. Lingering with *Billboard* for 56 weeks, the album was certified Platinum by the Recording Industry Association of America (R.I.A.A).

Singles from *Surrealistic Pillow:*
'My Best Friend'/'How Do You Feel' (7-inch 45; *Billboard*: 103)
'Somebody To Love'/'She Has Funny Cars' (7-inch 45; *Billboard*: 5; Cashbox: 5)
'White Rabbit'/'Plastic Fantastic Lover' (7-inch 45; *Billboard*: 8; Cashbox: 6)

'She Has Funny Cars' 3.11 (Kaukonen, Balin)

Bo Diddley's signature 'shave and a haircut, two bits' hambone beat percussively demonstrates how things have progressed since *Takes Off*, Dryden's rumbling syncopation accompanying Casady's and Kaukonen's descending theme ahead of Balin's opening vocal. Marty is joined by Paul and Grace in the first recorded instance of the 'classic' Airplane lineup's trademark, the three core voices in close harmony: an acid Peter, Paul & Mary for a radical generation.

The accents pound their way through the first verse, before an abrupt interruption for a cheery, almost ragtime bridge and early evidence of two more Airplane tropes: the band's often oblique lyrics and Grace's jazzy instinct for ad-libbing, with great lateral agility, around Marty and the words of the song. A strangulated guitar solo from Jorma, more primal, cymbal-blasted hambone from Spencer, and in barely three minutes, Jefferson Airplane has delivered its mission statement.

Jeff Tamarkin opined that 'She Has Funny Cars' defined psychedelia. True, and I'd go further: from the livewire jungle rhythm to the dynamic, effortless changes of pace; from the spacious interplay of bass and guitars to the fat, three-part close harmonies (and out of those the darting vocal fandangos);

from the strange lyrics to the stranger title (as Marty confessed, 'She Has Funny Cars' was 'surreal nonsense'), the song is pure, concentrated Jefferson Airplane: a nourishing, energy-filled taste of the feast that was to come.

'Somebody To Love' 2.58 (Darby Slick)

'Somebody To Love' is the first of the brace of songs Grace brought to her new employers. According to Summer of Love chronicler Joel Selvin, Darby Slick wrote the song 'in a depressive fog around dawn one morning, coming down on L.S.D. after spending the evening waiting for his girlfriend to come home.' Grace explained that the song was not about the affection one enjoys from another, but that 'a more satisfying state of heart might be the loving you're giving'. Years later the man himself explained that the song was his response to the murder in 1963 of President John F Kennedy. '[The lyrics were] very much about assassination and loss,' Darby posted to Facebook in 2016. 'They took away somebody we loved.'

What cannot be argued is the bittersweet, acidic flavour to the words, this unconventional love song expressing sentiments that suggested a tincture of vitriol ran through the talents of even Grace's non-blood relatives. The song could have issued from the writer's sister-in-law herself:

When the truth is found
To be lies
And all the joy
Within you dies
Don't you want somebody to love?
Don't you need somebody to love?
Wouldn't you love somebody to love?
You better find somebody to love.
When the garden flowers
Baby, are dead, yes
And your mind, your mind
Is so full of red...

Rearranged by Jerry Garcia, 'Somebody To Love' took thirteen takes before everyone was satisfied. The result was faster, more urgent than The Great Society's version, Grace intent on making Darby's lines her own and delivering them with a verve that leaves the original – fine in itself – plodding in its wake. It's also tailor-made for a lead guitarist on the cusp of transitioning between two instrument setups of varying attack. (Geek note #1: in 1965, inspired by Lovin' Spoonful guitarist Zal Yanovski, Jorma bought a Guild Thunderbird six-string and a Standel Super Imperial, a solid-state amp with two 15-inch speakers; this rig can be heard on 'Somebody To Love' and 'White Rabbit'. For most of the balance of *Pillow* and for the rest of his Airplane career, Jorma used a Gibson ES-345, putting the neck pickup through a fuzztone and the other through a wah-wah. Amplification was two – and later an ear-shattering four – Fender Twin Reverbs).

Subject to ever-greater degrees of swooping extemporisation by both singer and instrumentalists, 'Somebody To Love' would be played by the band more frequently than any other Airplane song. It survived the transitional 1970s and became integral to the stage shows of Airplane's successors, even after Grace – the one singer who could do it proper justice – had left the mothership far behind.

'My Best Friend' 3.01 (Alex Spence)

Sweet as it is, 'My Best Friend' little hints at what Jefferson Airplane were really all about. The album's first single feels strangely out of place on *Surrealistic Pillow*, as if its true home were really *Takes Off.* Unsurprising, since this innocent pop song was written by Airplane's ex-drummer, for whom straitened circumstances had prompted the band to generously include it on the new L.P. Following a rat-tat-tat snare intro, the song effectively out-Balins Balin as a simple expression of love. Ironic, then, that it would be Marty who bore the brunt of band criticism for over-sentimentality in *Pillow's* wake. Those fans who had come to Airplane by way of their fierce live performances were nonplussed, but 'My Best Friend' *is* insanely pretty.

'Today' 2.59 (Balin, Kantner)

For a father proud of his baby's countercultural heritage, Marty was admirably even-handed when choosing potential collaborators. One day, Airplane busying themselves with the new album at R.C.A. Studio B and various Rolling Stones ensconced in A, Tony Bennett was recording in Studio C. Marty was keen to meet the veteran crooner, perhaps even talk Tony into covering 'Today'.

That the meeting never happened is surely our gain; with due respect to Mr Bennett's unquestionable talents, one can only speculate over the orchestral suffocation his people might have visited upon this surpassing song had the singer optioned it. In 'Today', Airplane forged something truly special, one of those exquisite *Surrealistic Pillow* tracks that would so exercise those in the band bent on a more daring musical journey. The innovations were to come; in the meantime, Marty and Paul created one of the Airplane's most expressive love songs; a luxuriant, atmospheric ballad which the sophomore album wore as snug and sexy as a second skin.

'Today' begins with gentle acoustic guitar – Paul or Marty, although before the end, both would be in attendance – which is soon joined by Jerry Garcia's sweet electric lead and a jingle of tambourine. Like everywhere else on *Surrealistic Pillow* there's abundant reverb as Marty's keening vocal advises that:

> Today, I feel like pleasing you, more than before
> Today, I know what I wanna do, but I don't know what for
> To be living for you is all that I want to do
> To be loving you, it'll all be there when my dreams come true.

From the page, the words are unexciting, banal even. But these are meant to be sung, not read. Voiced by the King of Yearn, they become tear-jerkingly poignant and heartfelt; there's no doubting the sincerity, that to relinquish the object of his affection would surely crush him, and that only by loving another could he discover his own potential, his 'best self' empowering him to take flight. The arrangement is simply gorgeous: at 1.05, Spencer's drums arrive, distant and echo-drenched. The drama builds as, almost supernaturally, the way opens for Grace's oh-so-subtle vocal harmonies, a chorale of such stately, ghostly beauty her voice could be resounding from the depths of a cathedral.

'Comin' Back to Me' 5.18 (Balin)

Airplane's response to 'Today' and 'Comin' Back to Me' spoke to the early seeds of a schism that would one day crack the band asunder. The song is a perfect example of what Jorma and Jack, and to a lesser extent Grace and Paul, would criticise as an overly sentimental streak in Marty Balin's songwriting. Indeed, it could be argued that Marty, less keen than the others on the radical, often daunting new musical landscapes to be excavated on *Surrealistic Pillow's* follow-up album, never completely left behind Airplane's folk-rock roots.

A colourfully Balinesque tale attends the creation of 'Comin' Back to Me'. With the new album percolating nicely in the studio, sundry Airplanes and Garcia on duty, Marty departed for his motel only to chance upon Paul Butterfield's bandmates, who charitably passed him a spliff of rumoured rare strength and quality. In his room afterwards, Marty, who by then couldn't find his legs, took all of five minutes to pen an absolute corker of a love song, which he immediately took up and ran with back to the studio, intent on recording before the expiry of his high. For accompaniment, he grabbed Grace, Jack and Jerry and had engineer Hassinger run the tape. The result was one-take, five-minute perfection: Garcia's and Balin's arpeggiated acoustic guitars plotting an autumnal, sublimely beautiful melody, immaculately decorated by Grace's recorder and Jack's restrained bass. Marty, rock's own Nabob of Sob, delivered a vocal that couldn't be more emotive, defying any listener not to well up as he watches his loved one return to him. It's every fabulous love-story movie finale you ever cuddled up to, its lyrics the poetry of pure dream:

The summer had inhaled
And held its breath too long
The winter looked the same
As if it never had gone
And through an open window
Where no curtain hung
I saw you, I saw you
Comin' back to me.

Marty later claimed to have given the song little thought following its recording, 'Comin' Back to Me' by consensus deemed too intimate to be sympathetically slotted in amid the *sturm und drang* of a typical Airplane gig. Given the band's ongoing live output was running on 100 per cent kerosene, he probably had a point; Airplane simply weren't given to the gentle, mid-concert acoustic interlude beloved of so many troubadours who found themselves in rock'n'roll bands. The song was later covered by Ritchie Havens and Rickie Lee Jones.

'3/5 of a Mile in 10 Seconds' 3.42 (Balin)

An internet search of the title reveals much fevered speculation. Marty's later denial of any meaning failed to dissuade overtired folk from calculating that '3/5 of a Mile in 10 Seconds' not only corresponds to 216 mph, but that 216 is six cubed: 6 x 6 x 6, geddit? Assuming Balin wasn't a black witch in league with Aleister Crowley and Judas Priest, attributing Judeo-Christian numerology to nothing more esoteric than random word-association – he spotted *3/5* and *10 Seconds* separately on a newspaper's sports page and 'combined the two in a sudden flash' – is probably a step too dumb, even for interpreters of an imagination as fancifully transcendental as Marty's. Once past the title and its fabricated controversies, '3/5 of a Mile in 10 Seconds' is really a plea from the composer to be left alone to live his life as he wants; a standard ask from lyricists of any period:

> Do away with people blowin' my mind
> Do away with people wastin' my precious time
> Take me to a simple place
> Where I can easily see my face…

Marty then comes up with some vivid, if ambivalent imagery:

> Do away with things that come on obscene
> Like hot rods, pre-cleaned real fine nicotine
> Sometimes the price is sixty-five dollars
> Prices like that make a grown man holler
> 'Specially when it's sold by a kid who's only fifteen.

A kilo of weed was then on Haight Street for around $65. While the writer unsurprisingly bemoans the price, he also appears to adopt an unusually high moral position over the age of the average vendor, revealing a conservatism often absent among the era's drug ambassadors. Musically the song pounds urgently along, finding an almost martial route to the middle eight and Jorma's pained solo, Marty swapping the vocal lines with the chorale throughout. Like so many Airplane songs of the period, onstage '3/5 of a Mile in 10 Seconds' was a work in progress, its velocity and intensity increasing with almost every live rendition.

'D.C.B.A.-25' 2.37 (Kantner)

In Paul Kantner's first solo credit for Jefferson Airplane, the writer approaches territory for which Marty Balin was about to be hit by a mountain of ordure. With 'D.C.B.A.-25', Paul produces an unabashed love song (albeit with – literally – an acid tinge). Yet unlike Marty, whose lyrics usually reflect either the fearful torment of letdown or the tearful relief of reconciliation, Paul here glides away from a close liaison almost shrugging his shoulders. In a manner befitting the times, over the manacles of a single relationship he's choosing freedom to roam. Or is he on lysergic comedown? By 1967, Paul was a seasoned acid-voyager; he could as equally be releasing a companion from trip-chaperone duties as suing for personal liberty. But whatever was in Paul's mind at the time (other than the obvious) 'D.C.B.A.-25' is a triumph, delivered with the most delicate harmonic counterpoint by Paul and Grace:

It's time you walked away, set me free
I must move away, leave you be...
Time's been good to us, my friend
Wait and see how it will end
We come and go as we please
We come and go as we please
(That's how it must be).

At 0.45, Grace's harmonising behind Paul's lead is subtle and unforgettable:

Here in crystal chandelier, I'm home
Too many days, I've left unstoned
If you don't mind happiness
Purple-pleasure fields in the Sun
Ah, don't you know I'm runnin' home...
Don't you know I'm runnin' home...
(To a place to you unknown?).

I take great peace in your sitting there
Searching for myself, I find a place there
I see the people of the world
Where they are and what they could be...

I can but dance behind your smile...
I can but dance behind your smile...

By letting his friend go, Paul's really handing out a favour; as if to invite any companion to accompany him on his current journey could expose her to all manner of freakishness (prescient, perhaps, given Paul's trajectory over the coming years). Overall 'D.C.B.A.-25' is an exercise in moderation, Jack inputting the descending theme – his bass takes a less forceful role than usual – followed by light percussion, a jangling, classically folk-rock guitar melody and a solo break in the middle from Jorma that is sweetness itself.

The song's title comes from its chord sequence, D-C-B-A, together with Paul's sly wink towards the drug culture. '25' was L.S.D.'s originally synthesised batch number; some suggest it's also the average microgrammage necessary for acid's full effects to kick in. Naming a song after its musical infrastructure plus a gratuitous dope reference might normally suggest an afterthought, a throwaway that could be attached to a wordless piece with no intrinsic meaning. That is not the case here; had they ever sussed, R.C.A.-Victor's po-faced bosses would surely have had kittens over yet another knowing drug allusion. Doubly to be cherished as both writer and band entered a difficult, more searching phase, in 'D.C.B.A.-25' Paul Kantner had realised a small masterpiece. It's also one of the author's two or three all-time favourite Airplane songs. 'I can but dance behind your smile'? Wish I'd written that.

'How Do You Feel' 3.31 (Tom Mastin)

The recorder must be every other musician's formative instrument. As played here by Grace, it's all over this love song from the schoolyard, a contemplative accompaniment to a sonnet to adolescent angst. 'How Do You Feel' is a featherlight soufflé that's filled with so much cool, unassuming air it struggles not to float away from the record player. Confused about what to do about a girl he clearly fancies, the gangly singer can only stand back, observe and wistfully wonder what might be:

Look into her eyes
Do you see what I mean
Just look at her hair
And when she speaks, oh-oh what a pleasant surprise
How do you feel?
Just look at her smile
Do you see what I mean?
She is looking away.

'How Do You Feel' was written by a little-known singer-songwriter friend of Paul Kantner and Rick Jarrard called Tom Mastin, who would suffer chronic depression before taking his own life in the 1990s. The song's minor-key melancholy and awkward neediness betray the author's innate sadness. Like 'My Best Friend', 'How Do You Feel' might have felt more at home on Airplane's first album (appropriately, the songs comprised *Surrealistic Pillow's* first single), but the band happily channel folk-rock antecedents The Mamas & The Papas and make it work. Even if it's against Airplane's direction of travel, it's delicious, with several acoustic guitars, an electric lead (possibly Garcia again) and lashings of echo on the chorale.

'Embryonic Journey' 1.54 (Kaukonen)

Jorma had been kicking this solo blues around since he composed it at a Santa Clara guitar workshop, followed by its earliest public airing at the Offstage Music Theater in San Jose in 1962. After Jarrard heard Kaukonen idly fingerpicking the complex pocket instrumental during a break in the *SP* sessions, no one was more amazed than the guitarist when the producer insisted it be included on the record. 'I thought he was out of his mind,' Jorma said later, the band themselves unsure if it would fit. Mismatched with the album's overall tone or not, 'Embryonic Journey' is a beautifully atmospheric acoustic vignette, packing immense drama into less than two minutes as Jorma dextrously picks and hammers the liquidly dreamy theme. Four repeated descending chords form a delicious middle before Kaukonen closes out with brief, assertive strumming. Short and unassuming as it is, the tune places the soloist easily among the elite guitarists of the period. With a staying power that saw it through Hot Tuna and beyond, 'Embryonic Journey' is as eloquent a testament to Jorma's range and prowess as anything he recorded.

Kaukonen (and even Airplane) completists might be interested in an eponymous 1995 album which Jorma cut with sometime Grateful Dead keysman Tom Constanten. The record comprises no fewer than 11 takes on 'Embryonic Journey', from a straightforward solo to a 'MIDI Orchestration'. It's not unlike those remastered classic CDs larded with originally discarded material, except that this time an entire album has been made from what were all outtakes from a 1993 Constanten solo outing, *Morning Dew*. Unsurprisingly it's bitty, but there's no faulting the musicianship or the obvious fun the two West Coast vets had doing it. Also worth tracking down is a YouTube clip of the early San Jose reading accredited to Jerry Kaukonen, the guitarist's preferred ID back in his pre-Airplane coffeehouse days.

'White Rabbit' 2.31 (Grace Slick)

The second song on *Pillow* salvaged from The Great Society, 'White Rabbit' references Lewis Carroll's 1865 novel *Alice's Adventures in Wonderland* and its 1871 sequel *Through the Looking-Glass:* stories which, though ostensibly written for children, were according to Grace anything but. It's a dark, exploratory bolero; in addition to L.S.D. and Carroll's storytelling, Grace acknowledged the influence of French composer Maurice Ravel, composer of the ballet 'Bolero'. A number of her future songs would be similarly Spanish in flavour.

More than any other song before or since, 'White Rabbit' crystallises the prevailing mood in Haight-Ashbury. The first explicitly drug-related single to be aired on mainstream radio, 'White Rabbit' codifies the entire psychedelic experience: a hint of the wonders and mysteries of hallucinogenic research and sensory adventure, and the evocation of a dreamscape recalling Carroll, J. M. Barrie and *The Wizard of Oz*, all folded into a compact, darkly-fascinating three minutes that would become the ultimate soundtrack to the Summer of Love.

Written in just half an hour in late 1965 or early 1966, after an acid trip accompanied by the Miles Davis/Gil Evans masterpiece *Sketches of Spain* on continuous loop, 'White Rabbit' was already a live favourite for Grace's old band by the time she joined Airplane. As evidenced on The Great Society's album *Conspicuous Only in Its Absence* (the first of two recorded in concert at the Matrix, the band on those nights possibly second-billers to Airplane themselves) the tempo was originally slower, with a meandering, Eastern-tinged guitar/sax preamble providing a raga-like springboard for lengthy improvisation. For Airplane's version, Grace relocates from India to Iberia, dropping the long intro, upping the pace and compressing a song that's driven from the beginning by Jack's ominous bass and Spencer's tattooing snare. Jorma's guitar snakes in at a low pitch, chiming out the curlicues of the main theme before Grace's wintry contralto slices through the darkness like an icebreaker. As the song starts to build, a delicious tension alongside, famously the singer tells of how:

One pill makes you larger
And one pill makes you small
And the ones that mother gives you
Don't do anything at all.
Go ask Alice
When she's ten feet tall.

Grace namechecks the White Knight, the Red Queen and the hookah-smoking caterpillar, and the bolero intensifies its march towards an anthemic crescendo:

Remember
What the dormouse said
Feed your head
Feed your head.

And there it is: Airplane's embroidered expansion of Timothy Leary's famous directive to 'turn on, tune in, drop out'. Thousands would do just that, as the song drilled into daytime mainstream AM radio schedules and became symbolic of an era. Grace later asserted that 'White Rabbit' was pitched at parents who happily reared their children on Carroll's proto-lysergic fantasies only to be horrified by the kids' later adolescent experiments with drugs. Despite its cross-cultural appeal and its status as *the* song of praise to flower power – remembering that the early architects of the San Francisco hippie utopia declared the movement dead just as everyone else thought it was in full bloom – 'White Rabbit' was deemed by its author to have failed. 'It's an interesting song, but it didn't do what I wanted it to,' Grace told Jeff Tamarkin. Others disagreed. Marty Balin – who later criticised both his singer and the pervasive influence of Class-A drugs on his bandmates – was big enough to call the song 'a masterpiece'.

39

Coupled with 'Plastic Fantastic Lover', 'White Rabbit' was Airplane's second single to chart, peaking on the U.S. *Billboard* Hot 100 at #8 and in the U.K. at #94. *Rolling Stone* ranked the song at #478 on the magazine's list of 500 Greatest Songs of All Time and it's listed in The Rock and Roll Hall of Fame's 500 Songs that Shaped Rock and Roll.

'Plastic Fantastic Lover' 2.38 (Balin)

It's hard to square this surreal ode to/critique of 20th-century consumerism with the love ballads Marty's colleagues had given in evidence of the founder's dereliction. It's also difficult to believe his accusers would have submitted 'Plastic Fantastic Lover' as proof that Balin was anything other than a superb wordsmith:

Her neon mouth with the blinkers-off smile
Nothing but an electric sign
You could say she has an individual style
She's part of a colorful time
Secrecy of lady-chrome-covered clothes
You wear cause you have no other
But I suppose no one knows
You're my plastic fantastic lover.

Marty claimed thathe wrote the song about a television set following a visit to a Chicago factory. Others aver that this 'aluminum finished, slightly diminished' wonder of modern technology is really the new stereo rig the composer had recently bought. Still more – albeit from the unedifying deeps of today's internet – insist that it's a dildo or an inflatable doll. Then there's the expression 'plastic fantastic', used in dragster-racing circles to refer to improbably-customised 'funny cars'; a term which itself references another Balin composition, the opening track from *Surrealistic Pillow* whose title was supposed to be meaningless. Are the coincidences here too delicious to resist?

The clue lies in 'plastic', this being a pejorative term for society's obsession with acquisition and disposability. For Marty, The Man is the market, sucking up the outcomes of mass-production, accumulating more stuff than he'll ever need, thereby unconsciously feeding the beast. The singer spits the words, a far and passionate cry from the bland minstrel he was later erroneously painted.

Rhythmically 'Plastic Fantastic Lover' is insistent and mechanistic; imagine a soundtrack to the robotically-toiling workers in Fritz Lang's 1927 film *Metropolis*. Jorma's lead guitar is tortured and howling throughout, driven remorselessly by Spencer's stirring beat and punctuated by crashing cymbals. In a couple of years, the song will be an exemplar of Airplane's ability to seamlessly co-opt funk into their stage show. For now, it closes out a majestic second album with aplomb.

Associated tracks

'In the Morning' 6.22 (Kaukonen)

In his memoir *Been So Long*, Jorma wrote that 'Last Wall of the Castle', from *After Bathing At Baxter's*, featured his first words for an Airplane song. Records reveal that his debut as a lyricist was actually this slow, moody blues, dropped from *Surrealistic Pillow* and resurrected for the 1974 *Early Flight* compilation. The song was the result of an evening jam during the *Pillow* sessions, when Jorma, Marty, Jack and Spencer kicked back with Kaukonen's old school buddy John Paul Hammond (son of the noted bluesologist John H. Hammond) on harmonica, guitar from Jerry Garcia and piano courtesy of Goldie McJohn, soon to join Steppenwolf.

'In the Morning' is perfectly decent musically and lyrically – the slow 12-bar was already a template for Jorma's regular blues interludes onstage – and while the song is derivative, Hammond's fine rootsy harp and Kaukonen's excellent guitar solo invest the smack of authenticity. However, Jorma's singing feels mannered and overwrought. He delivers the song, as he would continue to throughout his career, in an excessively bluesy drawl with a pronounced vibrato. The style echoes his former bandmate Signe Anderson, and even in places the early, forced R'n'B efforts of Mick Jagger.

'J. P. P. Mc Step B. Blues' 2.38 (Alex Spence)

Airplane enjoyed an abundance of superlative songwriters in Grace, Marty, Paul and, waiting patiently, Jorma. So it's easy to overlook the contributions made by Skip Spence before his erratic personality saw him sacked and sent forth to Moby Grape. 'J. P. P. Mc Step B. Blues' is an unresolved gem. It feels slight and unfinished, but no less delightful for that. Its title is as vague, and probably as meaningless, as numerous others in Airplane's world, although something may be gleaned from the words:

A love for you my friends that I can't hide
And on these words that come I hope you ride.

Craig Fenton and others have suggested that Skip might have been evoking the unseen, unknowable bond between musicians and their audience, enjoining everyone to take a ride, affirming hope and that things will change. In that respect, 'J. P. P. Mc Step B. Blues' is a perfect adjunct to 'Wooden Ships', a story of water-borne survivors of a cataclysmic war. A key track on 1969's *Volunteers*, this will occasionally be extended onstage to accommodate Skippy's charming song.

'Go to Her' 4.01 (v2) (Kantner, Irving Estes)

A punchy version of a song Airplane had been trialling since Signe Anderson. Taken faster than earlier readings, it's a stonker of a rocker, with vocal parts for Marty, Grace and Paul and all three together, and a steaming solo break from Jorma. 'Go to Her she waits, she lies, lonely for you', urges the lyric, the

41

singer suddenly remorseful for having left his lady for other diversions. If only he can palm her off onto his pal, the less caddish he'll feel about himself. Like Airplane's other early co-operative songs, 'Go to Her' accommodates all three singers with a verse each. Grace takes a solo part of the woman scorned, the lines previously delivered by Signe equalling the original's power but with Anderson's overstated vibrato substantially pegged back.

'Come Back Baby' 2.57 (Trad; Arr Kaukonen)

Driven by insistent drums and assorted percussion, this spirited rocker is a straightforward plea from Jorma to his artist wife, Margareta, with whom he would weather 19 years of turmoil, riven on both sides by dope, booze and Nordic temperament. Implicitly Margareta would make a frequent appearance in Jorma's songs. Years later, he'd include 'Come Back Baby' in early Hot Tuna sets.

'White Rabbit' 5.21 (original mono version) (Grace Slick)

Monaural reproduction aside, nothing distinguishes the single from the album version. The extra length accommodates a phantom track, the instrumental backing to Paul's 'D.C.B.A.-25'. This reveals some lovely lead-guitar noodling and is simply perfect for your local bar and its Friday night psychedelic karaoke sessions.

We're doing things that haven't got a name yet - After Bathing At Baxter's (1967)

Marty Balin: vocals, guitar
Grace Slick: vocals, piano
Paul Kantner: rhythm guitar, vocals
Jorma Kaukonen: lead & rhythm guitar, vocals
Jack Casady: bass
Spencer Dryden: drums
Produced at R.C.A. Hollywood by Al Schmitt & Richie Schmitt
Released: November 1967
Highest chart place: U.S. *Billboard* 200: 17

The success of *Surrealistic Pillow* fanfared Jefferson Airplane's rise to superstar status. The band was awash in record company cash, everyone buoyed by the knowledge that two huge, era-defining hit singles meant they could do little wrong. Yet all of Airplane's subsequent music would be distanced by orders of magnitude, not only from the debut album but from the sophomore on which the band's success was founded.

In September 1966, the Scots folk-rocker Donovan Leitch namechecked Airplane in an album track entitled 'The Fat Angel'. Airplane returned the compliment by seeding the song into their live set. A committed stoner and proficient hitmaker – his 'Sunshine Superman' made #1 on the *Billboard* singles chart the same month – Donovan's imprimatur mattered; he'd already scored serious street-cred as the first British pop artist to be arrested for cannabis possession. Over the coming months, Airplane's visibility at ur-hippie events, such as January's Human Be-In – a 'tribal gathering' of poets, performance artists and groups before more than 30,000 people in Golden Gate Park – and June's Monterey International Pop Festival, along with the commercial and critical successes of *Surrealistic Pillow* and its two breakout singles, would see the band's primacy confirmed, Jefferson Airplane now *the* name to drop by fashionistas on both sides of the Atlantic.

Matthew Katz was done by the end of 1966, although legal issues would long outlive his tenure. While the charge sheet against the manipulative manager lengthened with each passing month – topless dancers and pom-pom girls aside, nobody in the band had seen a bank record or a balance sheet, not to mention a cent of R.C.A.'s $25,000 advance – the last straw concerned the whereabouts of Marty Balin's beautiful Martin acoustic guitar, which for some reason he'd loaned to Katz. Unsurprisingly Marty was furious when the manager breezily advised that he'd given the 40-year-old instrument to his girlfriend and that there was little chance of any comeback. Birthed there and then, the enmity between Balin and Katz would drag on, in and out of court, for decades.

Katz's duties were assumed by Bill Graham, a forthright impresario from New York. Bill's introduction to the Bay Area scene had been as manager of the San

Francisco Mime Troupe. In November 1965, Marty had convinced Graham to mount a benefit concert for the Troupe. Purely coincidentally, Airplane would be included on the card (see *Fly Translove Airways,* Live Albums chapter for appraisals of Airplane's three surviving tracks). A successful event convinced the streetwise businessman that a combination of rock'n'roll management and show promotion was likely an excellent route to personal prosperity. Within a year, Bill's Fillmore Auditorium and Winterland ballrooms were regularly hosting acclaimed all-night concerts, where Airplane refined their act to dizzying new heights of musical intuition and intensity, networking with likeminded souls the Dead, Big Brother, Quicksilver and Country Joe and often sharing billing, prodded by Jack and Jorma, with established blues and jazz masters such as Muddy Waters, B.B. King, Charles Lloyd and Rahsaan Roland Kirk.

Visual drama added to the heady mix. If audiences at the Fillmore, Winterland and Avalon wondered at the pulsating infernos of birthing stars, collapsing universes and other cosmic cataclysms in which the bands were engulfed, it was thanks to a man on a platform behind the stage-sheet sliding old glass clock faces of water and heated coloured oils over a light projector. Between 1967 and 1970, Glenn McKay's Headlights worked closely with Airplane, action-painting the thermonuclear spacescapes that illuminated the band's immersive sheets of sound. Allied to the dope and the atmosphere of stoned, transcendental togetherness, the totality of sensory overload could literally be mindblowing.

Over on CBS Television, the Smothers Brothers, a politically irksome comic duo with a nationwide reach, promoted Airplane alongside the likes of Buffalo Springfield, Steppenwolf, The Doors, Joan Baez, Pete Seeger and The Who. So commanding was Airplane's prestige the band were even granted an audience with rock royalty: in April, Paul McCartney walked among the Haight's finest raving about Airplane's music, fellow bassist Jack Casady's playing in particular. At the subsequent bassman's congress, southpaw Paul struggled with Jack's right-handed instrument and declined an opportunity to test-fly a freshly-minted, fast-acting Owsley psychoactive called DMT. Before he left, the Beatle alerted Airplane to an unknown guitarist from Seattle called Jimi Hendrix who was making waves in London, before introducing his own radical new product: a test pressing of the box-fresh Beatles album *Sergeant Pepper's Lonely Hearts Club Band.*

With more than 100 gigs logged by the close of 1967, Airplane were on top of the world. Yet the world was in bad shape, the San Francisco that nurtured the counterculture now in unmanaged decline. Although the year is popularly remembered for the sprouting of flower power and hippie libertarianism, the first wave of psychedelia was on borrowed time. As far as the earliest adopters were concerned, the dream died that same year, from the moment Chet Helms officially codified the 'Summer of Love'. Texan Helms, a gentle Yin to Bill Graham's aggressive Yang, had managed Big Brother and now promoted shows with the Family Dog collective at the Avalon and other venues. At a

May press conference, Chet predicted that, by June, 100,000 people would be flocking expectantly to San Francisco. His soothsaying was bang on. Convinced a re-run of the 1849 Gold Rush was imminent, Los Angeles was wising up to its northern neighbour's rock scene and attendant brouhaha. The aims of The Mamas & The Papas' John Phillips and his manager Lou Adler may have been more altruistic than those of the hard-nosed money-men in L.A.'s boardrooms, but it was this duo who came from the south seeking the Bay Area's hippest and coolest. And they were canvassing for what would become one of the Summer of Love's flagship events.

As a flower-power lodestone, the Monterey International Pop Festival sat alongside the era's other exemplars: the acid tests, the Trips Festival, the Human Be-In and, two years on, Woodstock. Judged on the music and the patchouli-scented good vibes that wafted across the County Fairgrounds between 16 and 18 June 1967, Monterey suggested Helms' sanctified Summer was in rude bloom. However, San Francisco's original radical underground thought differently: flower power had wilted and was ready for deadheading. Three months after Monterey, the Diggers (a San Francisco community activists' group modelled on the 17th-century English protestant anarchists of that name) staged a mock funeral procession dubbed 'The Death of Hippie', publicly burning underground news-sheets and freak paraphernalia with the aim of discouraging any more media coverage of whatever was going down in the Haight.

The Diggers had been wary of hippies for ages. The Be-In had sewed such panic that in February, they mounted their own happening: a dope-fuelled, orgiastic, determinedly un-protestant bacchanal called the Invisible Circus. Now these relentlessly pamphleteering graduates of the class of '65 scorned Monterey as a symbol of everything that had gone sour, a monstrous hi-jacking by cynical corporate interests. Excellent music notwithstanding, in this they were right: the moguls were abroad, dangling enticing recording contracts – Big Brother and Janis Joplin were among the event's main beneficiaries – along with manufactured hippie accoutrements and spurious, right-on empathy for all. Meanwhile, stoned incomers begged and starved on Haight Street. Teenage brains fried like fritters on a manhole cover at noon. Bells and beads were now shrinkwrapped and sold to kids seen by the tycoons as nothing more than numbers in ledger columns. After Monterey, it took about six to eight months for the rest of the world to cotton on: not much had really changed after all.

But with or without the Diggers' affront, the flower-power lifecycle would always be fleeting and finite. Skipping blissed-out around the Golden Gate Panhandle in a diaphanous kaftan (or not) while a rock group played from a flat-bed truck and everyone got heroically wasted was obviously great fun, but it was never going to stop the war. No matter how elevated the group consciousness, how colourful the tie-dyed threads of communitarian oneness, obsolescence was baked into the euphoria. The hippie scene had all the durability of a 1967 Corvair, its negative energy born of Haight-Ashbury's reputation going global. To the disgust of true believers, sightseeing coaches cruised the overcrowded district as Mr & Mrs Amerika gawped incredulously at the animal life on the streets. Hippies were at once tourist attractions and the tourists themselves. Teen runaways from across the nation, lured by Scott McKenzie's soaraway summer hit, 'San Francisco (Be Sure to Wear Flowers in Your Hair)', were attracting a darker entrepreneur, as dealers of hard drugs spotted a lucrative marketing opportunity of their own. By autumn, the damage wrought by perilously addictive amphetamines, barbiturates, cocaine and heroin could be seen slumped, hollow-eyed, on the same sidewalks which only recently had run rich with psychedelic nectar.

To cap it all, the Bear was jailed for possession. For some reason, a jury didn't buy Owsley's claim that the 500,000 doses of banned hallucinogenics he'd synthesised at the Factory were for his personal use. The 'good' stuff was now impounded (and was probably still destined for the streets via the honest brokers of law enforcement), fatally compromising what passed for quality control on the Haight. With Owsley up the steps, the way was clear for peddlers of Woodstock's notoriously impure 'brown acid' and other products of dubious provenance to ravage the compromised hippie paradise.

So where were Jefferson Airplane in all this? If the Diggers' coffin lid was about to slam down on the latest youth movement, the increasingly inclement Summer of Love apparently did Airplane no harm whatsoever. A fine performance at Monterey was justly praised, opening up wide new avenues of exposure. (For more on Airplane at Monterey, see Live Albums chapter). Worked ever harder on the live circuit by the hustling Graham, however, the band were dealing with their own inner demons. Grace and Spencer were amorously absorbed with each other; Jorma and Jack were increasingly eager to tear down instrumental barriers; Paul was happy just to bust through anything that got in the way. All were doggedly tailoring their music to suit *their* times, and no one else's. Among those no-one elses appeared to be Marty Balin, whose songsmith's instincts for courtly love and romantic entanglement – qualities now seen by the others as conservative sentimentality bordering on the trite – were downgraded.

Marty saw first-hand the *nouveau-riche* hubris as five-sixths of his band surfed the waves of fame and came dangerously close to wipeout: 'I got disgusted with all the ego trips,' he said. '[They were] so stoned I couldn't even talk to them. Everybody was in their little shell.' Unfortunately, his colleagues appeared to be falling prey to the same shady market forces as the kids on the Haight, as cocaine and its attendant paranoia became the chemical diversion of choice. Kaukonen and Casady were also lunching on fistfuls of a dangerous prescription pick-me-up called Eskatrol, its fast-acting rush inimical to any more talk of folksy Balin ballads. At the height of their fame and their powers, Airplane's very soul seemed as fractured as the environment from which they had spawned.

Given the bad blood between the founder and the rest, it's remarkable that Airplane were able to produce a single coherent note, let alone one of their best and bravest albums. But while nothing had captured the Summer of Love ideal quite like *Surrealistic Pillow*, the overall mood of *After Bathing At Baxter's*, released in November 1967 but written and recorded in intermittently long, stoned sessions from May through the doomed flower-power summer, was a challenging step-change from its predecessor. For *Baxter's* production, Airplane, high on the hog (and much else) and free to do whatever they liked, rented a Beverley Hills mansion recently vacated by The Beatles for $5,000 per month, all paid for by R.C.A.-Victor. With the lengthening series of rehearsal sessions soon looking like an extended pyjama party on nitrous oxide, glacially an album fruited from the exploratory instrumental workouts and languidly instinctive tinkering at the state-of-the-art desk (*ABAB* was one of the first American albums to be recorded on eight-track).

Producer Al Schmitt (replacing Rick Jarrard, due as much to Jarrard's perceived over-production of *Surrealistic Pillow* as his alleged liking for a drink) went along with the band's laughing gas-propelled agenda. Schmitt noticed that Grace, every inch as innovative as the instrumentalists, would imitate Jorma's guitar sounds with her voice. 'She would turn her head from left to right to create weird but interesting nasal noises,' he said. 'On other days, she would keep changing her position from left to right in front of the microphone to see what changes she could create in her own tonalities.' But Marty Balin declared himself unmoved by his singing partner's inventiveness, which he felt too often skewed the vocals' natural harmonic flow. Creatively brilliant or not, the band's endeavours were lost on Schmitt's employers at R.C.A. But if the bosses figured they were getting another runaway commercial proposition a la *Pillow*, they thought wrong.

The new album, broken into five unconnected and purposely undefined 'movements', remained unequivocally trippy, a still more explicit white paper for chemical mind-expansion than its predecessor. This was as much due to a musical rebooting as the lyricists' unchained response to the era's permissiveness and the latitude R.C.A. now permitted its biggest sellers. Though *Jefferson Airplane Takes Off* was a fine record and *Surrealistic Pillow* a magnificent one, both albums remained relatively digestible. If the drug references were obvious by the time of 'White Rabbit', the instrumental arrangements framing the words, as inventive and beautiful as they frequently were, were unlikely to scare the children.

All of this was to change with the new album. The result of Airplane's six months of imaginative overindulgence was exactly as intended: a hardline push against whatever was left of folk-rock's orthodoxies. The studio coup engineered by Marty's bandmates was so consuming that the band's founder and first songwriter could claim but one composition on the new record. And even this, 'Young Girl Sunday Blues', was co-authored with Paul Kantner.

Now effectively Airplane's principal writer, Paul gleefully extolled the joys of pharmaceutical adventure at every opportunity. The new album's very title, coined by the band's co-conspirator Gary Blackman, was a euphemism for acid comedown. To ears more attuned to *Pillow's* antebellum air of sunny lysergic optimism and longingly personal statements of love, the record's eschewal of accessible, standard-length ballads in favour of multi-part suites, instrumental jamming, more complex song structures, surreal lyrical imagery and even a convulsive, sub-2min jolt of *musique concrète* was strong meat indeed.

Daunting enough to reveal its treasures only slowly. Nothing is immediate about *After Bathing At Baxter's*. Yet the listener's perseverance is rewarded with an immensely exhilarating ride, an excursion through soundscapes and wordplay no contemporary artists had yet attempted. It took me a while, too. *After Bathing At Baxter's* was the first Jefferson Airplane L.P. to which the author's paper-round wages ran after the epiphany at Satan's Rejects. Mainly I was drawn to the cover: an eye-catching illustration of a hybrid flying machine by Ron Cobb, who'd later work as a designer on box-office hits such as *Alien* and *Raiders of the Lost Ark*. Reminiscent of Bruce McCall's collection of comic paintings, *Zany Afternoons,* an imposing Haight Street Victorian townhouse sprouts the wings and rotary engines of an antiquated triplane and chugs pleasingly above the tangled scrappage of American consumerism, a police helicopter keeping a watching brief. Unlike the usual miserly British release, the U.S. sleeve was a stiff gatefold, the black background of its inside spread peppered with hand-scrawled credits and ghostly individual vignettes of the band. Spencer is bathed in blood-red, appearing to smoke a pencil-thin joint; Paul's imprisoned in a Cubist mess of electronic shards; Jorma peers out in half-lit disdain; Jack's bobbing in space, an ejected astronaut from *2001;* Grace looks like a lobotomised nun. Marty, tellingly, is so abstract it might not even be him. At least the tracklisting remained the same.

Happily for the band's underground kudos, the inky imagery on the inside dust jacket shook the record company from its slumbers. One of the drawings, a vague black hole that could be either an eye or part of an exclamation mark, was judged as – what else? – female genitalia.

After Bathing At Baxter's remained on the U.S. *Billboard* chart for 23 weeks, its highest position a modest #17. It didn't chart in the U.K. The new album's failure relative to *Surrealistic Pillow* prompted words from Bill Graham, whose commercial instincts had long convinced him that its cerebral iciness would freeze out record company and record buyer alike. The band, of course, were unmoved. Spencer and Grace issued Bill with a 'you or us' threat to quit (the initiative was mainly Spencer's; Grace later conceded the asset-value of a 'shyster from New York or Los Angeles – or at least someone who could add'). Much to Paul's chagrin, Graham was let go two months after *ABAB's* November 1967 release. But even as personal hostilities compounded and malign tidal forces amassed ominously in the world outside, Airplane was flying high and set fair for a creative zenith.

Singles from *After Bathing At Baxter's:*
'The Ballad of You and Me and Pooneil'/'Two Heads' (7-inch 45; *Billboard*: 42; Cashbox: 24)
'Watch Her Ride'/'Martha' (7-inch 45; *Billboard*: 61; Cashbox: 37)

Streetmasse
'The Ballad of You and Me and Pooneil' 4.35 (Kantner)

The song that since May 1967 had been a staple of Airplane live sets comes screaming in with an atonal blast of electric guitar feedback. It's as if every last atom of scorn Jorma Kaukonen has put by as payback for what he considers the previous album's shortcomings is compressed into an anguished, thirteen-second singularity of contempt. Brief as it is, nothing like this had been attempted on *Surrealistic Pillow*.

The shrieking judders to a halt and a jaunty guitar-snare-hi-hat rhythm trips swiftly in, punctuated by short interjections from Jorma. The vocalists enter over Casady's walking bassline. If in 'White Rabbit' Grace favoured Lewis Carroll for the requisite acid allusions, Paul's fairytale author of choice is A. A. Milne; the song's title merges Milne's Winnie the Pooh with folksinger Fred Neil, an early Kantner touchstone. For the first and last verses of what would arguably become Airplane's live signature piece, Paul unblushingly plunders Milne's poem 'Spring Morning', throwing in for good measure the 'Halfway down the stair' line, also Milne's. (Paul would later deny accusations of plagiarism, confessing: 'I have thousands of influences in literature and find it a turn-on to leave a little thing like that for people to find and then go to the writer who it came from and read him. I never thought of it as plagiarism.')

The words are rousingly declaimed by Paul, Marty and Grace, the latter's contribution a kelpie's wail swirling around, above and between her cohorts, mainly wordless until delivering a classic Airplane non-sequitur: 'Armadillo!' Jack plays a short, overdriven bass solo which, like Jorma's statements as the song plays out, would be extended, often to sublime effect, for live performance. In concert, the band could draw out the song for anything between seven and fifteen minutes, some longer readings later evincing enough spatial generosity to have folded into them elements of other songs, notably Paul's 'Starship' from the forthcoming album *Blows Against the Empire*. In its studio guise, 'The Ballad of You and Me and Pooneil' is as much a statement of intent as 'She Has Funny Cars' was for *Surrealistic Pillow*, but with the lysergic content ratcheted up accordingly.

'A Small Package of Value Will Come to You, Shortly' 1.34
(Dryden, Gary Blackman, Bill Thompson)

A jarringly explicit statement of where certain well-fed heads are headed. Credited to the Walking Owls, an off-the-cuff collective comprising Spencer Dryden, Bill Thompson and Gary Blackman (according to Jorma, an 'extremely eccentric' friend of Thompson's), 'A Small Package of Value Will Come to You,

Shortly' is a brief blizzard of percussive and vocal cacophony. Spencer happily channels his inner Zappa, even if access to the trio's brimming medicine cabinet would never have got past the famously drug-free leader of the Mothers of Invention. If anything, it's 'Three have plenty of fun in a recording studio with lashings of L.S.D.', as the chums playfully assault the mixing desk with whatever's in reach, from piano and assorted blunt instruments to a rented compendium of movie FX and Webster's Dictionary of Quotations. 'No man is an island,' Blackman screams (after Donne) at the end, to which Thompson replies, 'He's a pie-nin-sula,' and the whole thing collapses into stoned, helpless laughter. There's even a briefly tinkled extract from the Christmas carol 'Joy To The World'. 'I don't understand,' bemoans Bill at 1.16. Neither do we, agreed a thousand *Surrealistic Pillow* fans, but it's a splendid racket nonetheless.

'Young Girl Sunday Blues' 3.36 (Balin, Kantner)

The cackling closure to 'Package' segues comfortably into Marty Balin's sole contribution to *Baxter's*. That 'Young Girl Sunday Blues' succeeds is largely due to Jack Casady's splendid running bassline and some typically serpentine Kaukonen soloing. In fact, much of the song comprised music that had already been recorded in concert.

'Young Girl Sunday Blues' is a blend of studio performance and one they made earlier. Between September 1967 and the following March, The Grateful Dead would wreak studio havoc with a spaghetti of live tapes for the whole of their second album, *Anthem of the Sun*. In the Dead's case, it was all done in an intensely lysergic spirit of experimentation. Airplane's own mix'n'match, according to Jeff Tamarkin, was more practical. Despite several stabs, they weren't happy with their early studio demos of 'Young Girl Sunday Blues'. Finally, they decided to use a backing track recorded at a Fillmore gig with Marty's new lead vocal mapped over it.

Apparently the subject of 'Young Girl Sunday Blues' had also inspired 'Come Up the Years' from *Jefferson Airplane Takes Off*. This suggests that Marty, rather than Paul, wrote the lion's share of its lyrics, which are suitably poetic, although the result is a fairly generic, if trippy, love song. The writer seems to be sufficiently smitten with the young woman that he's decided to wait patiently as she reaches her age of majority. Whether his forbearance has paid off is debatable; the words suggest that although he's supposed to be with her, she's coquettish and still playing hard-to-get.

The War Is Over
'Martha' 3.26 (Kantner)

Befriended in 1965 by David Crosby, Paul Kantner and Marty Balin, Martha Wax had been a teenage runaway, well-known among the Haight-Ashbury set. As a pal of Janis Joplin who later shacked up with Grateful Dead manager Rock Scully, it's safe to say that little of Ms Wax's lifestyle will have found its way to the election manifestos of Martha's father, the mayor of Sausalito. Following a brief romantic interlude, Paul wrote Ms Wax this wistful poem to a passing fancy, perfectly summing up the Airplane's relaxed approach to making music in the most laid-back city in the world. Once again, lyrically the song evokes a sunny and bucolically-stoned San Francisco afternoon:

> Martha she calls to me from a feather in the meadow, 'Fly to me;'
> You can dance and sing and walk with me
> And dreams will fade and shadows grow in weed;
> She does as she pleases, she waits there for me;
> She does as she pleases, her heels rise for me.

In places, 'Martha' is so casual it could be mistaken for a demo or a run-through, punctuated by Spencer's rimshots and eased along by Grace's pensive recorder and almost nagging lead guitar from Jorma. Easy going until the instrumental bridge, that is, when Kaukonen's sharp, reflexive solo briefly burns off the summery haze. As with most of *After Bathing At Baxter's*, instant gratification takes a pass – but time reveals of 'Martha' a lovely, dreamily lysergic vignette.

'Wild Tyme (H)' 3.10 (Kantner)

On 3 June 1967, a fortnight before the Monterey Festival and with Airplane the doyens of hippiedom, the host of the TV show *American Bandstand* Dick Clark asked Paul Kantner whether parents had anything to worry about. 'I think so,' Paul confirmed. 'Their children are doing things that they didn't do and they don't understand.' Which was what he was talking about on 'Wild Tyme (H)': another fairly standard-issue love song coupled with a simple evocation of youthful change. One of the shorter and more straightforward songs on the album, with Jorma's guitar snaking its way around the vocalists and breaking loose for an excellent middle solo, 'Wild Tyme (H)' was probably a more obvious choice for a first single than the longer, more complex 'Pooneil'. Perhaps Bill Thompson worried the nation's deejays might have trouble with the song's name.

The oddball title has, of course, thrown up any amount of chin-scratching. Positing that 'Tyme' is marijuana and 'H' is heroin, as if the opiate were naturally a 'breakaway' correlation to its softer counterpart, is spurious; while the Airplane were happily imbibing weed, speed and L.S.D., the darkest narcotic shadow was yet to fall, and no-one was willing it to do so. Another view has Paul referring to The Byrds' 'Wild Mountain Thyme' – itself a wistful song of change. However, this does not explain the parenthetical 'H', which may have been another typical JA non-sequitur designed to set tongues wagging.

Hymn to an Older Generation
'The Last Wall of the Castle' 2.41 (Kaukonen)

With the help of the band's three main singers, Jorma dwells on what he describes in *Been So Long* as 'the unfolding disaffection' of his marriage.

Logically such a mindset would have affected not only Kaukonen's lyricism but his playing; from the start, his guitar darts out like a sidewinder from under a desert rock and coils angrily around the song. In the writer's own words, 'The Last Wall of the Castle' is 'an amphetamine-fuelled barn burner'; it certainly rips along, the writer's incisive lead rarely far from the action. At 1.09, there's a short break for seven solo seconds of Spencer's tom-toms, before the song is reawakened by a fuzztone guitar solo that scrapes like silver foil on a dental filling, pepped up even more by Gary Blackman reportedly blowing his nose. As would be proven on *Crown of Creation*, it wasn't the last time Blackman's volcanically overactive proboscis would feature in an Airplane song.

'rejoyce' 4.04 (Slick)

In 1968, The Beatles launched Apple Corps, their proprietary retail-to-records-to-hey-let's-give-it-all-away conglomerate. Much was made of the proposed artists' roster for the Fabs' exciting new vanity label. Among the touted releasees was Grace, who, as Signe Anderson's replacement, had not been obliged to sign a contract with R.C.A. (a freedom she shared with fellow newcomer Spencer).

Apart from the amusement value of Grace Slick sharing a label with Mary Hopkin (a briefly successful singer-songwriter bound for the Eurovision Song Contest) one can only speculate about what might have occurred had Apple's A&R skills transcended the well-meaning but indolent rock'n'roll ligging that characterised much of the imprint's early business model. 'rejoyce' was another track on *After Bathing At Baxter's* whose link with Airplane was really in name only. The song suggested that its author could mine a depth of abilities rich enough to sustain solo material at once complementary to, and distanced from, the band's own nominal output, with everyone the better for it.

Post-Airplane, Grace would make a quartet of solo albums: *Manhole* (1974), *Dreams* (1980), *Welcome to the Wrecking Ball!* (1981) and *Software* (1982). Other than the excellent *Dreams,* however, these were of varying quality. Had Grace the opportunity to strike while the iron was hot – and in 'rejoyce', as chilly a chamber-piece as the song is, her inspiration couldn't have been at a more scorching pitch – a fascinating solo work might have emerged much sooner.

For most of the first side of *After Bathing At Baxter's,* Grace is relatively muted. Now the balance is reset. With 'rejoyce', Grace nails for ever any lingering notion that she is somehow an inferior substitute for Signe Anderson (a few misguided worthies, such as ex-Airplane bassist Bob Harvey and even, briefly, Marty Balin, inclined to this view) or, worse, that Grace was merely another female cypher in an era in which, despite the groovy new freedoms and slackening of uptight prejudices, women were still dismissed by a not-so-liberated patriarchy as 'old ladies' or even – heaven forbid – 'chicks'.

Here, however, her prodigious talents are full-frontal, coalescing like glistening beads of liquid mercury on a mirror, fusing volatile and disparate elements to realise a gleaming compound of musicality and wordcraft. Born of skills that until now have been occluded – the two hits notwithstanding – 'rejoyce' is Grace's most inspired and powerful statement yet; a song that time would confirm as one of the finest in Airplane's repertoire. She dials up imagery and characters from James Joyce's *Ulysses* with a bookish rigour equal to the novel's formidable literary conceits, extending the narrative to a masterly declaration against war. 'rejoyce' – in a Joycean touch, the lower-case initial is deliberate – is instrumentally mainly the composer's piano (much, much more proficient than the self-deprecating Grace ever allowed herself credit for) alongside Jack's bass, Spencer's touches at the kit and the drummer's own horn arrangement. The song begins with ominously discordant piano, thrumming bass notes and gentle washes of cymbal as Grace opens her chilling vocal:

Chemical change (like a laser beam)
You've shot the warning amber light
Wake me warm
Let me see you
Moving everything over
Smiling in my room
You know you'll be inside of my mind soon.

With the first of the several key changes that structure the song comes a smeared garnish of brass, as Jack quickens the pace and Spencer adds a limber pattern on the snare. In places, the percussionist discreetly withdraws, leaving just piano and the faithful Casady behind Grace's bell-clear voice. A jazzy break at 1.50 eases into a serpentine soprano sax, relocating the mood to North Africa. Another jazzy bridge from the core three-piece, then back come the brass, ushered in by progressively insistent bass guitar. At last, a French horn and a flute accompany Grace's final stanza:

Sell your mother for a Hershey bar
Grow up looking like a car
There are;
All you want to do is live,
All you want to do is give but
Somehow it all falls apart.

So what does 'rejoyce' actually mean? According to Grace, 'Joyce was making a statement about the middle-class... I was simply touching one side of its relevancy.' Following that, any further interpretation ought to be taken with a pinch of salt. Much of the famously difficult *Ulysses* is a blurred stream of consciousness, particularly the unpunctuated, 90-page final chapter, on which 'rejoyce' seems to be based. Grace, who would prove herself no stranger to lyrical meandering, perhaps saw herself and the Irish author as kindred spirits; her most effective tribute could only logically be through a songwriter's affectionate paraphrasing, with word structures that echo the spirit of Joyce's opaque prose rather than attempt to unravel them. Certainly, *Ulysses* has an anti-war component; in a move which may have contributed to radio bans on 'rejoyce', Grace expresses her sentiment by provocatively subverting John F. Kennedy's famous 'Ask not...' speech:

> War's good business so give your son
> And I'd rather have my country die for me.

'rejoyce' is the first and only Jefferson Airplane song to include a brass accompaniment. Without a Kaukonen in sight, it's a remarkable departure for a group theoretically wedded to electric rock guitar. Initially cold and forbidding, ultimately rewarding, this important contribution to Airplane's boldest album is living proof that, in Grace Slick, the group had found its most intellectually searching and mature writer.

How Suite It Is
'Watch Her Ride' 3.11 (Kantner)
This was *Baxter's* second single, another conventional love song – by Airplane's lights, at least – with Paul's usual twists of candy-coloured psychedelia. 'Watch Her Ride' is basically and unambiguously about balling:

> And I would really like to watch you ride
> And always feel you by my side
> I would really like to watch you ride
> All on me.

Were the record barons finally coming around to the dreaded permissive society they'd heard so much about? Perhaps R.C.A., at last, accepted that the more they fretted over Airplane's lyrical content, the more these disruptive but profitable youngsters would poke the hornets' nest. For it's unlikely a Kantner lyric so transparently imbued with sex, drugs and rock'n'roll would have got past the smutwatchers if the song had been on *Takes Off*. It's a decent, if chaotic rocker, speaking as closely as any Airplane track to Spencer's 'six musicians looking for an arrangement' comment. Paul takes the lead vocal slightly off-key, as he does so often. Put together with the (deliberate?) dissonances in the backing tracks, this makes the whole song rather unsettling, although the middle eight is terrific, with big feedback chording from Kaukonen and a stunning Casady bassline. That the single stiffed at #61 on *Billboard* is no real surprise; its B-side, 'Martha' is the better song and might have been the superior choice as a commercial 45.

'Spare Chaynge' 9.13 (Casady, Dryden, Kaukonen)

'Probably the single most important event was when Eric Clapton came over and played the Fillmore.' Thus Jack Casady summarised precisely where he and Jorma Kaukonen thought Airplane should be going. Since the end of 1966, two U.K. power trios, Cream and the Jimi Hendrix Experience, had been demonstrating to the Californians the possibilities of extended, massively amped-up improvisation. Cream's guitarist, Clapton, at the time as driven by John Coltrane and Ornette Coleman as by B. B. King and Robert Johnson, was inspiring Jorma to stretch out and explore new pathways for the electric guitar, and the heady delights that might be uncovered assisted by wah-wah, fuzztone, unconstrained playing time and a megalithic amplification stack. As recently as 2019, Jorma continued to sing the praises of Eric, Jack Bruce and Ginger Baker, enthusing on his website: 'No one transliterated the work of the acoustic blues masters into an electric format better than Cream.' Given his admiration for Clapton and for America's own blue-eyed blues guitar maestro, Michael Bloomfield, it's remarkable that Jorma sounded nothing like either player. In fact, as soaked in the devil's music as Kaukonen was, he only ever sounded like himself, a trait he shared with a different musician again, Jerry Garcia.

With Airplane's vocalists indisposed elsewhere and Jorma taking time out from touring the studio on his Harley-Davidson, 'Spare Chaynge' was the result of one of the many bouts of jamming which diverted Airplane's three principal instrumentalists as the album came together. Influential Cream might have been, but the piece bears little resemblance to anything the British power brokers were unleashing at that pivotal moment. Live, Cream took blues standards, such as 'Crossroads', 'Spoonful' and 'I'm So Glad', and remade them as launchpads for long, fearsomely heavy instrumental workouts, the three musicians unquestionably brilliant and hugely empathetic, but also seemingly bent on blasting each other off stage in a nightly ego-war that would be the band's undoing.

Airplane's moment for such brinkmanship was to come. But for now, 'Spare Chaynge' suggests something different, rejecting the usual blues progressions for a loose bolero that seems to bely Kaukonen's later denial that the group were in any way 'telepathic'. Irrespective of how much 'Spare Chaynge' was really a product of blood, sweat and rehearsal time, it sounds as if the band are cautiously building a fresh improvisation from the ground up. As with their heroes, it's just guitarist, bassist and drummer; but instead of speed, volume and power from the off, Jorma, Jack and Spencer steal their way into the tune, Casady's strummed intro accompanied by Kaukonen's carefully controlled feedback before Dryden arrives with his tom-toms. For a while, the trio tentatively orbit around each other, until at 4.17, after another harsh smear of feedback, the playing intensifies and the bolero takes shape.

Just as Grace and Marty love to challenge each other's vocal moves, the instrumentalists prod and poke, one sometimes attempting escape altogether until another brings him to heel. There's a fabulous moment at 7.55 where, after several bars of baiting each other, Spencer draws the line with an emphatic fill and everyone comes back together for a juddering finale. It's a terrific jam that manages to parallel Airplane's regular live instrumental excursions while sounding nothing like any of them – or, indeed, the British band of whom they were in such awe.

Shizoforest Love Suite
'Two Heads' 3.13 (Slick)

No sooner do Jorma, Jack and Spencer finish dancing brazenly around each other than Grace contributes her own quixotic helping of invention. Among a tranche of songs whose lyrical conceits range from psychedelic whimsy to recondite abstraction, 'Two Heads' may be the most oblique piece Grace ever wrote. She told Barbara Rowes she'd been inspired by a volume of cartoons belonging to Spencer. This might have been a pamphlet of eighteenth-century political sniping by James Gillray, in which the satirist depicted Louis XVI and Marie Antoinette as a double-headed cartoon beast, reflecting a belief held in pre-revolutionary France that Mlle Antoinette wielded more influence than the King might have liked. How this image aligns with the rest of Grace's cryptic narrative is hard to fathom, however, particularly when Marty adds to the murk by repeating a line so low in the mix it's just short of backmasked: 'Reflections in the door of a green Volkswagen,' indeed. Others have suggested that Spencer's book was the work not of Gillray but of an obscure 20th-century French illustrator, to whose depictions Grace alluded in her lyrics:

You want two heads on your body
And you've got two mirrors in your hand.
Priests are made of brick with gold crosses on a stick
and your nose is too small for this land.
Inside your head is your town
inside your room your jail
inside your mouth the elephants trunk and booze,
the only key to your bail.

Grace told Rowes that 'Two Heads' was 'an anti-WASP, anti-alcoholic, anti-war, anti-frigid, anti-middle-class-morals song against the suppression of the free soul inherent in every individual'. This may very well be so, but the stream of consciousness with which her anti-ideas are conveyed is too puzzling to permit any sensible line-by-line interpretation. But if unlocking apparently random, acid-inspired wordplay is a shot to nothing, great pleasure may still be derived from the shapes of the phrases and the unearthly worlds Grace so coolly conjures. Still more enjoyment is to be had from the music, which is dominated by Grace's treated harpsichord, Spencer's stop-start percussion, Jack's nimble six-string bass scuttling underneath like a spider after a fly and the kind of studio messing that realises trippy audioscapes best heard through headphones.

And soaring above everything, of course, those strange hypotheses peerlessly intoned by Grace, as ever the voodoo priestess holding court.

'Won't You Try/Saturday Afternoon' 5.07 (Kantner)

On 14 January 1967, 30,000 people mustered in Golden Gate Park's Polo Field for the 'Gathering of the Tribes for a Human Be-In.' As official a start of the Summer of Love as the first tube of Factor 40, the event was a colourful pageant of youthful rebellion and freedom, a celebration of L.S.D. and a mass protest against its criminalisation a few months earlier. The new law had taken candy from a baby; the hippies were now determined to make up for lost time. As Rock Scully remembers: 'There was so much dope rising in the air, Jerry [Garcia] and I thought we'd walked into a geodesic dome.' Allen Ginsberg, the man responsible for the term 'flower power', danced and chanted alongside fellow Beat poet Lawrence Ferlinghetti, while Timothy Leary stuck flowers behind his ears and harangued the throng. 'Turn on, tune in, drop out,' demanded Leary, which they did eagerly, thanks to Owsley's premium White Lightning acid, distributed gratis by the Bear like confetti at a wedding. Most importantly, the crowd were entranced by the Bay Area's finest rock groups – among them Jefferson Airplane.

Paul Kantner wrote a straightforward narrative about the joyousness of it all. Essentially two songs in one, 'Won't You Try/Saturday Afternoon' is transparently an offer to the uninitiated to partake of whatever he's having; and a more poetic (and suitably more psychedelic) transcription of what the acid evangelists were going on about:

Saturday afternoon
When your head is feeling fine
You can ride inside our car
I will give you caps of blue and silver sunlight for your hair
All that soon will be is what you need to see, my love.

The song is steeped in hallucinogenics, from the liquid bass and heavily-distorted chordal guitar intro and the time-honoured and majestic choral vocals, to Jorma's fingernails-down-a-blackboard middle solo and the insouciance of the song's message. R.C.A.'s dope inspectors must have missed Paul's reference to 'caps of blue' and 'sunshine', but perhaps they thought he meant the ladies' hats and the jolly nice weather. Paul concludes with a pithy 'acid, incense and balloons', a line he may have adapted from Ralph J Gleason's account of the Be-in in the *San Francisco Chronicle,* but which nevertheless perfectly summarises the day's merriment.

Associated Tracks
'The Ballad of You and Me and Pooneil' 11.08 [live] (Kantner)
Recorded live in the studio three days before Airplane's outing to Monterey,

and around a month after its first concert performance, *Baxter's'* intro was drawn out to eleven minutes and briefly earmarked for inclusion on the album. With the L.P.'s total running time already exceeding 43 minutes – and given Airplane's steadfast commitment to the best possible standards of audio reproduction – that the studio version made the cut instead was likely due to the constraints of vinyl, optimally regarded as 20 minutes per side. This version remained unavailable until BMG-Heritage's 2003 reissue of *Baxter's*.

'Martha' 3.29 [mono] (Kantner)

To promote the 'Watch Her Ride'/'Martha' single, Airplane waved their freak flag by making a movie that looked like an outtake from The Monkees' TV show. But then, so did most promo films of this period. Subjects would be shot in a park or on a beach, happily frolicking and tumbling and bottling the whacky spirit of the times, studio chicanery later making everyone run backwards, roll up hills and materialise magically out of bushes and tree trunks. The piece for 'Martha' recalls a film produced by The Beatles for 'Strawberry Fields Forever' early in 1967. In brief snatches – rapid jumpcuts were a favourite editing trick – we see the band looking contemplative or frisky, here and there garbed in strange masks, wigs, hats and what looks like a 1930s lampshade. Two years later the props would be dusted off for the cover of *Volunteers*. This 'Martha' is a brighter mix than on the album release, with Casady's bass more prominent, but otherwise no real change.

'Two Heads' 3.19 [alternate version] (Slick)

With little to choose between the backing track on this and the version of 'Two Heads' that made the album, the only real differentiator is Grace's vocal, and only because her delivery here is too deliberately mannered, as if the singer is unnecessarily keen to show off her chops. The right choice was made for the release.

'Things Are Better in the East' 6.41 (Balin)

Given its inclusion as an extra on the 2003 BMG-Heritage CD edition of *After Bathing At Baxter's,* it's easy to assume this undiscovered Balin gem simply failed to make the cut. By September 1967, when this demo was recorded, the third L.P. was largely in the can and Airplane talk was turning to a fourth. Two new tracks were taped: 'Things Are Better in the East' and another Balin song, 'Don't Let Me Down', a soulful shouter that occasionally popped up in the Airplane's live show. Both songs were shelved, remaining mothballed even as the spadework began on *Crown of Creation* early in 1968.

Why the brush-off? One factor might have been the absence of the band's biggest commercial asset. But Grace Slick wasn't involved with other songs that *did* make it to *Crown of Creation,* and anyway, Airplane didn't kowtow to such industry pressures. More likely is the reluctance of dissenters within the band to indulge their founder, particularly with songs like 'East' that are just so, well,

Balinesque; too saccharine for Dryden, Slick and Kantner, absolute kryptonite to Kaukonen and Casady. A mismatch for *Baxter's,* 'East' might have sat better on *Crown,* given how the latter would see a rapidly maturing Airplane sanding away some of the harsher edges of the former, as well as Marty contributing more songs. So between these pivotal mid-period albums, the two tunes can be seen as a natural bridge.

With the song running to around two-and-a-half minutes, Marty accompanies himself on acoustic guitar. (The balance is a hidden track, unlisted on the sleeve, of an early band run-through of the instrumental backing to Marty's 'Young Girl Sunday Blues'). A superior version of 'East' by the whole band eventually surfaced on the 1992 box-set *Jefferson Airplane Loves You,* as did a studio demo of 'Don't Let Me Down'. Of the latter song, much the better reading is Marty unleashing his full inner Otis Redding for a propulsive 1966 live version on *Grace's Debut,* part of Sony's Collectors' Choice quartet of Airplane archive releases (see Live Albums chapter).

They cannot tolerate our minds - Crown of Creation (1968)

Marty Balin: vocals, guitar
Grace Slick: vocals, piano
Paul Kantner: rhythm guitar, vocals
Jorma Kaukonen: lead & rhythm guitar, vocals
Jack Casady: bass
Spencer Dryden: drums
Produced at R.C.A. Hollywood by Al Schmitt & Richie Schmitt
Released: September 1968
Highest chart place: U.S. *Billboard* 200: 6

For those in the know, it had been dead since 1966. For the casual observer unexposed to Diggers and down-and-outs, the cream of Hippie in the Haight began to curdle in December 1967, when a star of Monterey, the soul giant and Marty Balin's idol Otis Redding, died in an air crash. A month later, the Vietnam war was escalated by the Vietcong's Tet Offensive, one year on to be avenged by a hawkish new Republican president. 1968 saw the flames of insurrectionary unrest licking at the barricades from Paris to Prague, assassins' bullets silencing the hopeful voices of Bobby Kennedy and Martin Luther King Jr (the latter murder precipitating race riots in more than 100 U.S. cities) and Chicago Mayor Richard Daley's cops tear-gassing unarmed protestors at the Democratic National Convention.

With the Haight in disarray and some eighteen months before Joni Mitchell's lyrical celebration of Woodstock, musicians were getting back to the garden. In March, practised acid testers The Grateful Dead and their extended family, tired of wasted flower-power *arrivistes* camped ceaselessly outside 710 Ashbury, gave up their famous commune for the rural idylls of Marin County. Airplane were not far behind, a newly promoted adviser taking steps to ensure that everyone in the band would be comfortably insulated from whatever was being ignited, lobbed, struck, exploded, imploded, ducked or lying around smashed out on the streets.

Airplane confidante Bill Thompson – happily relieved of his responsibilities for Lilith Anderson's diapers and a man who, according to Grace Slick, 'knew how to talk to straight people' – now assumed Bill Graham's managerial mantle. Among Thompson's first initiatives was to create Icebag Corporation, bringing in-house the band's publishing rights. Expansion was in the air; although the split with Graham was amicable, this did little to avert a joint Airplane-Dead concert-hall venture that might threaten his near-monopoly on big S.F. rock shows. Sumptuously appointed and twice the capacity of Graham's Fillmore Auditorium, Market Street's old El Patio dancehall, in its new guise as the Carousel Ballroom, would host San Francisco's biggest groups during the tyro partners' brief tenure. Graham needn't have worried; the venue was soon haemorrhaging cash, its naïve new lessees duly distancing themselves from rock promotion's time-consuming management, dealmaking and general skullduggery. Meanwhile, Graham fretted about his Fillmore Auditorium's location; with America a racial powderkeg, he couldn't ignore the security issues of running mainly white shows out of the city's biggest African-American neighbourhood. Surrendering his old lease, Bill remade the Carousel into what would become one of the most famous venues in rock'n'roll history: the Fillmore West.

Airplane's next instruction to Thompson was to ink a $73,000 deal on a prime piece of San Francisco real estate: a seventeen-room colonial townhouse at 2400 Fulton Street, on the desirable north side of Golden Gate Park, and close – but not *too* close – to the Haight-Ashbury warzone. Full of elegant period features, the three-storey 'Big House' was roomy enough for Airplane and acolytes to desport themselves to their Dionysian hearts' content; less the idle acquisition of wealthy rock stars – everyone retained their own homes elsewhere – than a component, like Icebag, of the canny Thompson's strategy to financially featherbed his clients.

Like most rock bands, Airplane wanted little more than to get high, make music and screw around. Number-crunching and future-proofing were for the hired help, even if that assistant was also a friend who contributed his own creative input and liked to party as hard as anyone. Stimulants, of course, were never far away; most of the band were consuming acid by the bucketful, alternating (and sometimes coinciding) their regular intake of L.S.D. and weed with worrying volumes of crystal meth, nitrous oxide and cocaine. By fitting out the Big House with a 4-track recording studio, office facilities for Thompson and his assistant Jacky Watts, individual apartments and sundry playthings for the band (David Crosby had the pleasure of personally stress-testing a medieval torture rack, converted to a $2,000 dining table, which the group installed in the basement), Airplane created an iconic palace of excess that would pass into Bay Area folklore.

Despite their status as darlings of the love'n'peace generation, like most good ol' fashioned Americans, Airplane would not hesitate to defend their patch if they needed. When squatters invaded the L.A. mansion Airplane rented during the *After Bathing At Baxter's* sessions, Jorma Kaukonen and roadie Bill Laudner chased the interlopers away with pellet pistols. 'We all – Paul, Jorma, Grace and myself – had guns,' Spencer Dryden later confessed. He also denied the band were hippies, adding disdainfully: 'We were basically musicians... into guns and machinery. [They] were the people who lived on the streets down in Haight-Ashbury,' momentarily forgetting that the same great unwashed who still had a few bucks for records and Fillmore tickets were among the reasons why he and Airplane's household could live in such armed and isolationist splendour.

Although the writer of 'White Rabbit' by now largely avoided L.S.D., Grace had liked a drink ever since she secretly quaffed cocktails at high school.

While most of Airplane were concentrating on tripping and hoovering, Grace – now undoubtedly the star of the show – was letting alcohol get the better of her. In public, on TV and onstage, the booze would release her infamously sharp tongue and she'd turn vitriolic, often hurtful, gallows humour on anyone within sight. Where went Grace, so went a sometimes graceless irascibility. And having found an enthusiastic champion and fellow juicer in Spencer, Grace felt no external pressure in her immediate milieu to contain her extravagances.

As increasingly Grace was glorified, Marty Balin was debased. In a 2016 interview, Jack Casady said: 'Marty was dealing with the fact that there was another hugely strong personality in Grace Slick. At the time, hardly anyone had seen a woman in a rock band really strong like that.' Signe Anderson opined that Grace suffered from stage fright. 'She and I talked about this,' Signe told Craig Fenton. 'It is possible that fear caused her to have some problems with drugs and alcohol. If she felt comfortable in her space, you may have seen more from her.'

Helmed by Al and Richie Schmitt, *Crown of Creation* was begun at R.C.A. on 20 February. Although it's hard to see how the band could have outdone the unrestrained behaviour of the previous summer, the new album exhibited an unusually disciplined studio approach. Perhaps R.C.A. had demanded a moratorium on the frosty experimentalism that had prevented *Baxter's* from selling as well as *Surrealistic Pillow*. The result was a fourth album that would sit happily between the two Airplane extremes: exploratory and psychedelic enough to satisfy any trekker through inner space, but with the rough edges sufficiently smoothed out to ensure that no horses would be spooked en route. Airplane were forced to bend the album's sessions around their gigging commitments; that such an erratic recording pattern didn't terminally compromise *Crown of Creation* – to these ears, their greatest studio achievement – is remarkable.

The corrosive discontent that had been eating away at Marty since *Baxter's* hadn't yet reached totality. To some extent, his singing and compositional talents were even back in favour, the band's founder writing or co-writing four of *Crown of Creation's* strongest tracks. Indeed, the album was the band's most collegiate since *Surrealistic Pillow*, the songs often built from scratch in the studio. As Marty told Jeff Tamarkin: 'Sometimes Jack and Jorma would have some grooves they'd put down and then Grace and I would write lyrics over it. Or we'd have a lyric or an idea. Someone would show the others a thing and we'd all build upon it.'

This said, Paul's palace coup was proving a keeper; increasingly he was now the band's main writer and spokesman, while the martial intensity of *Crown of Creation's* title track was early evidence of a militancy that would expand over the next few years. With the astounding 'In Time' (co-written with Balin), Paul proved that his muse was still capable of inspiring great subtlety and lyricism. Grace, too, was on imperious form, now unquestionably rock'n'roll's most accomplished female singer, both of her own songs and as an interpreter of others'. Jorma's songwriting continued its slightly detached, contemplative path, while escaping the studio floor was just one of Spencer's progressively Zappa-fixated sound collages.

By the time *Crown of Creation* hit the stores, the Airplane were in Europe for the first time. The band performed at a private party at London's Revolution club on 29 August, followed by headlining the first Isle of Wight festival and, on 4 September, a rain-soaked free concert in Parliament Hill Fields. On the weekend of 6-7 September, Airplane played two consecutive nights with The Doors at London's Chalk Farm Roundhouse. In Amsterdam, Jim Morrison munched a large chunk of hash as if it were a cupcake, then washed it down with Dutch hootch, after which the head Doorman lumbered onto the Concertgebouw stage for a crazed, Dervish-like dance while Airplane blasted out 'Plastic Fantastic Lover', before collapsing at Marty Balin's feet in a tangle of cable.

Back in Manhattan on 7 December, Airplane became the first rock band to play an 'impromptu' live gig atop a city building (The Beatles famously set up above Apple's Savile Row HQ for the Fabs' final live performance on 30 January 1969). Occupying the roof of the Schuyler Hotel, the band rendered a powerful, suitably desolate version of 'The House at Pooneil Corners' for the never-to-be-finished Jean-Luc Godard-D. A. Pennebaker film, *One AM*. The band followed up with 'Somebody To Love' – missed by the filmmaker – before the NYPD moved in and blew the whistle on the permit-less band.

Crown of Creation remains Airplane's darkest album. While its predecessor was unnervingly cloudy in places, *Baxter's* was still bathed in enough Owsley sunshine to allow lysergic optimism to peep through just when it was needed, the album's key first and final tracks guileless sonnets to the Summer of Love. On the new record, the bookends respectively echo wry reflection and nihilistic despair; in between lies a sequence of complex, superbly crafted songs that are mature yet downbeat, the writing, singing and playing now informed by the realities of 1968, reflecting both the immediate hippie decline and a more global sense of impending doom.

This was underlined by another striking sleeve: a full-colour U.S. Air Force photograph of the Hiroshima inferno consuming an interesting double exposure of the band by Yasuhiro Wakabayashi, a fashionable *Harpers Bazaar* photographer better known, with appropriately bleak irony, as Hiro. On the back, the two images are replicated, their relative sizes reversed, the mushroom cloud apparently whisking, genie-like, from Jorma's fingers.

Commercially, *Crown of Creation* bettered its predecessor, rising to #6 on the *Billboard* chart.

Singles from *Crown of Creation*:
'Greasy Heart'/'Share A Little Joke' (7-inch 45; *Billboard*: 98; Cashbox: 77)
'Crown of Creation'/'Lather' (7-inch 45; *Billboard*: 64)

'Lather' 2.58 (Slick)

Spencer Dryden is long held to have been the subject of *Crown of Creation's* stunning opening track, as Grace Slick characterises Airplane's oldest member as a fragile man-child, turning 30 and finding the adult world challenging. Grace will have been intimately acquainted with her then beau's state of mind, detecting in Spencer an overall frailty and road-weariness, the very antithesis of the clichéd rock drummer.

Yet according to Bill Thompson, Grace's bittersweet character in 'Lather' – representative of shaving cream, a commodity not in common demand among pre-teens – is a composite of Spencer, Gary Blackman and Jack Casady. In a sleevenote to BMG Heritage's 2003 CD reissue of *Crown of Creation,* Bill wrote: 'Jack was given a pill called STP made by Owsley. Only Owsley made a mistake and made the STP twelve times too strong. Jack was arrested on the beach in Santa Cruz, California, naked, drawing pix in the sand.'

But Lather still finds it a nice thing to do
To lie about nude in the sand
Drawing pictures of mountains that look like bumps
And thrashing the air with his hands.

Casady and Slick had also briefly been an item – Jack's reward, it is said, for bringing Grace into the band. Though Blackman is hard to discern in the lyrics, it's possible that Lather the individual is a fusion of discrete character traits that Grace had respectively spotted in all three men, which she then amalgamated to create a composite adult with behavioural issues. While there's never been evidence of anything similar in Casady's makeup, the very image of the stoned, buck-nekkid bassist making childlike images in a public space and getting busted for indecent exposure plays readily to the demeanour of an adult of arrested development, an innocent abroad. If the song's less about Dryden, Casady or Blackman – or all three – than about a universal archetype, evoking Jack's misadventure would seem to make sense, while acting as a side comment on how psychoactive drugs can regressively release any adult's inner child.

Grace, who despite the apparent celebration of Jack's acid-fuelled imaginings insisted the song was solely about Spencer, had been pondering society's expectations and reasons why adults should be deterred from maintaining a childlike playfulness and receptiveness to new ideas. As she stated in her autobiography: '['Lather'] was a concerted effort to stay seventeen years old emotionally for as long as possible.' What cannot be doubted is that the song is exceptionally poignant and touching, despite lyrical imagery that, like much of Grace's work, seemed tailor-made to unsettle:

But wait, ol' Lather's productive you know
He produces the finest of sounds

Putting drumsticks on either side of his nose
Snorting the best licks in town.

This indelicate but striking image precedes one of the oddest instrumental
breaks in rock history. What sounds like a heavily treated Kaukonen solo –
perhaps it's Jorma's 'electric chicken', although this credit could refer equally
to a brief burst of wah-wah at the close – is, according to Thompson, a 'nose
guitar' played by Blackman. This deeply strange gentleman, and his endlessly
adaptable schnozzle, pops up with the Airplane as the band lip-synchs 'Lather'
on the Smothers Brothers' TV show, although the irritatingly 'groovy' effects
of the surviving video obscure precisely how Gary mimes whatever it is he's
miming; the audial effect is of a jaw-harp played through his nose and put
through a synthesiser. If anything spoils 'Lather', it's the over-egged studio FX
(apparently appended by Dryden and Blackman) designed to correspond with
the lyrics: a clattering typewriter depicts Lather's school chum turned bank
executive, an exploding shell portrays a tank commander and so forth. Airplane
were rarely predictable; that – at the height of their powers – the band feel they
must resort to the bleedin' obvious for 'Lather' adds nothing to an otherwise
brilliant opener.

'In Time' 4.14 (Kantner, Balin)

'It's not the notes you play, it's the notes you don't play.' Miles Davis' famous
aphorism was never more convincingly validated by an Airplane song. Delicate
and understated, each bar as carefully considered as the last, 'In Time' bears
a stillness that's almost tactile, every judicious rest as crucial to structure as
anything in the composer's toolkit; a song that has casually materialised of its
own volition, belying the work that Paul and Marty put into it. It's like bottling
time and space.

This deceptively leisurely overall mood was a defining trait of so many
Airplane compositions and arrangements from this profoundly creative
1967-68 period. The bass is vitally important; as usual, Jack Casady is high in
the mix, bubbling away from the intro alongside sombre minor arpeggiated
guitar chords. With slight reverb, Paul opens the vocal and plays a recurring,
bluesy background pattern, countered by Jorma's penetrating but always
judiciously placed lead. Announced by Spencer's crashing snare, Paul is
joined by Marty and Grace in close harmony for the chorus and the full
ensemble connects in thrilling contrast to the earlier restraint. There's
enormous latent power here, demonstrated when Jorma's wah-wah guitar
bounds out of the increasingly busy background architecture for an explosive
middle eight.

The lyrics are as sexy and lithe as the music, suggestive of an affair that is at
once physical and cerebral. The singer and his companion drift on a pillow
of colour and sensuousness, liquidly connecting inside and coming out of a
psychedelic haze of expanded consciousness:

Orange, blue, red & green
Are the colors of what I feel
And my mind y'know it starts to reel in time
To know your flesh layin' by my skin
And I wonder whenever I'm in
Warm, soft, nice & now
Are the word things of what I know
And my body y'know it's so in time.

To take the words of 'In Time' literally – not something necessarily recommended for an Airplane song – does the narrator hint at the identity of his friend?

I see you at the same place that I play
Ah darlin' tell me what can I say...

She might be a groupie, or a friend of the band, a bandmate's lady or even a bandmate herself. Is this Paul reaching out in song to Grace, with whom he's not romantically involved but will be within the year? Whoever the couple are, the tenderness is freely and mutually given; a perfect, caring transaction for the Summer of Love even as the season fades away. The ending is incongruous, a nod towards the Wyndhamesque escape of the album's title track. Ambiguous or not, 'In Time' shows how far ahead of every other rock group Jefferson Airplane has travelled in just two years.

'Triad' 4.56 (David Crosby)

David Crosby's haunting invitation to a fashionable threesome between himself and two younger, less sophisticated companions was originally scheduled for his own band's 1968 album *The Notorious Byrd Brothers*. Unfortunately for the L.A. group, 'Triad' became a casualty of the internecine warfare then raging between Croz and his bandmates, especially Byrds' founder Roger McGuinn and bassist Chris Hillman. On whether 'Triad' was excluded because the devout McGuinn considered it too irreligiously risqué, or because Hillman saw no merit in the song, or because by then the pair simply detested the sight of their abrasive colleague and would have dumped the Lord's Prayer if it had Crosby's name on it, the jury's out.

But The Byrds' loss was Airplane's gain. With its trendy mix of unencumbered sex and literary conceit – Crosby's old friend and fellow sci-fi buff Paul Kantner will have enjoyed the 'water brothers' line from Robert A Heinlein – 'Triad' crystallised the spirit of the times. And in 1968, there wasn't a singer in the world better equipped to express it.

At her best, Grace Slick was able effortlessly to hone to a diamond edge a simultaneously affirmative, gentle, girlish, occasionally vulnerable vocal purity. She could toggle between, and accommodate equally, the shrillness of a banshee's wail, the extemporised swoop and swell of a seasoned jazzer, the raunchy, whiskey-soaked blues shout of a Janis Joplin, the sweet lucidity of a Joni Mitchell or a Judy Collins. And it's no insult to any of those great singers to say Grace had the measure of each; an accolade I can think of applying to no other artist.

'Triad' is one of Grace's finest vocal performances. She comes in after Jorma's and Paul's acoustic guitars, Jack's quietly percussive bass and a sprinkling of Spencer's ride cymbal. With the gentlest of vibratos rippling out from her cool, ice-clear invitation to 'try something new', Grace advises her two naïve, embarrassed young suitors that she has no problem with a threesome and that, furthermore, neither should they, despite the outrage of an older generation:

> Your mother's ghost stands at your shoulder
> Face like ice, a little bit colder...

With those lines, almost imperceptibly, Grace's voice hardens. It might have been our parents' way to suppress a natural and very beautiful instinct, but it is not ours. Yet despite the heartfelt and empathetic delivery, Grace later stressed that she was never into multitasking; the song's sentiments were entirely those of its famously party-loving writer, who later maintained that he'd enjoyed several similar *menages*. 'Doing two people at once would be confusing for me,' Grace assured *Relix.com*. 'I wouldn't like it because there's too much going on.' Notwithstanding, this is a solo vocal performance of true majesty. McGuinn and Hillman could relax: David Crosby could have written 'Triad' for Grace Slick, and no one else.

'Star Track' 3.12 (Kaukonen)

As Jorma later put in his memoir, his wife Margareta was 'all over' his lyrics at this time. But 'Star Track' suggests issues other than his marriage were equally distracting him. Appropriately for a musician so devoted to the rustic austerity of Delta blues – and simultaneously paradoxical, given that the promise of toying with electronic widgetry had attracted him to Airplane in the first place – Jorma is fearful of a loss of identity, obliquely conflating his marital woes with the attendant disorientation of technological progress. Concerned 'that life can be hard when you're holes in a card in some electronic hand', he seeks to slow down and find an inner route to peace and fulfilment:

> You can fool your friends about the way it ends
> But you can't fool yourself
> Take your head in hand and make your own demands
> Or you'll crystallize on the shelf
> The freeway's concrete way won't show
> You where to run or how to go
> And running fast you'll go down slow in the end.

For the next couple of years, Jorma's songwriting would exude such introspection, as the winds generated by Marty's steady disaffection and the increasingly standoffish Slick/Kantner creative axis blew Airplane off course and the band atomised. But for now, everyone still holding together, the band fashion a splendid acid blues from the chord progression to Rev. Gary Davis' 'Death Don't Have No Mercy', then a regular on The Grateful Dead's setlist and later covered by Hot Tuna. The guitarist lets rip with a merciless solo break so squallingly intense it's as if he's just unearthed his wah-wah pedal after losing it in the Mississippi mud, psychedelising a traditional form more adeptly than most rock musicians engaged in updating the blues.

'Share a Little Joke' 3.10 (Balin)
Although Marty Balin was co-credited for 'In Time', the bigger stamp on that masterpiece was probably Paul Kantner's. Which effectively makes 'Share a Little Joke' Marty's first complete writing donation to a Jefferson Airplane album since *Surrealistic Pillow*. It's a happy return if a poignant one: although Marty once explained that the song was about, and part-composed by, Gary Blackman, 'Share a Little Joke' might equally be about Balin himself, referencing what, not unreasonably, he believed had become his outsider status within his own group:

> A friend of mine asked me
> Where has he been
> Where is he now?
> I said he'd been set free
> Shares a little joke with the world somehow
> Sounded like he'd make a halo
> When I heard his laughter floating
> It's all for fun you know
> He said he just let go
> Shares a little joke with the world.

If so, Marty's remarkably nonchalant about it all, musically and lyrically shrugging his shoulders should anyone question his current relevance to Jefferson Airplane. The song kicks away with a brief, distant clap of thunder from Spencer, then it's over to Marty's guitar (rather than Paul's) for an ominous intro, the solemn chords as rich and sonorous as an ancient clock. Spencer keeps time as Jack fades in, his high bass notes drenched in sustain, followed by Jorma with the main theme.

Aligning with Marty's wistful lyrics, which are delivered by the vocalist with his usual passion despite the wry messaging, there's much dynamism and musical drama. At 1.24, his voice soars for the chorus; a declamatory 'Your heart's never been satisfied', followed by an otherworldly vocal shriek. An instrumental break, in which the accompanists move on from the spartan main passages to briefly take off, then Spencer's great snare-drum fill settles everyone back into the song. 'World around you, never catching up with you', Marty observes, and the shared little joke ends with an accelerated rhythm and a scream of guitar feedback. 'Share a Little Joke' is a welcome comeback, even if the song's only a Band-Aid over Marty's broader band concerns.

'Chushingura' 1.21 (Dryden)

'Chushingura' was the second Airplane piece attributed to Spencer Dryden following the crazed 'A Small Package of Value...' on *After Bathing At Baxter's*. For another short, startling sound collage – although edited down from a seven-minute original – Spencer again wears on his sleeve the disquieting influence of Frank Zappa, whom the drummer had visited during the recording of the third Mothers of Invention album *We're Only In It For The Money*. 'I watched this madman work and it impressed me so much,' Spencer later said. 'You don't smooth off the edges and go for perfection, you go for this attack... taking sounds that are totally opposite and placing them against each other and playing with them. That made a great impression on me.'

'Chushingura' – with impeccable literary affectation, the title was lifted from an obscure 1962 Japanese film – fades in with a single, ominous, high-frequency tone. In Sidney Lumet's 1964 doomsday movie, *Fail-Safe*, a similar screech transmitted over the presidential hotline signalled the unintentional explosion of a U.S. thermonuclear bomb over Moscow. Here it's the grim echo of *Crown of Creation's* sleeve image and a precursor of the ruined future to be graphically explored later on this surpassing album.

After 0.12, a disparate flurry of electronics multiplies and envelopes Dryden's funereal bass drum, as atonal guitar and piano bob and weave around each other. Following more otherworldly bleeps, as if an episode of *Star Trek* were being shot next door, 'Chushingura' is done and dusted after a compact 1.20. In creating music from audial chaos, Spencer had learned well at the feet of the master.

'If You Feel' 3.22 (Gary Blackman, Balin)

This cheery sidebar to *Crown's* uneasiness about arrested development, personal alienation and nuclear war feels as if it were created solely as a springboard for extended concert improvisation. In fact, Airplane usually kept the length of the song to below five minutes, and although Marty recalled frequent inclusions in live shows, the song is hard to find on bootlegs (although its final outing, at Amsterdam's Concertgebouw in September 1968, is captured on *Nothing in Particular* – see Live Albums chapter).

'If You Feel' begins with Paul's tentative rhythm guitar and sharp stabs from Jorma, Jack's bass only coming in on the second verse. Marty's and Gary's lyric is a simple, classically hippie exhortation to enjoy life; whatever you wanna do, go ahead; you're only young once, you're a long time dead, etc, etc. Once Marty's made his opening assertions, he's joined by Grace and Paul, after which the instrumentalists take over. Spencer's drumming is loose, open and jazzy, he and Jack leaving Jorma and Paul the space to improvise for as long as they like, or at least until the Eskatrol wears off. If they'd continued jamming away for long after the fade, it would have been no surprise; as it is, 'If You Feel' is a briefly-glimpsed ray of sunshine ahead of the gathering storm.

'Crown of Creation' 2.54 (Kantner)

In *Crown of Creation's* title track can be deduced the early seeds of where Paul Kantner's literary inclinations were leading him. Rarely again would he so eloquently express them. Paul once spoke of how science fiction had seen him through a harsh Jesuit military schooling; now the works of Robert A. Heinlein, Isaac Asimov and – most pertinently to 'Crown of Creation' – John Wyndham, were liberally salting his adult songwriting.

In his 1955 novel *The Chrysalids*, Wyndham tells how a small band of telepaths, led by David Strorm, elude a dour, primitive theocracy that statutorily banishes to the fringes of the 'Badlands' anyone perceived as godlessly different. That these 'Deviations' are usually innocent victims of genetic mutation (and here telepathy is a sufficiently outré transfiguration as to be considered terminally sacrilegious) suggests Wyndham is portraying a post-nuclear, agrarian dystopia, possibly thousands of years after the scripturally euphemistic 'Tribulation' zapped most of the world back to the Stone Age. Although unstated, this is given further heft by images of the Badlands as an irradiated hell of ruined, still eerily-glowing cities, black glass and gene pool chaos.

Paul, with a little help from Marty, will have more to say on this album about the apocalyptic consequences of thermonuclear war. For now, he echoes the novel, illuminating the optimism of escape from the biblical retribution of the neighbourhood elders. He tracks the telepaths as they're rescued by a more advanced species of humanity, the cavalry arriving in the flying saucers David has foreseen in a dream. More broadly, this is the release of the tolerant and the visionary (golden youth? The hippies?) from a stern, stagnated and uncomprehending *ancien regime (*Amerika, in all its Old Glory). For this doctrinal community, unwilling to see idiosyncracy as anything other than blasphemy, has sewn the seeds of its own downfall, the cycle of change endless as one decrepit society dies out in the face of another more vibrant... and so it goes.

Having diligently obtained the novelist's permission, Paul borrows and paraphrases freely from Wyndham's text:

Soon you'll attain the stability you strive for,
In the only way that it's granted:
In a place among the fossils of our time
In loyalty to their kind, they cannot tolerate our minds

In loyalty to our kind, we cannot tolerate their obstruction
Life is change
How it differs from the rocks
I've seen their ways too often for my liking
New worlds to gain
My life is to survive and be alive for you.

On 15 December 1968, Airplane returned to the Smothers Brothers' TV show and played a live version of 'Crown of Creation'. Disingenuously Grace claimed that she'd only worn the black full-facial makeup because she thought it rude not to empty her dressing room's complimentary cosmetics box. However, at the end of the song, she'd also raised her fist in an earnest Black Panther salute, much like the Olympic athletes Tommie Smith and John Carlos, with deeper resonance, had done in Mexico City two months before. Suddenly the black-&-white minstrel gesture felt less comical, more political/ironic in intent.

Then on the cover of January's *Teenset* magazine, an edition themed around minorities' experiences in America, Grace posed awkwardly in identical blackface and with a similar clenched-fist salute. In an article, one of the many reasons Grace gave for her Smothers Brothers stunt was an elucidation she would often repeat: 'If you listen to the words of 'Crown of Creation', think about a spade [sic] singing it. It makes a lot of sense'. Leaving aside an anachronism that today might be found offensive – although few fussed in 1968 – perhaps Paul had repurposed David Strorm's telepaths as African-Americans: a 'different', historically maligned community, more than ready to decouple itself from moribund and racist old values that are bound for the scrapheap.

The next instalment of Kantner's odyssey to other worlds will follow on the sixth album, *Volunteers*. After that, he'll find it increasingly difficult to contain his instinct to strident excess. For now, 'Crown of Creation's stirring militancy – apparently he'd been kicking around the martial rhythm since his days in the soldiers' seminary – is the making of this superb arrangement, sung for the whole of its sub-three minutes by Airplane's fabulous three-up chorale. Driven by Spencer's furious toms, Jack's commanding bass and a brief, perfectly composed solo from Jorma, it's important, magnificent stuff.

'Ice Cream Phoenix' 3.03 (Kaukonen, Charles Cockey)

In his autobiography, Jorma described his approach to songwriting: 'The guitar tends to tell me what to do. Words tend to follow, one after the other.' Sadly it's beyond the remit of this book to precis the guitarist's preceding account of what configurations of strings, frets and fingerings he employed to compose 'Ice Cream Phoenix'. It's also difficult to definitively review the song itself, although I'm grateful to its writer for letting would-be interpreters off the hook: 'It was written during the stream-of-consciousness years,' he confirmed. 'I'm just having fun with vocabulary.' He certainly is:

You don't know just
When to stop and when to go
City streets in the dead of winter
Stop your mind with dirty snow
Walk at night and
Touch your hand to the golden lights
And let them show
Feel the shadows disappearing
I'll smile and say
I told you so.

It's tempting to read drug resonances into the lyrics (*dirty snow* for cocaine?) or a pessimistic deliberation on the passing of time and the futility of love in a world that could end at any time. If this is so, 'Ice Cream Phoenix' sits right alongside the apocalyptic shadings that blanket *Crown of Creation* like lowering clouds. But maybe that's just freighting the song with more meaning than Jorma intended, so it's with some relief that I defer to the composer and dwell no further. Although the songwriting is Jorma's, its vocal expression falls largely to Grace, whose steely voice cuts through the Airplane chorale, high in the mix. Kaukonen's bluesy guitar curls behind and through a relatively spare arrangement, while Paul strums rhythm and Spencer pounds at his toms as if he's driving a gang of galley slaves. An infrequent inclusion in Airplane's stage show, 'Ice Cream Phoenix' was drawn out to a ten-minute jam at the Matrix on 1 February 1968 (see *Return To The Matrix*, Live Albums chapter).

'Greasy Heart' 3.27 (Slick)
Grace Slick was now unquestionably Airplane's focal point, the charismatic Aquarian-age goddess to whom fandom and a drooling press corps were drawn like moths to a spectrally dark flame. Yet, for all her radical peacenik leanings, she shared much the same choleric view of the day's posturing as others in the band. She was no enemy of fame and its trappings *per se* – always a sharp and sexy dresser, she unblushingly enjoyed the good things in life and once paid $18,500 cash on a whim for a brand-new Aston Martin – but Grace was smart enough to understand stardom's transitory nature and that it all just came with the territory anyway.

In *Crown of Creation's* first single, Grace tears mercilessly into the cult of beauty and vacuous adoration that now surrounds Airplane. Typically detached, the writer casts herself as the song's subject; the model-turned-rock icon turns in a vitriolic excoriation of style's triumph over content, the new superficiality measured in fashion, cosmetics, the resetting of identity to suit whim or expedience, the decadence of valuing art in lines of cocaine:

Ladies eyes go off and on with a finger full of blue
Lips are drawn upon her face in come-to-me tattoo

Creamy suntan color that fades when she bathes
Paper dresses catch on fire & you lose her in the haze
Don't ever change lady, he likes you that way because
He just had his hair done and he wants to use your wig
He's going off the drug thing cause his veins are getting big
He wants to sell his paintings but the market is slow
They're only paying him two grams now
For a one-man abstract show.

'Greasy Heart' proved not only Grace's vocal dexterity *in situ* with Marty and Paul. As Al Schmitt had correctly noted, her ability to duet with an instrumentalist was natural and instinctive. Following a fuzzed-up guitar intro that sears through the headphones like a dentist's drill, Jorma and Grace engage in a fascinating conversation, his wah-wah twisting sinuously through the song, complementing vocal inflections that are so venomous the listener is left in no doubt how Grace feels about this strange world she and the band inhabit.

Grace would claim that 'Greasy Heart' was her own take on Marty's messaging from 'Plastic Fantastic Lover'. 'I am essentially telling plastic people not to take acid,' the Acid Queen assured Barbara Rowes. 'It would blow their whole charade and they would be left in a marathon run without crutches.' A pragmatic view, to be sure, although but for White House security in 1970, the same challenging race might have been graced with an entry from arch plastic person Richard Nixon (see *Bark*).

'The House at Pooneil Corners' 5.55 (Kantner, Balin)

If 'Chushingura' wrapped an audioscape around the grating, single-tone electronic howl that might attend atomic misadventure, 'The House at Pooneil Corners' forewarns of what could follow in the starkest manner imaginable. A frightening evocation of nuclear apocalypse, it's one of Jefferson Airplane's most powerful achievements.

Crown of Creation's final track can be read as a metaphor for the demise of flower power, the moment that irreversible pressures gain a terrifying ascendancy. It's an audial cataclysm, the evil twin to an earlier song. If 'The Ballad of You and Me and Pooneil' celebrated the world as a candystriped Nirvana, sweetened with acid and A. A. Milne, barely months later the trip has gone terminally bad, the nursery-rhyme playroom putrefied to bullshit.

'The House at Pooneil Corners' begins with the same juddering howl of feedback as its cousin. But where the earlier song quickly bounced like a spring rabbit into a fairytale of green skies and positivity, here the mood instantly greys out to a nuclear winter, Jack's huge bass propping up Grace's reedy Farfisa organ chords, Jorma's squalling guitar flying overhead like an angel of death. In come Grace, Marty and Paul, inverting the optimistic sentiments of the earlier Pooneil. At 0.56, Paul injects a brief note of hope:

And you know I'm still gonna need you around...

...but he's brought down to the toxic earth by his co-leads as the instrumentalists skirl and swirl behind in mounting disorder. Accompanied by a warning siren that begins in the streets then spirals uncontrollably out into the acid rainfall, Marty delivers over the dirgelike backing the bleakest lines ever to appear in an Airplane song:

Everything someday will be gone except silence
Earth will be quiet again
Seas from clouds will wash off the ashes of violence
Left as the memory of men
There will be no survivor my friend.

Tension builds as everything falls apart, the musical deconstruction reflecting the severing of societal threads and the ensuing pandemonium. Jack's bass here is simply magnificent, at once anchoring the piece and frantically playing off Jorma as an equal partner. The End, literally, is nigh; it's the bitter legacy of nuclear-spawned genetic chaos, promised by the holocaust long after the mushroom clouds have dispersed:

The cows are almost cooing
Turtle doves are mooing
Which is why our poo is pooing
In the sun.

Other than for the forthcoming 1969 live set, for all future studio dates Jefferson Airplane would be, in effect, a different band. They were about to tighten up and toughen up, as Spencer Dryden found himself as embittered as Marty Balin and the band began to make tentative enquiries after a replacement.

For even if the personnel would remain relatively stable for a while longer, petty jealousies, cavalier musical and personal factionalism, huge drug consumption and general bad blood were rupturing Airplane's own social cohesion whenever they were away from their natural habitat, the stage. Given the travails, perhaps there was no other way to close out Airplane's finest studio album, by its best-ever lineup, than with the sonic collapse into madness embodied by 'The House at Pooneil Corners'.

Associated tracks
'Ribump Ba Bap Dum Dum' 1.32 (Dryden, William Goodwin)
With the musical inquiries and overall restlessness of *After Bathing At Baxter's* having weighed against broader commercial appeal, Airplane probably had no wish to muddy the newfound coherence exhibited by the fourth album. This

meant no place for some of Spencer Dryden's more Zappaesque amusements; perhaps 'Chushingura' was a sufficient token. 'Ribump Ba Bap Dum Dum' could have been part of that brief soundscape's original seven minutes. Insistent accents at the kit and other percussion are braced by absurdist scat singing and sock-it-to-mes voiced by the drummer's colleagues, everybody no doubt well-refreshed. Disposable.

'Would You Like A Snack' 2.40 (Frank Zappa, Slick)

Grace Slick had liked Frank Zappa for production duties on *Crown of Creation*. This was an interesting idea, particularly in light of Frank's fervent anti-drugs stance and his unalloyed contempt for San Francisco's flower children. Recently he'd ruthlessly skewered the Haight and all its works in the Mothers of Invention's satirical masterpiece *We're Only In It For The Money*. But as previously noted, by now Airplane no more considered themselves hippies than did Zappa himself. In many ways, Frank and Grace were kindred spirits; both were iconoclasts who revelled in notoriety, only too ready to puncture pomposity and cant with a savage putdown. Grace often visited Frank at his L.A. home, while Zappa had Slick pencilled as a 'celestial seductress' in his (later abandoned) film *Captain Beefheart vs The Grunt People*. Like the *Crown of Creation* production gig, time, availability and, possibly, money got in the way.

They did manage briefly to work together. 'Would You Like A Snack' is more like an atonal, free-jazz outtake from a Mothers album, perhaps *Weasels Ripped My Flesh* or *Uncle Meat*, than an apparent studio throwaway knocked up after the more serious stuff was in the can for a Jefferson Airplane record. Far from a random slice of improv, the piece was written on the piano by Frank while Grace supplied the words. It features Grace's double-tracked vocals accompanied by Mothers Ian Underwood (woodwinds and dissonant piano chording, not a light-year from Sun Ra) and Don Preston (keys), with Art Tripp weighing in with skittering marimba alongside Spencer at the kit. As for the subject matter, the titular 'snack' is what might be enjoyed by engaging in oral sex during a woman's menstrual period. What tastier a topic for a collaboration between two such uncompromising art terrorists?

'Share A Little Joke' 3.09 [mono] (Balin)

Marty's song here receives a different mix, ready for the B-side of the 'Greasy Heart' single, distanced from the album iteration in that it was recorded in monaural only – typical of the time, even if R.C.A. was pushing its artists towards its state-of-the-art 8-track. More importantly and, in the author's view, more effectively, the opening guitar chords are artificially slowed, then sped to the song's natural tempo. Though arguably a cheap studio trick, the affectation works, adding a decidedly unsettling dimension to one of Balin's best mid-period Airplane songs.

'The Saga Of Sydney Spacepig' 10.30 (Dryden)

Another outtake with Zappa all over it, but not in a good way. 'Spacepig' starts with Jorma, Jack and Spencer riffing on A. C. Williams' (via Albert King) 'Oh, Pretty Woman', but quickly plummets into a mess of piano chords, cymbal crashes and ambient spaced-out studio chitchat. At 4.00, the blues falls away and someone (Zappa?) taps out a piano tune similar to Frank's 'The Air', accompanied by whoops, raspberries and the 'snarking' that peppered Zappa's early albums. At around 7.50 it fades to silence, before another hidden track at 8.05, a Jorma run-through of Gary Davis's 'Candy Man', annotated with more studio nattering and general silliness. 'Spacepig' is probably little different from the countless lengths of tape rock bands have left on studio floors since Eric was God; Zappa obsessives might be interested, but *Uncle Meat* it ain't.

Captain High at your service - Bless Its Pointed Little Head (1969)

Marty Balin: vocals, guitar, bass on 'Fat Angel'
Grace Slick: vocals
Paul Kantner: rhythm guitar, vocals
Jorma Kaukonen: lead guitar, vocals on 'Rock Me Baby'
Jack Casady: bass, rhythm guitar on 'Fat Angel'
Spencer Dryden: drums
Live album produced by Al Schmitt & Richie Schmitt
Released: January 1969
Highest chart place: U.S. *Billboard* 200: 17

All right friends, you have seen the heavy groups, now you will see morning maniac music, believe me, yeah. It's a new dawn!

Even if Grace Slick was discombobulated from eight overnight hours waiting to take the Woodstock stage, the self-belief she expressed over the festival PA on 17 August 1969 reflected how Jefferson Airplane's onstage prowess had increased exponentially since the early days at the Matrix. Her rallying call put clear blue water between morning maniacs Airplane and almost every 'heavy group' of the time. For as the festival performance suggested and, six months earlier, *Bless Its Pointed Little Head* had decisively nailed, of Woodstock's many co-billers only a handful – Hendrix, Sly Stone, The Who and Santana – had Airplane's measure on stage. And with their diversity of talent and tendency to the unpredictable, bypassing such tedious conventions as rigid setlists and plans of attack, Airplane were ahead of the lot.

Offstage between 1968 and 1969, matters Airplane were less rosy. Since Thanksgiving 1968 Grace, never formally voice-coached, had suffered from throat problems. In January 1969 she underwent the first of three procedures in three years to remove polyps from her vocal cords, a condition caused by excessive strain on her singing voice in an era before onstage monitoring (see introduction to Live Albums chapter). A band hiatus of several months gave Jack and Jorma the chance to return to blues basics; along with Paul and session drummer Joey Covington, they began casually gigging around the Bay Area as Hot Tuna (R.C.A.-vetoed original name: Hot Shit, although Jorma has since denied this), performing Kaukonen originals alongside blues standards by Jelly Roll Morton, Blind Blake and the guitarist's hero, Gary Davis.

On checking out of hospital, Grace found her Sausalito home burgled, as was Marty Balin's in Mill Valley. Paul's car was stolen and Jack's was damaged by a break-in. Before the close of the year, thanks to groupie housesitters who really shouldn't have been left alone with matches, the Pacific Heights apartment Spencer shared with Grace and the Kaukonens was destroyed by fire. Factor in the ongoing resentment felt by an increasingly distant Marty, along with the kind of infra-band bedhopping Fleetwood Mac would one day raise to the level of art – Spencer was constantly diverted by drugs and groupies while Grace found herself drawn, more and more, to Paul – and it's safe to say Airplane was not in a good place.

But if the background to the recording of *Crown of Creation* had been the sound of a band beginning to crack asunder, no-one would have known it from experiencing Airplane live. For it was on stage that Jefferson Airplane could come together and make some of the most seductively powerful live rock music ever heard.

By 1968 San Francisco's great triumvirate of Summer-of-Love bands – Airplane, The Grateful Dead and Quicksilver Messenger Service – were showing what could be achieved whenever the instinct to improvise, and to journey to wherever the musicians were taken by the audience, the atmosphere in the room and the dope, were allowed primacy over the constraints of setlists and curfew times. Onstage, the familiar was becoming the radically new. And this spontaneity was reciprocated across the pond: Steve Winwood's elegant Traffic, whose expansive meadows of stoned, relaxed jamming could easily pass for West Coast in origin, would take a slender studio original and push it in concert to 20 minutes or more. Early Fairport Convention were unafraid to jam long and hard, the Airplane model taken to heart in both the band's personnel profile and its music. Merthyr Tydfil's Man, in time one of Britain's finest blowing outfits, extrapolated lengthy, cooking performances from similarly tentative, loose-limbed points of entry. (In 1975, Man's men were delighted to share stages with one of their guitar heroes, Quicksilver's John Cipollina). It was a haphazard M.O.; if the vibe wasn't right on the night, it's likely the music would follow. But at the shows which begat *Bless Its Pointed Little Head* (at Graham's Fillmore West in October 1968 and his New York City equivalent, the Fillmore East, the following month) Airplane conclusively demonstrated what could happen when all the boxes were ticked; six musicians not so much seeking an arrangement as magicking several out of thin air, one after the other, everything melded seamlessly into loose, liquid grooves few could match.

Bless Its Pointed Little Head largely comprises live interpretations of previously issued songs, but so sweeping are the overhauls they've almost morphed into different tunes altogether. The singers and the instrumentalists tempt, insist, even shoulder each other aside into new territories of sound. Old favourites are taken at a lick, yet the band never sound as if they're ticking off a list to please an audience jonesing for the same old live material. Modest studio rock songs such as '3/5 Of A Mile In 10 Seconds', 'Somebody To Love', 'It's No Secret' and 'Plastic Fantastic Lover' here become stormingly intense new stratagems for contained power and revved-up funk. The empathy between the instrumentalists is palpable, matched by the vocalists; never before or since would the voices of Marty Balin, Grace Slick and Paul Kantner be so sympathetically captured in a concert setting.

In equally brilliant form are Jorma Kaukonen, whose lead guitar with its arsenal of gadgetry sweeps like a tide of liquid fire through the densest forest of stewing improv; and Spencer Dryden, whose sense of timing and rhythmic patterns at the kit lock down his colleagues when required without ever inhibiting their broader adventures. As ever, Paul Kantner restricts his rhythm guitar to the colour infills behind the raging leads, in so doing often making the song. Completing the instrumental assault is Jack Casady, his 'roaring dinosaur' technique by now commonly praised as the equal not only of those modern masters of melodic rock bass-playing, Paul McCartney, Phil Lesh, John Entwistle and Jack Bruce, but of the distinguished sidemen behind the best in soul and funk, from Jack's old boss James Brown and Motown to the Memphis Group and Sly & The Family Stone.

Geek note #2: in Airplane's early days, Jack used a Fender Jazz bass. Having switched to a Guild Starfire II and seeking better upper harmonics, Jack asked Owsley to upgrade the instrument with new electronic circuitry. With his towering back-line augmented by a small, separately-miked 35w Versatone amp, the cumulative impact of Jack's experiments with amplification would be hammered thunderously home, track after track, night after night.

The album's cover is a monochrome line-conversion of a long dining table at the Big House. It's set partially for a banquet. A production line of virgin wine bottles marches down the plain tablecloth. In the foreground a slumped Jack Casady ponders the consequences of playing a bass after Owsley's monkeyed with its innards – or perhaps he's simply time-jumped to the later stages of the same party. He still manages to cling to one of the vintages. On seeing Jim Smircich's opportunist photo of the comatose bassist, Grace channelled the poet Philip Whalen and unwittingly concocted the album's title, exclaiming: 'Well, bless its pointed little head!'

Single from *Bless Its Pointed Little Head:*
'Plastic Fantastic Lover'/'The Other Side of This Life' (7-inch 45; *Billboard* Hot 100: 133)

'Clergy' 1.35

'Clergy' is actually the closing seconds of the 1933 movie *King Kong,* complete with its assertion that 'beauty', not the 'airplane', was guilty of killing the eponymous beast. Since this soundtrack finale was used to intro Jefferson Airplane's live shows, it seemed an obvious start to the concert album, besides giving the band the opportunity for some sly titling wordplay. To spare the blushes of the doubtless legions of Jefferson Airplane fans serving in the North Vietnamese Army, 'King Cong' was dumped by R.C.A., so Airplane found a more acceptable, if completely nonsensical name.

'3/5 Of A Mile In 10 Seconds' 4.39 (Balin)

As *King Kong* checks out, Airplane kick off with a live staple. Spencer releases a furious pattern at the kit, giving little clue as to where they're all going. Jorma arrives, and the song is revealed to be one of the high points of *Surrealistic Pillow*, pumped up to speedfreak velocity. '3/5 Of A Mile In 10 Seconds' feels like double the pace of the original, as Jack and Jorma, anchored by Paul's stabbing rhythm guitar, bound up and down their respective fretboards while Grace and Marty trade breathless vocal licks like cats in a sack.

In his memoir, the euphoria of the period leavened by the years, Jorma stated that *Bless Its Pointed Little Head* projected Airplane 'in absolutely top form'. An insightful, objective musician unafraid to self-analyse past errors, he also told Jeff Tamarkin: 'It really is a live album. There's no overdubbing. There are no redone vocals. That is Airplane at its peak.' Taking his word as gospel, this is an exciting, exhilarating intro, evidence that, provided their collective dander was up, Airplane required no gentle easing into a live gig. That night, on home turf at Fillmore West, the band hit the ground running; a well-tuned champion athlete nicely warmed-up and ready for all comers.

'Somebody To Love' 4.16 (Darby Slick)

In 2011 Jack Casady compared the live treatment of 'Somebody To Love' with *Surrealistic Pillow's* relatively gentlemanly original: 'It needed some continuous movement to add a sense of aggression, excitement, and flow,' Jack told *Bass Player* magazine. 'So we kind of reversed roles; instead of me laying a consistent pattern beneath lead guitar lines, I would move through the changes with a constantly evolving, connecting walking bass line against Spencer's furious backbeat and Jorma's accented fills.'

Jack could have been discussing Airplane's entire catalogue. But it's fitting that the bassist should exemplify the musicians' quest for improvement with the first J.A. song to have turned heads outside the Haight. 'Somebody To Love' had already journeyed far since The Great Society's February 1966 original. And Airplane's hit studio makeover had become a fixture of U.S. radio, leaving the band, if only within their own ranks, acutely aware of how familiarity can breed a sense of, if not contempt, certainly a wearying *deja vu*.

So Airplane redressed the balance on stage. From Avalon to Winterland, Fillmores West to East, every concert was a cauldron of reinvention, each night's experiments with structure, dynamics and the relative duties of instrumentalists and singers immediately upgrading any revisions of the evening before. In the case of 'Somebody To Love', by October 1968 the jaunty hit single of eighteen months previously had been reheated to a savoury gumbo of restless, exhilarating funk.

As usual with the Airplane, credit must go to every participant. While Casady and Dryden propel the band as if on a Montana cattle drive, Kaukonen keeps his powder dry until 3.15, when he lets go a buzzsaw solo. The vocalists are just as adventurous, Grace and Marty orbiting like binary stars, each refusing to be eclipsed by the other. Aggression, excitement and flow were never better expressed.

'Fat Angel' 7.37 (Donovan Leitch)

His famous 'Fly Jefferson Airplane' lyric had positioned composer Donovan Leitch as a notable British early adopter of the San Francisco scene. As included on Leitch's *Sunshine Superman a*lbum, the original version of the Scots singer-songwriter's gift to Airplane in 1966 was a real period-piece. 'The Fat Angel' (named for the sturdy Mama Cass Elliot, with whom Donovan had tarried when he visited L.A. the same year) was a dreamy paean to the joys of recreational narcosis; pleasant, gently swinging and wafted catatonically along by fashionable sitar courtesy of Don's friend Shawn Phillips. Couldn't you just savour that Lebanese Red?

More dubiously, 'The Fat Angel' also lauded the ever-helpful offices of the singer's dealer; a man who'll 'bring happiness in a pipe' then 'ride away on his silver bike' as if he were no more than a selfless, puckish sprite come among the hippie throng to spread unconditional comfort and joy. According to Leitch, the silvery cyclist was ex-New Christie Minstrel Barry McGuire, who hit solo gold in 1965 with P. F. Sloan's overcooked opus to nuclear anxiety, 'Eve of Destruction' (how many mics of California Sunshine the Glaswegian folk-rocker may or may not have procured from the pious troubadour is unrecorded). Dope-related songs weren't unknown for creating instant heroes of the shady characters who pushed the product, but this didn't make the idea any more palatable. Couldn't you just savour that Lebanese bullshit?

In Airplane's hands, the song knocks off the title's definite article and eases a stoned soul picnic of definitive jamming around Paul Kantner's suitably blitzed vocal. Though not normally at his best as a solo singer, Paul's approach is still preferable to the artifice typically advanced by the song's writer in the original, avoiding Leitch's ever-mannered 'I'm smashed, me' delivery for one that leaves you in little doubt that Kantner genuinely is. But if the original song itself is slight – from the fey affectation of the words to their tortuous and deeply irritating syntax ('he will bring orchids for my lady, their perfume will be of a very ex-cell-ent style...' and other horrors) – it's the performance of the instrumentalists that is the real delight here.

When Airplane performed 'Fat Angel' onstage – and after its first appearance in September 1966, the song became a favourite – Marty Balin would often don Jack Casady's Starfire bass while Jack busied himself playing rhythm on a Telecaster, the sounds Paul coaxed from his Rickenbacker ably sitting in for the sitar. 'Fat Angel' is another case study in how sharp the band's live edge had become; in earlier readings (such as the November 1966 Fillmore gig taped for *We Have Ignition* – see Live Albums chapter), the whole tune was informed by a woozy, mantric drone, creating little distance from the myriad Eastern-inflected pop songs of the period, Donovan's original included.

Here Airplane's performance is thrillingly dynamic, its tentative instrumental probings coalescing into shatteringly intense false climaxes before dropping back to the vocal verses ready for the next crescendo.

Spencer's percussive accents, mainly mallets on toms, are crucial in moving everything around. There's a great moment at 4.00, where Paul's vocal nudges into Spencer's fill a tad too soon and the drummer adroitly mitigates the intrusion. The seven-minute length of this 'Fat Angel' could easily have doubled and one would derive no less pleasure from it: it's a masterclass in spaced-out West Coast invention of which Traffic (who'd later jam with Airplane at Fillmore East and who typified those Brits looking towards San Francisco even as California gazed winsomely back at Cream) would've been proud.

'Rock Me Baby' 7.49 (Trad; arr Jefferson Airlane)

Most Airplane concerts had room for at least one classic blues for Jorma Kaukonen to get his teeth into. Whenever possible, the roots aficionado had kept the faith, essaying on stage such dependable workhorses as 'Kansas City', 'Uncle Sam Blues', 'Hesitation Blues' and his own 'In The Morning'. From gig to gig, these changed very little, the template a slow-burning 12-bar, the vocal delivered with Jorma's usual *faux*-Mississippi drawl, all affording the guitarist the opportunity to stretch out and go *mano-a-mano* with his soul brother, Jack Casady.

'Rock Me Baby' – attributed as traditional, but more likely the original work of B.B. King – starts typically tentatively, as Jorma's opening argument is countered by Jack and Spencer, Paul keeping to a quietly rhythmic comping beneath. The song gathers pace and intensity as guitarist and bassist relish playing off each other, much as did their Grateful Dead brothers-in-arms Jerry Garcia and Phil Lesh. While 'Rock Me Baby' is a straightforward slow blues, in theory little different from the countless thousands knocked out by rote in bars from Clarksdale to Clerkenwell, Airplane's instrumentalists shoot concentrated acid into a slumbering vein, the result a churning, molten manifesto for the side-project Jefferson Airplane would eventually pre-decease: Hot Tuna, and in particular Tuna's self-styled 'heavy' period of the mid-1970s.

Presumably to overcome the time limitations of vinyl, 'Rock Me Baby' is here shortened by one minute. *More Head,* a vinyl-only bootleg (reviewed in Live Albums chapter), restores the full 8.49, together with several other Airplane classics that didn't make *BIPLH* from the same gigs.

'The Other Side of This Life' 6.45 (Fred Neil)

In 1965, Jefferson Airplane chose Fred Neil's song to audition for Columbia Records. Although the band would never record 'The Other Side of This Life' in a studio, the piece would remain a staple of their live repertoire, while its author would loom large in the broader Jefferson Airplane story.

Following an introduction from David Crosby, Paul Kantner came to idolise the Ohio-born songsmith, detecting in Neil's music a soulfulness he felt was shared by few others. 'Freddie just led us to places that normal folksingers didn't go,' Paul explained. Yet despite the blessing of Neil's rich baritone, the songs seemed fated to be made famous by others. 'Everybody's Talkin', for example, was a hit for Harry Nilsson as part of the soundtrack for John Schlesinger's 1969 film *Midnight Cowboy*. Similarly, Tim Buckley, another mellifluous baritone, had adopted virtual ownership of 'Dolphins'.

It was working with the endangered inspiration for the latter song that took up the last three decades of Neil's life (he died in 2001 at the age of 65) suggesting his modest public profile, despite shedloads of raw talent, was evidence of an already unshowbizzy persona. But while Fred cared little for touring and its promotional opportunities, he was a frequent visitor to the Big House; Grace rechristened him 'Poohneil' and his Milne-influenced moniker was celebrated in the mirror-images of two of Airplane's greatest songs.

With 'The Other Side of This Life', which was also recorded by Peter, Paul & Mary and The Youngbloods, Airplane take Neil's American 'ramblin' man' archetype and turn it into an electrifying, bass-driven aural maelstrom, as far removed from the image of the gee-tar-totin' lonesome wanderer as could be. In January 1966, a barely three-minute version had been essayed at Vancouver's Kits Theatre. From there, the only way was up and out, and by October 1968 at Fillmore West, when this version was taped, the band weren't so much cooking with gas as cauterising everything in sight with an oxy-acetylene torch.

As usual, Casady's massive bass draws in the others, Kaukonen's prying guitar rinsed in Dryden's tentative cymbal work. The disparate strands gradually conjoin and start making sense at about 1.15 as the band settle into a vicious groove. Paul tentatively leads the vocal at 1.46, but Grace and Marty immediately come to the rescue. Midway through Jorma's solo at 3.59, Spencer sees his chance, machine-gunning two murderous snare fills, goading the band into upping their game even though everyone's already on the limit. As Paul later put it, 'We explore it all over the place.' He could have been talking about the Airplane's entire oeuvre.

'It's No Secret' 3.31 (Balin)

No sooner has 'The Other Side of This Life' done hopped that southbound train than 'It's No Secret' crackles away like a bag of Mexican jumping beans. Who knew, listening to *Jefferson Airplane Takes Off*, that Marty's subdued, down-the-line love ballad would just two years later turn into this barnstormer? Even if Balin had found the *cohones* to talk Otis Redding into optioning 'It's No Secret', it's difficult to believe the result would have bettered this careening, blisteringly effective rocker.

The original featured Marty duetting politely with Signe. Here Marty's done with being polite, amping up the urgency. Grace's sudden swoop after the first verse provokes him into a counter-attack, after which the two singers spend the rest of the song spitting at each other like a pair of angry cobras. Meanwhile, the instrumentalists go at the arrangement as if it's their last gig together, any residual veneration for the relatively staid original checked firmly at the Fillmore West's door.

'Plastic Fantastic Lover' 3.53 (Balin)

As elsewhere in this superlative collection, Jack Casady reminds us of the period he spent pre-Airplane with James Brown's band, along with a hint that one or two Sly & The Family Stone albums might have graced the decks at the Big House. Otis Redding had already turned heads at Monterey; two years later, it would take Sly's incendiary Woodstock assault to demonstrate conclusively that crossover rock-soul-funk could galvanise a hippie audience as effectively as any languorous, 20-minute space jam from The Grateful Dead – or, indeed, from Jefferson Airplane.

Much of *BIPLH,* perhaps most explicitly of all 'Plastic Fantastic Lover', suggests that the underground's ultimate house band was readily absorbing the best of contemporary black music as early as 1968. Good as *Pillow's* version is, just a couple of years and heaps of live renditions later it sounds decidedly pedestrian. Paul starts the bidding, his strummed rhythm from the original immediately crushed by Jack's piledriving bass. Spencer and Jorma arrive, the guitarist's clipped fatback protesting like a squawkingly resistant broiler chicken. The musicians feel their way to 0.30 before settling into the song's now savagely dismembered theme and another wicked groove, Marty donning his Ohio soulboy's hat and hissing the familiar lyrics. Barely one year later, Airplane would begin an inexorable drift towards harsher, more predictable, one-dimensional hard rock. But for the time being, audiences could listen to this stupendous retelling and savour cross-genre musical egalitarianism of the highest order.

'Turn Out The Lights' 1.25 (Kantner, Casady, Kaukonen, Dryden)

Less an album track than a brief break while assistants deal with a stage glare the musicians feel is compromising Airplane's light show. 'Turn out the lights...' sing-songs Grace, accompanied by a dark threat from Paul: '... or we'll send Owsley to get you'. The lighting wrongs righted, a short, jaunty, impromptu instrumental rag follows that probably turned into the easiest royalty points Paul, Jack, Jorma and Spencer ever racked up.

'Bear Melt' 11.27 (Kantner, Casady, Kaukonen, Dryden)

'You can move your rear ends now,' Grace tells her audience at the finish of 'Bear Melt'. It's as if the singer is reluctant to put the Fillmore East through any more of the blistering improvisation of the preceding eleven minutes. At any point in an Airplane show, the break for a lengthy jam had become a highlight. Subject to largely meaningless titles – the improv might be named 'Thing', 'Jam' or even 'Nothing In Particular' – it was that part of the programme in which the instrumentalists could let fly and cast off the armour of conventional song structure – not that an Airplane gig was overrun with stuff like that, to begin with. Years later, Grace explained Airplane's famously *laissez-faire* approach to live music: 'Sometimes we'd play for four or five hours,' she advised Relix.com. 'Jorma, Paul, Jack or somebody would yell out 'D minor!' and just jam. And Marty or I would make up lyrics.'

However, any idea that Airplane ran on pure thought-transference was dismissed by Jorma, who told Jeff Tamarkin: 'There's a lot of real complex stuff; it's not just a band telepathically jamming together; the arrangements are complex and rehearsed.' And the jam didn't always come off; as suggested earlier, for such blowing to work in a concert setting relied on a number of criteria, not all of which were necessarily within the players' jurisdiction. But when everything gelled, the results could be sublime.

Jorma's point is borne out by 'Bear Melt', its practised disciplines clear over 11 minutes of apparent extemporisation. 'Feel free to sing along if you like,' Paul says drily at the start, even if he's not yet sure where everyone's going. The first six minutes are dominated by Grace, as she riffs on lyrics that, while adlibbed, have a skeletal sense of structure and a definite theme, this time dealing with a Slick perennial, animal cruelty:

There's a man come along with a jacket on
Long gun in his hand
I said there was a man coming on
With a red jacket on
And a big long gun in his hand
Got a sledge hammer
All he needs is one head
Just one sledge hammer baby and all
All them animals is dead...

As with 'Spare Chaynge' it falls to Jack to establish an early direction: a slow, rising cadence, tentatively picked up by Jorma and Spencer. The creative tension becomes thrilling and furious; Grace's part for now done, the pace gathers as Casady expels frantic skeins of notes from high up on his fretboard, even threatening to overwhelm Kaukonen's lead until the guitarist ups the ante still more, as if to remind his bassist of the conventional pecking order. But in truth, there is no leader, just four instrumentalists and a singer who know each other inside out, turning on the taps of live improv as few other bands could. Those rear ends at the Fillmore East were probably nailed to the floor.

Bonus Tracks:
'Today'/'Watch Her Ride'/'Won't You Try'
The extra tracks on the BMG-Heritage CD remaster, standard inclusions in most Airplane shows of the period, were all taped at Fillmore West on 5 November 1968, putting them squarely between the San Francisco and New

York performances which comprised the original vinyl. This explains the raggedy sound quality and, arguably, less-assured performances. More tracks from Fillmore West, 26 October can be found on a vinyl-only bootleg, *More Head,* reviewed the Live Albums chapter.

Pick Up the Cry - Volunteers (1969)

Marty Balin: vocals
Grace Slick: vocals, piano
Paul Kantner: rhythm guitar, vocals
Jorma Kaukonen: lead guitar, vocals
Jack Casady: bass
Spencer Dryden: drums
Nicky Hopkins: piano
Stephen Stills: organ
Jerry Garcia: pedal steel guitar
Joey Covington: percussion
Ace of Cups (Mary Gannon, Marilyn Hunt, Diane Hursh, Denise Jewkes): vocals
Produced at Wally Heider's studio, San Francisco by Al Schmitt & Richie Schmitt
Released: November 1969
Highest chart place: U.S. *Billboard* 200: 13, U.K. albums: 34

Grace Slick once told wryly of how she and Paul Kantner called on Mick
Jagger at his London pad. The Airplane-Stones axis was convening to discuss
a joint free show earmarked for Golden Gate Park in December 1969.
Anticipating an orgy of Satan-worshipping debauchery – or at least the
kind of smack-drenched domestic gothic gloom Mick would soon be seen
haunting in Donald Cammell's *Performance* – the bohemian Californians
were surprised to be greeted by an urbane, booted-&-suited Gentleman
Jagger, who proceeded to talk business, amid his oriental carpets and elegant
Louis Quatorze furniture, over nothing more kaleidoscopic than a pot of Earl
Grey tea. (Lest we forget, Sir Michael was studying finance and accounting at
the London School of Economics long before Andrew Loog Oldham sculpted
him into a professional antichrist). 'Jagger's house was like my parents',' a
disappointed Grace wrote in her memoir. 'We had a formal chat and Altamont
was arranged.'

In March of that year, the ultimate hippie Armageddon was still but a
mote in the devil's eye. Grace and Paul officially became an item, prompting
the ever-alert *Rolling Stone* to appoint them 'the psychedelic John & Yoko'
(psychoactive drugs obviously having passed Mr and Mrs Ono-Lennon by).
And now, five months before the echoes of the world's greatest pop artists
resounded thrillingly beyond the leafy hills of Woodstock, Airplane were
ready to rock, to conclusively answer those who criticised the band for their
apparently insouciant approach to making records. In short, the Airplane were
about to knuckle down and toughen up.

Not that this mad rush of discipline quelled Grace's instincts to publicly
offend. At a Fillmore East show in November, she strutted on stage dressed
as Adolf Hitler, complete with Brylcreemed hair, toothbrush moustache and
a full S.S. officer's uniform. The charade seemed emblematic of a decadence
and decline that would gather pace as the 1970s dawned, although in the

same month a humbler Grace voiced *Jazzy Spies,* a series of short animations designed to help children learn to count, for the first season of *Sesame Street.*

Though earlier in the year Grace's problematic polyps had forced the band off the road, she could still play guitar and piano. And everyone was able and willing to spend time rehearsing the new record, toiling daily in the Big House's four-track basement studio and at a brand new local facility. Despite the ascendancy of San Francisco-based artists after 1965, in four years, none had cut a single record in the city, record companies preferring their charges to travel to studios in Los Angeles. On 28 March 1969, Airplane righted the glitch, booking into Wally Heider's newly-established 16-track studio in San Francisco's Tenderloin district to record their sixth album, *Volunteers.*

As usual, the output reflected the tenor of the times. Between 1965 and 1967, the gentle hippie dream of oneness had flourished by allowing its musical soundtrack, as if by osmosis, to structure itself. Jefferson Airplane, along with usual like-minded suspects the Dead and Quicksilver, had at their disposal a number of building blocks: instrumental dexterity, musical and lyrical inspiration, questing spirits and 'benign' herbs and chemicals, all supported by an accommodating ecosystem. As these ingredients fused in a recording studio or on stage, the weird alchemy of the times was left to compound everything together in optimal proportions, music of a rare and unlikely beauty emerging as if controlled by magic.

By 1969, this otherworldly state was dissipating fast. Representing the sounds of the new decade would rely no longer upon an intangible, unconscious assemblage of ideas and ideals. Drugs that had positively expanded consciousness given careful usage (not always the case, it's true) were supplanted by genuinely dangerous, tolerance-forming amphetamines, barbiturates and opiates. Added to the harsh external realities of war, racial unrest, bad politics and too much money, along with certain all-too-human traits bubbling up and embalming the taffeta and tie-dye like an ever-darkening cloak, a witches' brew was cooked up that was just as likely to contain and suppress the original optimism as to let it take wing.

But if the naivety of childhood was ended, life's new *realpolitik* still had room for positivity, even if in future it would be more obviously and precisely machined. *Volunteers* is Jefferson Airplane's last great album, coincidentally (or not?) the only one left, with two studio L.P.s yet to come, to retain the classic lineup. *Volunteers* signalled a sea-change in Airplane's attitude to making music, heralding the new mood of political urgency, a prosaically hard dose of agitprop muscling its way past the more poetic, abstract and psychedelic themes of the previous records. Once again Airplane showed they were one with the prevailing mood, even if this was more by accident than design. Punchy and self-assured, *Volunteers'* most famous and fiery tracks brimmed with joyous revolutionary fervour.

Following 'The House at Pooneil Corners', the fissured and desolate masterpiece that closed off *Crown of Creation,* the tone is now lifted, as if nihilistic desperation has been barged aside in favour of affirmative action. In two of *Volunteers'* best songs, 'We Can Be Together' and the title track, Airplane are marching confidently towards a new dawn, armed to the teeth with the rhetoric of youth and the righteous: 'We are obscene, lawless, hideous, dangerous, dirty, violent... and young.' 'Up against the wall, motherfuckers,' trills Paul Kantner, even as he refutes any impression that Airplane has suddenly gone all political. He told Jeff Tamarkin: 'Rather than a call to arms [Volunteers was] a call for attention to what's going on around you.' By giving more thought to what was happening on the streets now, he was saying, we all might better consider the alternatives for the future.

Originally the album was to be called *Volunteers Of Amerika,* the deliberate misspelling a common countercultural trope (echoing Kafka's novel *Amerika* and German fascism) to emphasise discontent with the U.S. government. The idea was shelved after objections from the same body that had inspired Marty's title song. But more than ever, 'Amerika' is the album's theme and target of acerbic and often surreal lampoonery. Consistent with Paul's vow that he was reporting events rather than shaping them, the sleeve is a mocked-up newspaper, VOLUNTEERS splashed above a group photo of Airplane disguised in the strange masks, wigs, hats and prosthetics last seen in 1967 in the promo film for 'Martha'. The group is superimposed over a huge Stars & Stripes, while a caption refers to 'The exciting Paz Chin-in', setting the scene for more out-of-kilter business to come. Journalistic affectation continues on the back: sharing space with relatively sober album credits is a grotesque cartoon strip, an absurdist crossword that might have been compiled by M. C. Escher and a spoof news story. As usual for Airplane, the humour is *apropos* of nothing at all, less surreal than downright daft. But it's the inner gatefold image from the original vinyl release that drives straight to the heart of how the band perceives Amerika and its defining preoccupations: two huge halves of a peanut butter & jelly sandwich, captured by Herb Greene's faintly unappetising, full-out glory shot. The sleevenotes helpfully advise that the PB&J was eventually eaten by one Gut, a Hell's Angel known otherwise as Allan Terk, whose claim to fame was creating the DayGlo livery for Ken Kesey's Pranksters' bus back in 1964, and who would manage the San Francisco decibel peddlers Blue Cheer.

Hell's Angels figured elsewhere in Airplane's 1969 story. But if the year is remembered for anything in the annals of Hippie it's for all the wrong reasons, Woodstock notwithstanding. Barely weeks before the great festival, Charles Manson – charismatic commune leader, fairweather pal of Beach Boy Dennis Wilson, failed musician, homicidal psychotic, who claimed the Beatles' 'Helter Skelter' had inspired him to start a race war – incited his 'Family' followers to murder the actor Sharon Tate and eight others in their Hollywood homes. These venal, motiveless killings rekindled societal fears about hippies (which Manson and his coven clearly weren't) before all bets were cancelled a few months later by another tragedy.

Originally 6 December's huge one-day free concert, as idealised by prime movers Airplane, The Rolling Stones and The Grateful Dead, was to showcase rock'n'roll's demiurges – the principals plus Santana, The Flying Burrito Brothers and CSNY, with (naturally) the Stones topping the bill – to 300,000 fans at the West Coast's equivalent of Woodstock. But after Golden Gate Park and a second choice, Sears Point, fell through (the latter just 36 hours before the show was due to start) the organisers were forced quickly to adapt to the poor transport links, non-existent facilities and parched topology of the Aral Sea. Or, as it was better known, Altamont.

60 miles east of San Francisco, Altamont Raceway felt like a treeless, dust-blown moonscape, peppered with the rusting consequences of the demolition derbies the track had staged regularly since its opening. On the day, the hastily-assembled infrastructure proved inadequate, gridlock on the only access road forced thousands to trudge past abandoned hotrods and escaping livestock, paramedics were overrun by the damage wrought by cheap L.S.D. tabs cut with arsenic and strychnine, 'security' was courtesy of neophyte Hell's Angels infamously enlisted for $500-worth of beer and a massive crowd became more juiced and fractious by the minute. What could possibly go wrong?

Under the circumstances, Airplane acquitted themselves relatively well, investing the whole ghastly shitshow with a rock'n'roll statesmanship which the Stones, theoretically the era's chairmen of the board, would struggle to match. Rockist ego had placed Airplane uncharacteristically early on the bill; Ralph Gleason later reported that Jagger, peeved after Airplane's performance at November's Palm Beach Festival had bettered that of the Stones, toyed with the idea of dumping his business associates from Altamont altogether. Eventually, Mick regally conceded to a safety buffer of several other groups between Airplane and their Satanic Majesties.

As Airplane burned through a fierce opening of 'The Other Side of This Life', Marty stopped singing and jumped off the four-foot stage to have stern words with a group of poolcue-toting Angels and wannabes. The fists turned on him and he was knocked briefly cold. Onstage, Paul drily thanked the Angels for their kindnesses towards his lead singer, not flinching when a biker jumped up in a threatening defence of 'my people'. Grace attempted to calm the rabble, observing with rare understatement that the Angels had been hired to keep order, but that both sides were 'fucking up temporarily... let's not keep fucking up!'. Tragically the problem wasn't so transitory; later during the Stones' set, Jagger could only gape in satin-clad impotence as Meredith Hunter, a dope-wrecked fan allegedly wielding a handgun, died beneath a welter of switchblades and lead-weighted pool cues. By then, far above the melee, Airplane watched from their helicopter as the ideals of a generation were choked in the Altamont dust.

Altamont's intended festivities proved more like a giant Stanford field experiment in how readily human beings, given set parameters, can descend to savagery. The rock gods and their celebrants were now revealed in all their nakedness, apparently no more concerned for peace, love and the Woodstock Nation than a gang of drunken, tooled-up bikers. With the Manson murders its handmaiden, rightly or wrongly Altamont would become symbolic of the collapse of the 1960s dream; a travesty too imperfectly aligned with both the *fin-de-décade d*ate and the beginnings of Jefferson Airplane's decline as a creative force. Spencer Dryden, the finest percussionist the band ever had, took one look at the 'horrible, pink-sky Heironymous Bosch dustbin' and decided his days with Airplane were numbered. Hell, only minutes before Meredith Hunter's murder the Stones had been playing 'Sympathy for the Devil'.

Altamont's part in the decline of the counterculture was more nuanced than many accounts continue to suggest. Woodstock festivalgoers, so keen to get back to the garden they forgot to pick up their litter on the way, had infamously left Max Yasgur with a $50,000 bill to restore his fields. With the 1967 Summer of Love already stillborn, it could be argued that the flower-power ethos was so contrary to our more basic instincts that any disrupting force – such as Altamont – would only have been kicking at an open door from the start. But for the sake of argument, coincidentally, metaphorically, factually or otherwise, the 1960s really did end there.

Single from *Volunteers:*
'Volunteers'/'We Can Be Together (7-inch 45; *Billboard* Hot 100: 65; Cashbox: 60)

'We Can Be Together' 5.48 (Kantner)

Volunteers' opener sets the album's scene and tone, with an irresistably tight, powerful riff that sees Airplane in their most pugnacious mood yet. Gleason argued this was likely the band's most successful L.P. because 'it accomplished what it set out to do, both musically and with the lyrics'. Certainly, it takes no prisoners; there's no ambiguity on 'We Can Be Together', which storms along with extreme prejudice, the sometimes sleepy lysergic swoon of the early records duly expelled.

Lyrically it's difficult to give credence to Paul Kantner's denial that this song and others on *Volunteers w*ere calls to arms:

We can be together
Ah you and me
We should be together
We are all outlaws in the eyes of Amerika
In order to survive we steal cheat lie forge fuck hide and deal
We are obscene lawless hideous dangerous dirty violent and young
But we should be together...

Paul protested that 'If people saw us as political, then that's their misconception.' Yet the lyrics' sentiments allow little space for non-confrontational answers to the day's problems. As much as the anthemic tracks on *Volunteers* might be 'like news reports of what's happening out in the streets', Paul's detachment rings hollow. For he's nothing on this album if not fully engaged, locked and loaded; it's difficult to imagine lines such as these, wrapped up in arguably the most truculent music Airplane ever created in a studio, as anything other than implicit instructions to storm the barricades.

Back in 1964, Fred Neil, with Vince Martin, wrote a song called 'Tear Down the Walls'. As we've seen, Neil was accorded hero status by Kantner, who now co-opts the weighted phrase for one of the strongest songs of his career (and a bellwether for what would soon be flowing from his pen, if with waning inspiration). As ever, Paul is never knowingly under-plundered; for the stirring refrain in 'We Can Be Together' he attaches the thought to another battle cry, this time courtesy of the Black Power poet-activist LeRoi Jones, whose 'Black People!' poem contains the lines: 'All the stores will open if you will say the magic words/The magic words are: up against the wall, motherfucker/This is a stickup!'

Unsurprisingly, this latest lyrical outrage caused R.C.A. another dose of the jitters. Although the suits reluctantly agreed to leave the line unsullied in the recording, no way were they about to print it on the sleeve, which explains why the original lyric-sheet opted for Paul's own comment on the absurdity of censorship, its bathos entirely intentional: 'Up against the wall, Fred.' (For an alternative interpretation of 'Fred', see below).

'Good Shepherd' 4.23 (Trad; arr Kaukonen)

This beautiful reading of a traditional gospel hymn is one of Jorma's most memorable pieces of work. Apparently oblivious to whatever Airplane were doing back in 1965, he described 'Good Shepherd', which he learned from a friend, Tom Hobson, and a little-known folk singer called Roger Perkins, as 'psychedelic folk rock'. That its simple message of faith stands in stark contrast to the political-social comment of much of *Volunteers i*s no surprise; Jorma shied clear of politics, usually preferring whenever he wrote a song to externalise his inner feelings – perhaps as catharsis – rather than hold forth about the price of grass and the future of mankind. Coming straight after one of Paul's more overt (if denied) expressions of rebellion, 'Good Shepherd' feels spiritually sincere and positive. The tune would become a concert staple for both Airplane and Hot Tuna, often drawn out to eight or more minutes.

'The Farm' 3.14 (Kantner, Gary Blackman)

One of Airplane's more absurdist songs – although the silliness is defused by the fact that it lampoons country music – 'The Farm' loosely speaks to the desire of the band and fellow travellers to flee the dealer-infested Haight for the verdant delights of rural living, specifically (though the location is unstated) to the west of the city in Marin County. Jollied along by Nicky Hopkins' piano and Jerry Garcia's pedal steel guitar, the song is a townies' take on rural life;

apparently people living in the country have nothing to do all day but '[spend] time in the hayloft with the mice and the bunnies'. It helps, of course, if you're a wealthy rock star.

Unsurprisingly for the Airplane, the idyll becomes still more distorted; the urban escapees have been sure to pack plenty of stash, as evidenced by the loopy vision of the new next-door neighbour's mode of transport:

> He always looks so regal ridin' on his toad named Lightnin'
> The toad's name is Lightnin' he's ten hands at the shoulder
> And if you give him sugar you know he'll whinny like a boulder…

Going up the country, by amphibian or not, was fine for a while – simply *everybody* was doing it – but their metropolitan sensibilities would have Grace and Paul saddling up their frog and scurrying back to the smoke within a couple of years. Similarly, the song's pastiche C&W may be fitfully diverting for about ten minutes, but this slight, insubstantial throwaway is far from the Airplane's best look.

'Hey Frederick' 8.34 (Slick)

Of 'Hey Frederick', Grace told Barbara Rowes: 'I was talking to myself, but I wasn't listening to what I was saying.' This hint that the song was pure automatism, substance-fuelled or not, feels appropriate for a lyric whose meaning is teasingly hard to pin down. Interpretations vary: is the song a message from a 1960s biker-broad, advice for an inexperienced lover or a pensive letter-to-self about sex and relationships? The motorbike references are arguably metaphorical; the smart money here is on a veiled warning against abusing dope, specifically methamphetamine, whose popularity was gaining a dark traction, both on the streets and among Grace's peers. The stuff is dangerous enough to warrant a premonition of death:

> There you sit mouth wide open, animals nipping at your sides
> On wire wheels the four-stroke man opens wide
> The marching sound, the constant ride
> And the casket is mine, all mine
> One more peril
> Wire wheels bear down on you
> Gear stripping the willow
> How many machine men will you see
> Before you stop your believing that speed will slide down on you
> Like the brakes in bad weather.

The drug's main derivatives, speed and crystal meth, are highly addictive; the 'machine men' are the unfortunates who have developed mental disorders due to intemperate use. Typically, Grace's account of the song's meaning has varied over the years, raising more questions than it answers: 'Those lyrics are meant for the listener to use with whatever they've got going on with themselves.' Indeed.

If lyrically ambiguous, musically, there's no misunderstanding: 'Hey Frederick' is the closest Airplane has yet come to heavy metal. Nicky Hopkins' cascading, two-fisted piano intro, Jorma's huge, fuzz-toned block chords and Spencer's crashing cymbals pave the way for Grace to sing the two verses, after which all hell breaks loose, Kaukonen's wah-wah leading the whole ensemble at a frantic pace, a massive encasement of sound and fury. At 5.43, there's a let-up, as if to catch breath. Jorma and Nicky – whose contribution is worth every cent of his session fee – continue a meandering conversation, then everyone comes rushing back in at 7.03 as if Owsley has stopped by offering two for the price of one. Thereafter the ever-thickening tempo is relentless all the way to fadeout. It feels as if things could have gone on in the studio for a lot longer.

Although Airplane never performed the song onstage, Jefferson Starship (billed as Paul Kantner & Marty Balin) aired a live version in 2000. As for Frederick's identity, it's likely a nod by Grace towards one of her literary heroes, Friedrich Nietzsche. She might also have suggested its diminutive 'Fred' as the R.C.A.-friendly replacement for 'motherfuckers' in the lyric sheet for Paul's 'We Can Be Together' (see above).

'Turn My Life Down' 2.57 (Kaukonen)

For the first and only time during his Airplane tenure, Jorma drafted a colleague to sing lead on one of his songs. The guitarist was convinced that only Marty, possessor of the band's senior male voice, could do justice to 'Turn My Life Down', which was inspired by Smokey Robinson & the Miracles' hit, 'Tracks Of My Tears'. Accompanied by Stephen Stills' Hammond organ and Joey Covington's congas, Airplane turn in a gorgeous performance, the lilting sweetness of the arrangement a counterpoint to Kaukonen's typically downbeat and introspective words, which likely comprise another message to his wife:

When I see you next time round in sorrow
Will you know what I been going through
My yesterdays have melted with my tomorrow
And the present leaves me with no point of view.

Lyrically resigned Jorma may be, but there's no mistaking the fire of his guitar solo, which neatly breaks off from his proxy's soulful cry, that 'wishful thinking leaves me no place to hide'. The final verse, though, is chilling, a hint of trouble more serious than the writer might have cared to admit beyond the rhetoric and metaphor of song:

I see the shadows softly coming
Taking me into a place

Where they turn my life down
Leaving mourning with myself
And nothing to say.

History proved that, in due course, Jorma happily weathered his emotional travails. But 'Turn My Life Down' suggested – obliquely, given the song's jaunty, campfire feel – that first he must traverse a long dark night of the soul.

'Wooden Ships' 6.28 (David Crosby, Kantner, Stephen Stills)

The majestic 'Wooden Ships' is among the most right-on anthems of the hippie era. Combining the creative juices of Jefferson Airplane and Crosby, Stills & Nash, it's another hint of where Paul Kantner was lyrically and emotionally headed. Writers David Crosby, Stephen Stills and Paul co-opt and expand upon graffiti – 'If you smile at me, you know I will understand' – that Crosby spotted on the wall of an old church. The result is a science fiction story, pre-empting the moods and themes that Paul would explore on future records by both Airplane and their successors.

The song tells of how two refugees from opposing sides of the coming apocalypse are cast adrift and forced to survive on diminishing resources. As one gifts the other a lifesaving repast of purple berries – 'I been eating them for six or seven weeks now/Haven't got sick once/Probably keep us both alive' – the pair discover a utopian instinct for brotherly selflessness brought forth by extreme circumstances. Prior to being thrown together on the makeshift craft, they were at each other's throat, the cannon-fodder of remote ideological sorcerers and political destructivism which neither could comprehend. Neither knows nor even cares which side won. All that remains is the distilled essence of the human spirit and the opportunity, afforded ironically by Armageddon, for goodness to prevail and even, provided the lessons of history can be learned, reset our species. 'Silver people on the shoreline leave us be,' pleads the narrator; we can rebuild with less than you're offering us.

The loose, languid elegance of 'Wooden Ships' allowed plenty of space for improvisation, which the band took to onstage with the usual glee. During a reading of the song at Family Dog in June 1969, the players slipped easily into Skip Spence's buried treasure 'J. P. P. Mc Step B. Blues', an aggregation that was briefly considered for the album but was dropped, no reason given. YouTube has a rough but delightful film, possibly shot by Marty, of Grace, Paul, Jack and Croz kicking back at the Airplane mansion sometime the same year, the two songs similarly merged.

'Eskimo Blue Day' 6.36 (Slick, Kantner)

That a lyrical expletive would amass more muttering at R.C.A. than a song's overriding message speaks volumes for the priorities of corporate Amerika. With the line 'Say it plainly, the human name/Doesn't mean shit to a tree', far from the self-indulgent use of a profanity merely because the era permits it, Grace Slick nails the central, unarguable message of this epic song: that humankind's most pressing concerns are bent irrevocably out of shape. 'Eskimo Blue Day' is Grace's elegiac denunciation of the cavalier abuse visited by the human species upon a planet which, Gaia-like, will outlive us however much we mess with it. The natural world will prevail – but not without biting back at us with global warming and its baleful consequences:

Snow cuts loose from the frozen
Until it joins with the African sea…
Snow called water going violent
Dam the end of the stream…

Grace makes bold, unequivocal statements about the fate of the Earth while delving poetically deep into the metaphysics of our relationship with it. In the middle, she cleverly condenses a cosmic argument to the everyday by toying with the idea of a guitar's bridge, of which an adjustment in favour of a single string automatically affects all six, potentially knocking everything out of line. Once this idea is scaled up to a world interconnected in every respect, an apparently isolated act of environmental vandalism can be seen to contribute to global devastation – the butterfly effect, in other words. That Grace should raise the issue as part of the song's own 'bridge' is a brilliant example of the writer's gift for thinking laterally:

Change the strings and notes slide
Change the bridge and string shift down
Shift the notes and bridge sings
Fire eating people
Rising toys of the sun
Energy dies without body warm
Icicles ruin your gun.

'Eskimo's arrangement is suitably doomy, chimed in by Paul with pin-sharp interjections from Jorma, Grace accompanying her own contempt-laden lead vocal with recorder and piano. From the resonant, stately intro, the musicians speed up and intensify as if tracking the acceleration of climate change itself. Appropriately the song ends with the shuddering, peremptory slamming of the global sarcophagus, embodied in the crash of a felled giant redwood. As Grace later said: 'Our greed does mean shit to a tree. The trees are dying. All of our separating ourselves from the planet is stupid… [becoming] president of Bank of America has nothing to do with evolution.'

'A Song for All Seasons' 3.30 (Dryden)
For once, Spencer gains royalty points without recourse to SFX and Zappaesque tampering with the mixing desk. 'A Song for All Seasons' signals

Above: Airplane Mk2 at the Matrix, 1965-66 - earnest folkies all; from the left: Jack Casady, Marty Balin, Signe Toly Anderson, Paul Kantner, Jorma Kaukonen, Alex 'Skip' Spence.

Below: Up against the wall: Airplane Mk3, 1966; from the left: Jorma, Paul, Jack, Marty, Signe, Spencer Dryden.

Left: Maiden flight: Airplane Mk2 scrambled. From left: Marty, Jorma, Signe, Paul, Skip, Jack. Thankfully Jack had jettisoned his 'Okie Joe' moustache. (*RCA Victor*)

LPM-3584

Right: The writing's on the wall: Airplane's seminal second album, and the arrival of Spencer Dryden (front, right), Grace Slick (back, middle) and her White Rabbit (out of shot). (*RCA Victor*)

Above: Zany afternoons, evenings, nights and (very late) mornings: the third album and Airplane's code for their favourite recreational libation. The original U.S. sleeve in all its gatefold glory. (*RCA Victor*)

Right: Critical mass: Airplane's fourth album blew away the harsher edges of its predecessor, starting with a touching human portrait and finishing with apocalypse. (*RCA Victor*)

Above: The classic lineup goofing around mid-1967: Jorma, Paul, Spencer, Grace, Jack, Marty.

Below: Two huge singles and the Monterey festival pitched Airplane into America's spotlight.

Above: Pensive bandmates c1967 appear oblivious to Grace and Spencer's canoodling.

Below: On top of their game: Jefferson Airplane c1968.

Left: The ice-cool Acid Queen: Grace delivers 'White Rabbit' for the Smothers Brothers' Comedy Hour, 1967.

Right: Airplane guesting with the Smothers Brothers: Jack mimes with his old Fender, complete with fretboard fish.

Left: Windswept at Woodstock: Jorma Kaukonen.

Right: The day after Woodstock, Airplane featured on Dick Cavett's TV show.

Left: David Crosby (left) guests with Paul and Grace on the *Dick Cavett Show*.

Right: Grace and Marty testifying like they mean it on *Dick Cavett*, with guests Nicky Hopkins (almost out of shot far left) and David Crosby.

Left: Jack Casady ponders the wisdom of letting Owsley tinker with his bass: Airplane's finest live album, with candid Jim Smircich cover that begat a title. (*RCA Victor*)

Right: Standing up for Amerika: Airplane pump their muscles for the sixth album. It's great, but cracks are about to appear in the Big House. (*RCA Victor*)

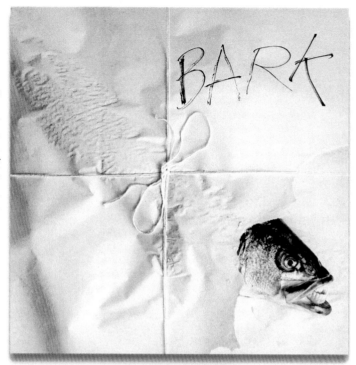

Right: That difficult seventh album: Now, with their own label, Airplane begin to atomise in the wake of Spencer and Marty bailing. The fish had more teeth than the music. (*Grunt / RCA*)

Left: Cigar humidor as stash box: arterial congestion was setting in on Airplane's studio swansong. (*Grunt / RCA*)

Left: Marty Balin at Monterey.

Right: Paul Kantner with go-faster Rickenbacker.

Above: Jack Casady with his customised Guild Starfire II.

Right: A casual Grace Slick relaxes in sepia.

Left: Airplane win The Man's approval and get *Life* in June 1968. The original hippies weren't impressed.

Right: San Francisco concert posters became an art form of their own.

Right: The irony might have confused them, but record company execs were relieved when this 1970 compilation hit #12 on the *Billboard* chart. (*RCA Victor*)

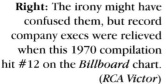

Left: The awkwardly-themed 1987 collection named after Airplane's Big House. (*Grunt / RCA*)

Right: 1974's compilation redressed the balance on outtakes, discards and banned substances from earlier days. (*RCA*)

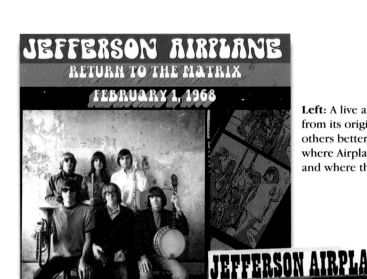

JEFFERSON AIRPLANE
RETURN TO THE MATRIX
FEBRUARY 1, 1968

Left: A live album repackaged from its original release, few others better demonstrated where Airplane had come from and where they were bound.

JEFFERSON AIRPLANE
CLEARED FOR TAKE OFF

Right: Not quite Monterey, but the band are on fire. Ignore the 'Live in 1961' claim in this boot's packaging.

JEFFERSON AIRPLANE | NOTHING IN PARTICULAR

The Lost 1968 Dutch Broadcast

Left: From Airplane's 1968 European tour: the recording did no justice to a fine Amsterdam performance.

Right: A document of one of Airplane's many free concerts at San Francisco's Golden Gate Park.

Left: Morning Maniac Music: Airplane's entire Woodstock set coupled with a reissue of *Volunteers*.

Right: No-nonsense 1971 bootleg from two TV specials: includes Airplane's greatest live performance in 'The Ballad of You and Me and Pooneil'.

JEFFERSON AIRPLANE

FEATURING · GRACE SLICK · PAUL KANTNER · MARTY BALIN · JACK CASADY · JORMA KAUKONEN

Left: The 1989 reunion album or your kid brother's wedding at 11.30 pm after the booze runs out. (*Epic*)

Right: Jorma models a fetching hot-water bottle for 1989 reunion publicity shot. (*Epic*)

that all is not well behind the Airplane's traps. Slight in musical endeavour, portentous in lyrical messaging, the song is effectively Spencer's 'Dear John' letter to the people who had brought the former jazzer into rock'n'roll in the first place. For some time, the drummer was known to have been unhappy with his Airplane colleagues, an idea given a powerful footing by the first two verses. But the target of Spencer's wry put-downs is no one individual or group. It might be the state of rock'n'roll itself.

As much as a personal jibe at his workmates, his words are a dry, barbed, allegorical and witty trashing of Haight-Ashbury and the spiritual insolvency into which hippiedom had sunk. And it's even more explicitly C&W in its musical framing than 'The Farm'. Hopkins couldn't sound any more honky-tonk if he wore sleeve-suspenders and an eyeshade. Meanwhile, the singers affect a rowdy barroom slur that suggests they stopped by a saloon on the way to the Grand Ole Opry. With the music circling the words like a Kentucky corral, it all adds up to royal lampoonery. And it's beautifully written, demonstrating that the lyricist in Dryden, underused by Airplane, was as skilled as the avant-garde soundscaper of 'Chushingura'. 'A Song for All Seasons' might not be about Jefferson Airplane *per se,* but the environment of which the band is inextricably a part, gets a thorough kicking.

'Meadowlands' 1.04 (Trad; arr Slick, Kantner)

Volunteers' penultimate track is one of those tunes you know from somewhere but cannot immediately place. A brief solo organ recital by Grace, 'Meadowlands' (in Russian, 'Polyushko-polye') was originally a Soviet army hymn/drinking song penned in 1933 by Lev Knipper and Viktor Gusev. Given the tune's deep Red pedigree, Airplane probably included it just out of sheer pseudo-revolutionary cussedness. In the background, and only heard with any clarity through a right-hand headphone channel, a huckster with a mittel-European accent hawks unidentified merchandise for 'dollar fifteen... come over here and get it'. A non-sequitur, probably, but perhaps aligning with the entertaining nonsense on the album's sleeve.

'Volunteers' 2.08 (Balin, Kantner)

Having been at loggerheads with most of Airplane for nigh on two years, Marty links arms with Paul and comes out of his corner fighting like Joe Frazier on steroids. Fist in the air, he spits feathers as he delivers an unambiguous call to arms:

Look what's happening out in the streets
Got a revolution, got to revolution
Hey I'm dancing down the streets
Got a revolution, got to revolution
Ain't it amazing all the people I meet...

On the song's ancestry, one morning Marty had been lying in his bed at 2400 Hilton. Roused by a 'Volunteers of America' charity van outside, he quickly penned some lyrics, later taking them to Paul for completion (although eventually the VoA organisation pressured R.C.A. into disallowing the album's original title, *Volunteers of Amerika*). The song's arrangement effectively turns 'Volunteers' into the bookend twin of the album opener, 'We Can Be Together', another rousing example of the barely-contained fury that Paul swore had nothing to do with politics. Often stretched in concert to accommodate Marty's additional lyrics (usually adlibbed variants on the singer's exhortations to revolt), here it's short, tight, punchy and to the point. With the big, anthemic set-pieces occupying the album's midfield, what better way to close the last truly important Jefferson Airplane record?

Bonus tracks
Good Shepherd/Somebody To Love/Plastic Fantastic Lover/ Wooden Ships/Volunteers

The extra tracks on the 2004 BMG-Heritage CD remaster of *Volunteers* were taped at Fillmore East, 28-29 November 1969, presumably swerving around Grace's graceless Hitler moment. All five cuts are dynamite, but on 'Somebody To Love' Jack's subterranean bass, Jorma's lethal guitar and Grace's by now outrageous vocal aerobatics are, quite simply, on another planet.

The following day saw the band supporting The Rolling Stones at Florida's huge West Palm Beach pop festival. With Airplane's live chops presumably still intact from the Fillmore, it's small wonder that Mick Jagger fretted the Californians might rain on his parade come Altamont one week hence. As long as the Airplane were generating the firepower of an armoured division, they remained too hot even for Jumpin' Jack Flash to handle.

Roll roll roll the rock around - Bark (1971)

Grace Slick: piano, vocals
Paul Kantner: guitar, vocals
Jorma Kaukonen: lead guitar, vocals
Jack Casady: bass
Joey Covington: percussion, drums, vocals
Papa John Creach: violin
Produced at Wally Heider's studio, San Francisco by Jefferson Airplane
Released: September 1971
Highest chart places: U.S. *Billboard* 200: 11, U.K. albums: 42

On Marty Balin's exit from Jefferson Airplane in April 1971, Paul Kantner later expressed regrets: 'Without Marty, there was no centrifugal force pulling all the parts together. Without that force, it just went... *whew'*. Long-term fans were similarly bemused that August when, after many months of uncertainty, Airplane's seventh album arrived.

In January 1970, Grace Slick had endured the second of three procedures to evict polyps from her embattled vocal cords. The op left her unable to talk for a month. Spencer Dryden, newly married to former groupie Sally Mann, quit in February, making *Bark* the first Airplane record since *Surrealistic Pillow* not to feature the band's classic lineup. (Some sources give 17 January as Spencer's departure date, although video evidence has him playing on 4 February at Family Dog).

Whether Spencer jumped or was pushed is moot. But reeling in the aftermath of Altamont, going strapped with a handgun was less the darkly playful conceit of the renegade rock star than the routine contingency of the paranoiac. Besides, he'd threatened to leave on 28 occasions before the band finally called his bluff. Fragile at the best of times, the drummer was wrung out from being musically pummelled nightly by his bandmates. Jack Casady and Jorma Kaukonen (whose earliest iteration of Hot Tuna concerned itself with the relatively gentle, acoustic-led Delta blues songs that comprised Tuna's first album) were playing out in live performance an unspoken notice period as they violently blew off the frustrated, pressurised steam of discontent. Seeking a more muscular presence behind the kit, they were ready to testify to Spencer's waning enthusiasm, doubtful that he had the physical capacity for their ever-more belligerent, Cream-topped musical intentions.

As Airplane's equivalents to the British power-trio's Jack and Eric, what Jack and Jorma really wanted was their own Ginger. But the fabulous Baker boy's role with Cream was one which, for many reasons not always related to drumming, Spencer could never have simulated. Small wonder he was no longer considered a sufficiently potent asset to his bandmates' heavier direction of travel. If he was unceremoniously fired from the band, it was a decision which Jack and Jorma would regret. Both later paid generous tribute to Spencer's talents.

Parachuted into the Airplane's drum seat even while Spencer was theoretically still warming it was Joey Covington, an ambitious soul heavy who'd been hanging with the band for several months. An onstage understudy for Spencer's occasional indispositions, he'd first played as Airplane's standalone drummer as early as June 1969. Interviewed for the post by Balin and Thompson, Joey had outdone even Ginger Baker's sixteen-minute 'Toad' by pitching a solo that went on for three-quarters of an hour, a marathon that won him a guest spot on *Volunteers*. When Spencer finally bounced, the departee was happy to ease the transition with support and advice for the new man. But when Joey proposed a double-drummer lineup for the 1970 tour, Spencer demurred with a knowing reference to Covington's loitering: 'If you can't do it now, you'll never be able to.'

By now massively disaffected by everything, Marty Balin suffered in relative silence until the dam broke that autumn. Drinking heavily and dismayed by his band's 'messed up cocaine music', he was also traumatised by the heroin-related death on 4 October of his friend Janis Joplin. Out of respect for Janis or disinterest in Airplane, he cried off a scheduled gig the following night. Airplane's Fillmore East show at Thanksgiving on 26 November 1970 was Marty's last as a fully paid-up member. Detoxing after the tour, he ceased all contact in those months before his official departure. In mitigation, almost inevitably Marty cited dope, saying: 'You could predict how a show would go according to the drugs lined up on the back of the amps.'

Then in May, as if removal of one-third of the classic lineup were not a severe enough body blow, Grace was almost killed in a car crash, effectively shelving the already fractured band's activities for most of the year.

Airplane were fast balkanising into separate factions. As usual things weren't so cut and dried, as loyalties became split over a number of different creative agendas. In the blue corner, Jorma and Jack were focused on Hot Tuna. Itself having toured with Airplane and with two albums in the bank by 1971, Tuna was now a 'proper' group; although for a while things remained fluid, a revolving door between Tuna and the mothership allowing Kantner, Covington and even Balin a measure of come-&-go as everybody saw fit.

In the red corner were Grace and Paul. In November 1970, the now family-centric couple – Grace was seven months' pregnant – quit the Big House and followed Marty to Marin County, 13 miles to the north-west of San Francisco. Their new home was a $150,000 converted nightclub (four bedrooms, swimming pool, dubious transport links, sea views to die for, geodesic dome) on an idyllic coastal bay at Bolinas. With the beaching of a non-album single, 'Mexico', and a baby on the way, the duo were routing their musical energies into a project that would again birth a completely new group.

Released that same month, *Blows Against The Empire* was a concept album accredited to Kantner and the earliest known sitings of Jefferson Starship. In these tentative early days as ductile as Hot Tuna, the conglomerate comprised most of Airplane, plus sessioneers and heavy friends from the Dead,

Quicksilver and CSNY, with Paul and Grace writing the bulk of the material. Perhaps surprisingly given his professed antipathy towards his old chums, Marty contributed to the lyrics of the album's signature finale, 'Starship'. Overall the tone is hopeful and idealistic, informed by radiant mother-to-be Grace and Paul's Asimovian dreams of interplanetary escape from a terminally compromised Earth. Remarkably, the sci-fi affectations netted a nomination (sadly unsuccessful) for a 1970 Hugo Award. Paul would explore similar themes, with less panache, on *Bark* and beyond.

Another newcomer dividing his loyalties between the two groups was 'Papa' John Creach. At 53, the tall, stooped jazz-blues fiddler had plenty of skin in the game, an adept journeyman who'd worked with Louis Armstrong, Fats Waller and Nat 'King' Cole. John was inducted into the Airplane by the energetic Covington, who'd first met the violinist at an L.A. union hall in 1967. By now, Spencer's successor was making his presence felt, his drumming muscular and enthusiastic. However, his quirky, disposable and, in places, downright antediluvian songwriting felt like overreach. Joey also inadvisedly insisted on singing lead on his own songs. Given the embarrassment of riches in Airplane's vocal department – theoretically, Marty was still on the team – this was palpably absurd. Perhaps they were ensuring Joey owned his indulgencies, establishing plausible deniability should awkward questions be asked later. Perhaps they simply didn't care.

But even if their behaviour still left much to be desired, they were having fun. By April 1970, the activist Abbie Hoffman had forgiven Airplane for their awkward foray into advertising three years before (see *2400 Fulton Street* under the Compilations chapter). Invited to a White House reception given by President Nixon's daughter Tricia – a fellow student at posh Finch College – Grace, squired for the evening by Hoffman, planned to spike Tricky Dickie's tea with 600 micrograms of L.S.D., theoretically leaving the leader of the free world sinking into the Blue Room's melting walls while coincidentally doing *Volunteers'* sales figures no harm whatsoever. The W.H. security people never caught on that the not-so-demure Miss Wing – alone among the twinsets and pearls, Grace was hipster-chic in see-through black crocheted top, miniskirt and boots – was the dreaded Acid Queen herself. With Kantner waiting in the car in a chauffeur's cap and Hoffman looking like a Mob hitman (which was apt, since Abbie was on the FBI's 'most wanted' list at the time) the interlopers' racy apparel and stoners' demeanour was enough to see them smartly turned around at the door.

June saw Airplane play two European pop festivals: Kralingen, near Rotterdam, followed by the Bath Festival of Blues & Progressive Music at Shepton Mallet in Somerset. In what could have been a trial run for future beanfeasts at nearby Glastonbury, Bath's richly-endowed card included Frank Zappa, Led Zeppelin, the Moody Blues, Colosseum, Dr John, Pink Floyd, and Hot Tuna (augmented by Marty, Joey and Paul Zeigler on rhythm guitar). It was past midnight when Airplane took the stage; as with the band's previous

U.K. outdoor gig at Parliament Hill Fields two years before, the weather was atrocious, forcing the Californians to curtail their performance to 48 minutes after Paul's mic handed him an electric shock. Grace was graciousness itself, joshing with the sodden crowd and thanking them effusively for their loyalty under such trying conditions. Airplane's set, though short and wet and with a fierce wind blowing the sound away to the Mendip Hills, was well received, with a particularly fine version of Jorma's blues workout 'Rock Me Baby'.

At home, Bill Thompson was renegotiating a multi-million-dollar deal with R.C.A. Effective immediately, the agreement gave band and family complete control over artistic output and who they partnered, from recording to release and beyond. Christened Grunt Records, the new company would be the freak scene's final victory over The Man, liberation from overbearing corporate governance that would seal the Woodstock Nation's resurgence after the nadir of Altamont.

Kantner and Thompson aside, Airplane were unmoved, taking little interest in the venture. Worse, a disgruntled Grace Slick saw Grunt as an example of capitulation to Big Brother Establishment, the final nail in the hippies' 1960s coffin. Far from beating The Man, Grunt was closer to beating The Wife, wearing the cufflinks and joining the golf club. As Grace said: 'We were becoming *them.*' And just as The Beatles had discovered with Apple, hard-nosed business could tolerate only so much idealism – not to mention some patently barking ideas. I'll leave it to the reader to judge whether conveying journalists by mule train to press calls in the Grand Canyon and creating demand with self-destructing records – both brainwaves of an early Grunt signing styled Reality de Lipcrotch – were ever likely to fly.

Following a drug-soaked $35,000 launch party, aptly held at the old Family Dog, *Bark* became the first official release on this new label that no one was taking terribly seriously – which was also appropriate, since no one was about to take *Bark* very seriously either. In fairness, *Bark* was less the disaster many have since insisted, but more a case of the Airplane atomising into six discrete creative elements of varying interest, with little binding them together. As a poet didn't quite say, when it was good, it was... well, pretty good, but when it was bad, it was horrid. *Bark* was evidence of wound-down disorder: an uncertain, unfocused mix of Paul Kantner's insurrectionary sci-fi wanderings and frankly wayward contributions from Joey Covington and even the usually reliable Grace Slick. Grace skidded from the sublime to the ridiculous, managing to include one of her best songs alongside another that was possibly her worst. On the plus side was more solid emergence of the songwriting skills of Jorma Kaukonen. Meanwhile, Papa John's greasy, yowling fiddle, though proficient, added an ill-fitting, outside dimension that would never have sat well with the classic Airplane.

In short, the record was a mixed bag – literally, given the conceits of the L.P.'s elaborate cover. This comprised a grocery-style brown kraft paper sack of the sort that would normally contain tomatoes and mushrooms, although much of the album's content was past its sell-by date and promised little in the way of cerebral nutrition. An inner cardboard sleeve depicted, as usual deserting all logic, a fishhead with dentures. An insert within carried the lyrics and a Gary Blackman-penned poem of more Airplanesque red herrings advising purchasers what they could do with the bag. Quite a few already knew.

Once inside the packaging, indecision reigned further, dividing fans to this day. An occasional gem shone through the mud, but the album as a whole lacked coherence. *Bark* proved that Airplane were no longer the sum of their parts, but six mismatched, self-absorbed individuals whose mutual antipathy had seemingly parked them in different studios. As Grace told her biographer: 'None of us was speaking the same language. Everybody was playing in their own dialects.'

Originally pencilled for *Bark* but passed due to the capacity limitations of vinyl were live versions of Grace's 'Mexico' and the single's B-side, Paul's 'Have You Seen the Saucers'. Also discarded until the CD era of remix/repackage were Marty's soulful 'Emergency' and 'You Wear Your Dresses Too Short', Peter Kaukonen's 'Up or Down' and two more from the workaholic Covington, 'Whatever the Old Man Does (Is Always Right)' and 'The Man (The Bludgeon Of The Bluecoat)'. (Live versions of all these songs are referenced elsewhere in this book).

Mysteriously, *Bark* outsold the vastly superior *Volunteers,* reaching #11 on the *Billboard* albums chart and certified gold by R.I.A.A. A single culled from the album, 'Pretty As You Feel', was Airplane's final Top 100 American hit. Critics were as riven as fans. In a November 1971 review for *Rolling Stone,* Lester Bangs, in his gonzoid pomp, gabbled floridly: '*Bark* is the 'Plane's most magnanimous opus since *After Bathing At Baxter's,* and even if its woof and whissshh ain't quite as supersonic as some of their other platters, it'll getcha there on time just like an amyl nitrite TV dinner garnished this time with a little Valium.' Er, quite. But 1979's *Rolling Stone Record Guide* editor John Swenson was less generous, deploring how Airplane 'literally fell apart' after Balin left: 'A cursory listen to the wretched *Bark* will prove the point.'

You choose. I have.

Single from *Bark*:
'Pretty as You Feel'/'Wild Turkey' (7-inch 45; *Billboard* Hot 100: 60; Cashbox: 35)

'When The Earth Moves Again' 3.58 (Kantner)

Paul Kantner was now officially installed as joint commander of an increasingly militant counterculture. On 1970's elegantly cluttered *Blows Against The Empire,* he and Grace Slick had drawn up a mission strategy for imminent escape from a dying Earth. It was all good knockabout fun, romantic sci-fi idealism light-years from the boulder-strewn reality of the streets post 1968. (Airplane's links to Abbie Hoffman and the Yippies, rather than any cod-revolutionary ranting from Paul, excited the F.B.I. enough to build a file on the band. Thus was one Grace W. Slick balanced upon the same commie pedestal as those other Fed-baiting irritants of the era, John W. Lennon and the bomb-loving future stockbroker, Jerry Rubin).

'When The Earth Moves Again' is Commander Paul's latest instalment in his long-running saga of stellar renewal. Unfortunately, this song and others suggest that his muse, ignited so incandescently by 'Crown of Creation', now requires fuel-sapping afterburners to retain any kind of momentum; oblivion must surely follow. As untidy as 'Mau Mau (Amerikon)', the song replaces the chaotic exuberance of *Blows'* opener with a tangled pudding of wheedling vocals, squeaking violin and drums that might have been recorded in the next studio. The singers, Paul and Grace in rousing unison, advise that:

Egyptian kings they sing of gods and pyramids of stone
And they left the deserts clean and they left the deserts golden.

To be fair, Paul's words have a certain poetic poise – and so they should, given his remarkable pedigree. But for once, they read better from the page than they sound, due mainly to the irritating harrying of the delivery; like with astrology-fixated strangers at parties who fix you in the eye and ask if you've been saved, you're just willing them to shut up and leave. If 'When the Earth Moves Again' is in any way prophetic, it is because it foreshadows the demise of Airplane as a creative force. Even Jack Casady can't get this one airborne.

'Feel So Good' 4.40 (Kaukonen)

'Feel So Good' is a simple, confident blues-rock workout of the sort Jorma and Jack could do with their brains in neutral and were regularly essaying with Joey as Hot Tuna. Paul strums rhythm and Grace's piano can be heard comping in the mix, along with her breathy vocal accents behind the guitarist's usual bluesy drawl. 'Feel So Good' features two drummers: Hot Tuna's Sammy Piazza and Santana's Michael Shrieve. Jorma's lyric departs from the former Sociology major's earnest philosophical musings and concerns itself with, yes, luurve: ironic, given Kaukonen's brutal dismissals of Marty Balin for the same misdemeanour a few years before. At 2.16, Jorma's wah-wah sears in for a splendid solo break that tells only part of the story: this 'Feel So Good' was chopped out of an original studio recording of more than nine minutes. It's well worth sniffing out the excellent compilation *Jefferson Airplane Loves You* for the full monty, although the unedited take has a slightly muddier mix (reviewed Compilations chapter). There's also a great 11-minute live version on *Last Flight/Thirty Seconds Over Winterland* (reviewed in the Live Albums chapter).

'Crazy Miranda' 3.28 (Slick)

It's likely that when Grace wrote this portrait of a 'liberated' woman, the same mindset prevailed as for 'Greasy Heart'. While 'Crazy Miranda' hasn't the earlier song's depth and deflating satirical bite, it does enable its writer to take another tilt at vacuousness, pretence and deception, poking fun at a young woman who:

Lives on propaganda
She believes anything she reads
It could be one side or the other
Free Press or Time Life covers
She follows newsprint anywhere it leads
But still she can't seem to read…

For all Miranda's craving for substance as a gadabout and gal about town, Grace sees an empty shell who lives her life according to the remit of magazines, her existence shaped, if only she knew it, by an unseen establishment patriarchy. Miranda is a typical child of the sixties, a period in which, apart from the wonders of so much of its popular culture, the ascendancy of a supposedly 'free' younger generation is propelled by corporate forces and the imperatives of Capital. Miranda, then, is a handy patsy, a fashionplate haunting the art galleries of Chelsea N.Y.C. and the boutiques of Chelsea S.W.3, whereby The Man allows everyone to bask in a newly delivered 'liberty' while continuing to accrue wealth by stealth.

The song begins with a dialogue between Jack's heavily fuzzed bass and the composer's sparkling piano, after which Grace arrives with her vocal. I don't know if it's me, but her voice seems less strong and assured than usual, perhaps as a result of her throat ops. There's a lovely change at 1.06, judged perfectly by a snapping assault and battery from Covington's snare, the stridency of Grace's piano pushed hard by Jack's superb control of feedback and the bassist's innate knowledge of exactly what should go where.

'Pretty As You Feel' 4.32 (Covington, Casady, Kaukonen)
At this point in his career, Joey Covington was rarely covering himself in compositional glory, despite his needily obvious wish to be taken seriously as a songwriter. 'Pretty As You Feel' at least bucks the trend, if only from the perspective of its musical framing. Originally a thrown-together, after-hours Hot Tuna-Santana jam charmingly dubbed 'Shitty as You Feel', the song features Carlos Santana on guitar and Carlos' drummer Michael Shrieve. The album's relaxed four minutes 32 seconds was filletted from an original of 30-odd minutes and released as *Bark's* only single.

Lyrically, 'Pretty As You Feel' is as oddball as most of Covington's songs. The butch-jock drummer is in touch with his feminine side, transitioning to a life-coach dispensing motherly advice to a teenage girl – a sort of 'What every young lady should know' column straight from the pages of *Jackie* magazine – assuring the wide-eyed colleen that it's probably a waste of time looking for guys in tubs of foundation cream: 'Beauty's only skin deep… go out there 'n' knock 'em silly girl/Go out there 'n show 'em how to thrill…' While it feels as out of place as every other track on *Bark,* musically, it's a loping, liquid delight.

'Wild Turkey' 4.49 (Kaukonen)

Though lacking any songwriting credit, John Creach's main contribution to *Bark* is on Jorma's instrumental boogie. 'Wild Turkey', named for Papa John's favourite tipple, is somewhat throwaway, mining a similar blues vein to 'Feel So Good' but lacking the solid direction evidenced by even the lengthy unedited version of the latter. Here, any rough edges are smoothed off, resulting in a strangely sterile, studio-bound blues-by-numbers. Creach sounds oddly pasteurised as his fiddle slithers and slides around the predictable themes. With every instrument in the mix polished to an antiseptic sheen – the audio equivalent of an especially nuclear-looking soft drink – it's a blues in name only.

'Law Man' 2.45 (Slick)

Life came close to reflecting art one evening in 1994 when police were called to Grace Slick's house. The raid followed complaints about a woman drunkenly discharging a firearm. Once the officers had subdued the distraught caller, himself worse for liquor, their attention turned to gunslinger Grace, who ordered them gone. After a brief standoff, her shotgun was confiscated and Grace was arrested and booked.

23 years earlier in 'Law Man', Grace is the aggrieved party, brought to her front door at an inconvenient moment:

> Law man, I'm afraid you just walked in here at the wrong time
> my old man's gun has never been fired
> but there's a first time and this could be
> this could be the first time…

The song chimes with the passive-aggressive nature of late-period Airplane. Its sentiments distance its writer still further from obsolete Summer of Love ideals, even superficially placing her alongside every self-sufficient midwestern homesteader with Deep State paranoia and a bomb shelter full of semi-automatics. Yet while Grace has the upper hand and her guest at gunpoint, the elusive lyric reveals less naked, N.R.A.-style belligerence, more a despairing world-weariness over the perpetual unwanted attentions of Amerika. Courted or not, this is the lot of the successful rock star. If she were Ted Nugent, you feel the cop would already be toast; being Grace Slick, her verities aren't quite so cut and dried. She's vulnerable, unhappy about the position she's in; and just as the arresting officers are able to 23 years on, her current visitor could probably wrest the weapon from her with relative ease. She'll even be willing to face the music tomorrow – the officer just got her at the wrong moment:

Well I'm tired and sweet from making love
and it's just too late, you'll have to wait
bring your business around here in the morning.

The sentiments expressed in 'Law Man' are inelegant. But if you can get past
the casual amorality of the words, the music punches through like a slug from
a forty-five. In unison with Grace's piano and Jack's massive bass, Jorma's
crashing, fuzz-toned, feedback-drenched guitar chords and Joey's battery of
tom-toms slam into one of maybe three tracks on *Bark* worth the candle. At
1.53, Grace's voice, multi-tracked throughout, hits a key change that will lift
your heart. Given a less prickly subject matter, 'Law Man' could have been a
huge hit single.

'Rock and Roll Island' 3.47 (Kantner)

It's just as well most rock lyrics aren't meant to be read. Try it with 'Rock and
Roll Island' and see how quickly you get lost in the aggressive, quasi-sci-fi
stream-of-consciousness that was beginning to possess Paul Kantner. This is an
ordinary rock'n'roll song, its vocal again delivered in an overly hectoring manner.
Coming from anyone else, there'd be nothing much wrong with that *per se,* but
we should be in exalted company; this song suggests a degraded Airplane and
typifies the schismatic malaise which was now overpowering the band.

'Third Week In The Chelsea' 4.38 (Kaukonen)

A stay at Manhattan's Chelsea Hotel is a rite of passage for rock musicians
visiting New York City. In 1970 the place was home to Jefferson Airplane
for three weeks, a sojourn recalled in 'Third Week In The Chelsea'. Jorma's
reflective lyric, which he wrote in his room one morning after a dream,
conveys the writer's melancholic sense of the hollowness and insincerity of the
rock'n'roll lifestyle, of how 'we go on moving trying to make this image real/
Straining every nerve not knowing what we really feel.' Like an addict dreading
the space from one fix to the next, Kaukonen fears those between-gig vacuums
that can only be filled with yet more music, even if this obsessive urge to create
is caused by rock'n'roll itself.

All my friends keep telling me that it would be a shame
To break up such a grand success and tear apart a name
But all I know is what I feel whenever I'm not playin'
Emptiness ain't where it's at and neither's feeling pain.

Drugs and alcohol were causing Jorma self-loathing, as he recounted in his
memoir: 'I was changing in a way that I was not pleased to see.'

Lines were drawn around a pair of eyes that opened wide
And when I looked into them I saw nothing left inside.

Jack Casady saw the song as an expression of fatigue: 'That's the story of us all... coming to grips with the weight of all those years there'd been, and how we had all been at it non-stop since 1965.' On the road with Airplane, Jorma and Jack would retreat to one or other's hotel room and strum at old blues and folk tunes. As well as grounding the nascent Hot Tuna, the duo gained more satisfaction from honing their already formidable musical chops just for the hell of it than any number of mudshark parties and other rock-star excesses. Here a sanguine Jorma is aware that, while he understands the burden of his responsibilities to and with Airplane, change is in the air and it's all going to work out fine, even if he isn't yet sure what 'it' will be.

Well now what is going to happen now is anybody's guess
If I can't spend my time with love I guess I need a rest
Time is getting late now and the sun is getting low
My body's getting tired of carryin' another's load
And sunshine's waiting for me a little further down the road.

Given its downbeat subject, 'Third Week In The Chelsea' is a carefree folk-blues, Jorma's ragtime melody coloured with delightful chromatic harp from sometime Hot Tuna colleague Will Scarlett. For the second successive album, it's a letter of resignation. Spencer Dryden's 'Song For All Seasons' from *Volunteers* conveyed the drummer's implicit statement that he was ready to quit. Marty Balin upped and left without even a valedictory song of loss. With Airplane on the ropes, now it was Jorma Kaukonen's turn. And although the guitarist would be around for one more studio album and a final long-playing testament to live performance, 'Third Week In The Chelsea' holds an elegant mirror to his disillusionment.

'Never Argue With a German if You're Tired or European Song' 4.36 (Slick)

What was it about Grace Slick and Germans? Following a late-night recording session in May 1971, a well-lubricated Grace crashed her car at 100mph while drag-racing Jorma's Lotus through a tunnel near the Golden Gate Bridge. Jorma, who was unhurt, pulled Grace from the wreckage. Briefly pronounced dead at the scene, her resulting hospitalisation and recovery period teamed up with her polyps to curtail much of Airplane's activity for the rest of the year (a schedule that should have included the final Fillmore West concert before Bill Graham shut up shop in June 1971, at which Hot Tuna deputised).

Happily, Grace's injuries proved relatively modest. That her trashed vehicle happened to be a Mercedes-Benz, however, appeared to be her cue for a cod-operatic, 'Teutonic' dirge, complete with a meaningless tirade in pidgin-Prussian and the first and only use by Airplane of a tape-replay keyboard. There's a vague oompah rhythm, even something in the backing that sounds like an accordion, which may or may not be deliberately evoking an unhealthy slab of 1930s Berlin decadence – you can almost see Grace tricked out as the Emcee from *Cabaret* – but this is probably to overthink one of the most unappetising songs Airplane ever made.

Incidentally, what sounds like a Mellotron is actually an American equivalent built by Chamberlin, which had loaded into its arsenal of pre-recorded brass and strings a male solo voice. It's used here. Perhaps for good reason, it's rarely heard elsewhere.

'Thunk' 3.01 (Covington)

Things go from bad to worse with Joey Covington's sole single-hander on *Bark*. Airplane fans of old will have their own take; but really, 'Thunk' is dire, giving not a clue as to how it was allowed to flee its author's pen. First there's Grace's desultory, minor-key piano, before Covington arrives with jokingly out-of-tune la-la-las and some worrying news: he's been sitting around thinking, and it ain't doin' him too good. It's no better for us, we think – or thunk – as we suddenly wake up in a whole roomful of Covingtons multitracking a nonsensically ruminative lyric. The already sparse instrumentation then falls away altogether in favour of acapella vocals that sound like the Bear's in-house barbershop quartet. The massed close-harmonising Joeys turn 'thought' into 'thunk' and the whole thing disappears down the barber's sink. Or sunk. Totally. Abysmal.

'War Movie' 4.44 (Kantner)

Airplane's least interesting album to date ends on a few brighter notes, largely because on 'War Movie' they're all less wildly assembled than those of Paul Kantner's other songs on *Bark*. The third here of Paul's apocalyptic sci-fi epics, the track barrels along at a rocket's pace, quickly leaving its dull predecessors in the dust.

The song describes the call-to-arms and massed ranks of future-tech ordnance being readied for the coming cosmic Armageddon – Paul's 'Battle of Forever Plains' – and how the forces of darkness are sure to be overcome, all jollied along by Captain High rousing his psychedelic troops like a New Age Churchill. After a menacing multi-tracked guitar intro, perhaps meant to sound like an air-raid warning siren in whatever parallel universe Kantner imagines everything kicking off, a semi-acoustic strumming brings in Paul and Grace in close harmony:

In nineteen-hundred and seventy-five
All the people rose from the countryside
Locked together hand in hand
All through this unsteady land...

Hmm. When, precisely, will this cataclysm occur? Predicting Childhood's End, or Mankind's Rebirth or whatever doomy soubriquet best characterises the visions that occupied Paul's frenzied headspace at the time was always an inexact science, and any fact-led provenance, no matter how fanciful, would have threatened the poetic speculation of the moment. It's all good nonsensical stuff, though, even if the song's stirring refrain:

Gonna roll, roll, roll the rock around
Lift the rock out of the ground.

...is basically complete eyewash. While the singers rattle on about 'mind raiders' and 'computer killers', the band actually sound as if they're having a good time. And if Jorma's lead is buried in the intergalactic rubble along with almost everyone else, 'War Movie' is driven mainly by Joey Covington, at the eleventh hour justifying his relatively recent arrival – although *not* mitigating the indefensible 'Thunk' – by underpinning it all with a thrillingly beefy rhythm pulse punctuated by thunderous double kick-drums. He comes crashing in at 1.49 and brooks no quarter as the air-raid siren swims and swooshes through the planetary conflagration to a final, dying resonance.

Associated Tracks

'Mexico' 2.07 (Slick) b/w **'Have You Seen the Saucers'** 3.41 (Kantner) (single)
Recorded at Pacific High Studios, with Phill Sawyer at the desk and featuring the classic Airplane lineup, 'Mexico' was a fine and sadly underrated tune, in which Grace bitchslaps Operation Intercept, a Nixon brainstorm designed to stop marijuana trafficking into the U.S. For once, R.C.A. appeared to have no problem with lyrics that were nonetheless relatively transparent; about both the 'tons of gold and green' coming up from south of the border and the man who sought to expunge it all:

Mexico is under the thumb
of a man we call Richard
and he's come to call himself King.
But he's a small-headed man
and he doesn't know a thing
about how to deal for you...

It was left to certain states of the Union to mobilise against the sentiments of 'Mexico', imposing bans on radio play which effectively scotched any progress beyond #102 on the *Billboard* chart. Once again, Jack Casady's bass drives a memorable tune that might have had more chart success if Grace could quell her constant urge to take potshots at Trickie Dickie.

The same band is augmented by Joey Covington's percussion for 'Have You Seen the Saucers'. It's less successful than its 'A'-side, another example of Paul escalating his lyrical reliance on science-fiction abstractions. Increasingly paranoid over where humanity is bound, he implores we 'star children on the back road to salvation to come and join us on the other side of the sun' and other sexy but unconnected phraseology. The arrangement is less boxy and dense than much of Airplane's newer material; happily there's still a sense of space between the instrumentalists, of whom Kaukonen and Casady acquit themselves with their usual aplomb. The saucers of the title recall Paul's John Wyndham leanings, as expressed on the far more successful 'Crown of Creation'.

Twilight All Around You - Long John Silver (1972)

Grace Slick: vocals, piano
Paul Kantner: rhythm guitar, vocals
Jorma Kaukonen: lead guitar, vocals
Jack Casady: bass
John Barbata: drums, percussion
Joey Covington: drums on 'Twilight Double Leader' and 'The Son of Jesus'
Sammy Piazza: drums on 'Trial by Fire'
Papa John Creach: violin
Produced at Wally Heider's studio, San Francisco by Jefferson Airplane
Released: August 1972
Highest chart places: U.S. *Billboard* 200: 20, U.K. albums: 30

It was like a rerun of the Korean War. Despite the increasingly entrenched hostilities between its frayed and fractious personnel, Jefferson Airplane were never officially declared over. Instead, they drifted into entropy. Marty and Spencer were long gone. Spencer's successor Joey Covington was a dead man walking; in April 1972, sessions for the new album already underway, he either self-ejected for a solo career (his telling) or he was forced out by Jorma and Jack. Playing on just two tracks out of the new record's nine, Joey was replaced, for the rest of the album and whatever time Airplane had left, by ex-Turtle and sessioneering heavy-hitter, John Barbata.

Grace and Paul were distracted by parenthood (their daughter, China, was born in January 1971), homebuilding and what might lie beyond *Blows Against The Empire* and its November 1971 follow-up, *Sunfighter.* The pastoral arcadia to which the couple had relocated on the rebound from the Haight in 1970 proved temporary; apart from feeling cut off from whatever action remained in the post-SoL big city, there was only so much Grace and Paul could stomach of the relentlessly hip residents of trendy, bucolic Bolinas. In June 1972, the family moved to an extravagant $500,000 house closer to town, the only Bayside residence in San Francisco. Just as the hippies' flagbearers had passed that nightmarish point of implosion, its two most visible members would be living the dream in one of the most desirable properties on the West Coast.

John Creach remained dutifully on call to Airplane and Hot Tuna. Keen to concentrate on their new band, Jorma and Jack stopped coming out to play with their old pals in 1972. Inspired by that year's Winter Olympics, the duo took up competitive speed skating (Jorma had learned to skate as a ten-year-old). The first excursion would be repeated every winter for several years, the pair keen to purge themselves of the habits and toxins that had metastasised through years of internal Airplane angst. As Grace explained: 'Paul and I didn't know what was going on because Jack and Jorma took off... They didn't call back, and they were just gone.'

Airplane's power plant was shutting down. Like a spent Catherine wheel on a damp Fourth of July, the band's unpredictable psychedelic energy was finally sapped. In 1974, after various solo projects, it would sputter back to life – but as a lesser being. 'Paul and I started making records as Jefferson Starship,' Grace said. 'We had to rename it because you couldn't call it Airplane unless all of the original members were making the record. It was the end of Airplane.'

Would things have been different if Marty Balin hadn't left a year earlier? The originator was nothing if not a dynamic, driven enabler, a man as willing to pour heart and soul into designing and building a revolutionary new take on 1960s folk-rock as he was, at the end of that tumultuous decade, to courageously face off against a seething swell of drunken Hell's Angels. But long before the fall, the band's prime mover was past caring. Janis's death was the decider; by April 1971, he was off. He could see the way ahead; as far as he was concerned, it wasn't pretty.

Neither was Airplane's final studio album. If its predecessor showed symptoms of declining health, *Long John Silver,* delivered six months late, indicated the condition was probably terminal. *Bark* had comprised a series of disparate statements that struggled for coherent form, as if the pieces of six jigsaw puzzles of different views of the Golden Gate Bridge were packed into the same box. Though *Long John Silver* at least had the virtue of aural uniformity, it lacked the all-important dynamic subtleties and contrasts which, in better times, were life's blood to Airplane. Now that thickening consistency was threatening a musical thrombosis, the listener assaulted with a churning, viscous soup of sound. Though neither playing nor production could technically be faulted, the music's overall effect was one of arterial congestion.

No one in the band much liked the new album, either. Grace confessed that she'd been drunk for most of the sessions. 'Everybody was so disassociated it was kind of pathetic,' she told Jeff Tamarkin, who noted the irony of Grace having contributed more songs than usual, both solo and, against type in each case, collaboratively with Jack and with Jorma. Meanwhile, Paul continued his life's mission to irritate Amerika with controversial content, albeit now clad in the immunity – theoretically from the clutches of R.C.A. – conferred by the stewardship of Grunt. Eyebrows were also raised over the album's packaging: by way of artful origami – or by just following the folds – the happy consumer could convert what looked like a tray of Havana cigars into a useful stash box for a still more illegal leaf.

Airplane played only a handful of shows in 1971. By early 1972 the band were once more gigging in earnest. Following Marty's departure, Grace had reminded everyone of the importance of a second male Airplane vocal, Balin's voice already known to be an exciting complement and foil to her own. Ex-Quicksilver vocalist/bassist David Freiberg came in as Marty's replacement. In July, Barbata on board for Covington, the band embarked on a tour to promote the new album. Causing as much hullabaloo as in the good old days – Grace stripping off her top at Gaelic Park, N.Y.; Chick Casady (Jack's brother and Airplane's equipment manager) charged with disorderly conduct in Akron, Ohio; Grace busted for slapping a cop at the same gig – a largely ill-humoured tour ended at Winterland on 22 September with a surprise appearance by none other than the band's founder.

But, if anyone thought the second coming of Marty Balin heralded a rapturous resurrection, they would be disappointed. Jefferson Airplane were effectively done; they'd not perform another concert, nor release another album of new material save a record of the Winterland show, for seventeen years.

Perhaps it's the slow decline, rather than the cataclysmic full stop, that explains why Jefferson Airplane and Jefferson Starship so often occupy the same breath, as if one were the logical outcome of the other. And perhaps, in reality, there *was* reason. After all, people change. Much as a great gig by the classic Airplane was so often in the gift of circumstance – each musician's respective condition, the room, the audience, the dope – didn't context govern the broader action or inaction of band members, as the hippie ideal was buried in the sclerotic hardening of the Haight and the blackened ashes of Altamont? As posited in the foreword to this text, in everything save a diminishing corps of characters and a few song reiterations, these two groups were poles apart. As Airplane's last hurrah, *Long John Silver* was a bridge spanning two very different shores. If on one side *Bark* had already shakily signified an identity crisis, *Long John Silver* on the other suggested the predicament had been definitively resolved in transit. Decisions had been taken about where to go, and the crossing would be one-way with no return. With the impetus mainly Paul's and, to a lesser extent, Grace's, Airplane's personality was subsumed. Later that decade Jefferson Starship would rally, aesthetically and, in particular, commercially. But in an odd way, Jefferson Airplane's final studio album was Jefferson Starship's first.

Singles from *Long John Silver*:
'Long John Silver'/'Milk Train' (7-inch '45; *Billboard* Hot 100: 104)
'Twilight Double Leader'/'Trial by Fire' (7-inch '45; did not chart)

'Long John Silver' 4.22 (Casady, Slick)
The album's title track celebrates a perennial pop-cultural favourite: the anti-hero. With his earrings, talking parrots, drunken singing and other clichéd jolly ribaldry, this eponymous buccaneer serves no one, eager to keep well beyond the Establishment's freedom-inhibiting redoubt.

In 'A Child Is Coming', from *Blows Against the Empire,* Grace and Paul suggested non-registration of their baby's birth as a way to keep 'Uncle Samuel' at bay. Here the sentiment is echoed:

> But all men are ruled by a flag or a game
> And he knows nobody's got you if you don't sign your name.

If the 'freedom' theme had been on Grace's mind for a year or more, its clunky manner of expression fell grimly short of the inspired brilliance of which she was capable. Likewise, the music (written by Jack Casady) is busy and clotted, with too much happening at once. Even on the 2020 remaster, Grace's lead vocal sounds hemmed-in and muddy, as if she's been clapped in irons and forced to record her parts from the *Hispaniola's* bilges. Everyone crashes in together, a full-frontal assault from the word go, Jorma's lead and Jack's bass in each other's death-grip across the stereo channels.

Interestingly Grace was positioning Robert Louis Stevenson's fictional pirate as a swashbuckling libertarian – in *Treasure Island* Long John was actually only the ship's cook – not long after she and Paul were allegedly threatening to call their newborn daughter 'God'. They weren't, of course; the fiction came about after Grace's mischievous response to a midwife's question about her baby's name. But the affair lingered in American consciousness for long enough to play to Grace's and Paul's renegade personas; the couple by now not so much a psychedelic John & Yoko as a post-psychedelic Bonnie & Clyde.

'Aerie (Gang of Eagles)' (Slick)

Once more, a lyric celebrates freedom; this time embodied by the eagle, famously symbolic of everything America thinks good about itself. Given Airplane's oft-expressed animus towards their homeland, eulogising the majestic predator as an exemplar of the freedoms they sought was hugely ironic. But like 'Eskimo Blue Day', 'Bear Melt', and a number of songs Grace would pen post-Airplane, 'Aerie' relegates the human species as the inferior to the animal kingdom, as the raptor stares warily down upon his would-be nemesis:

Well you can't fly, human master
No you can't fly – fly by yourself
You can't fly, dying master
Without a rifle on your shelf.

Grace sings powerfully on one of the album's better tracks. Although slightly anonymous – which might be taken as the author's code for 'not as good as classic Airplane' – the instrumental backing of 'Aerie' might feel more at home on a solo album such as *Manhole*. But it's nonetheless pleasingly doomy and portentous, with sonorous black chords from Kaukonen, stolidly heavy drumming from Barbata and Papa John's violin flying overhead, as high as the song's title.

'Twilight Double Leader' 4.42 (Kantner)

Paul's preference for the shouty sci-fi sagas that have now gained ascendancy over earlier masterpieces plummets to rock bottom. 'Twilight Double Leader' is energetic enough, but only in the sense that so is 'Rock and Roll Island'. His songcraft has become lazy, too often falling back for atmosphere on the meaningless buzz-phrases which now lard so much of his work. In preparing this book, the author, rightly or wrongly, chose not to investigate every writer whom Paul idolised, so it's entirely possible that apparently standalone fancies such as 'Determination structure' and 'Citadel redeemer', and indeed the song's title, have been repurposed from the works of Heinlein or any other of Paul's literary heroes. If so, it is all to no avail; they feel thrown in because they happen to fit, to scan, or at best to 'evoke' the 'spirit' of whatever it is he's banging on about. This is thin gruel, and preferably not consumed anywhere near what Kantner had already proved he could achieve.

'Milk Train' 3.18 (Creach, Slick, Roger Spotts)

Another abnormal collaboration for Grace, this time with Papa John and his near-contemporary Roger Hamilton Spotts, a 44-year-old arranger/composer who had worked with Count Basie, Ray Charles, Dizzy Gillespie and Lionel Hampton and whom Creach knew from the old days in L.A. In concert, the bluesy 'Milk Train' not unnaturally showcased Papa John's soaring, sawing fiddle and Jorma's ever-fine guitar, while you can almost see an assertive, sexy Grace as a sassy nightclub dame, throwing the shapes, one hand on her hip, the other clasping a cigarette as she wags an admonishing finger, delivering three verses of barely-disguised innuendo. Fun and inessential.

'The Son of Jesus' 5.27 (Kantner)

If the Daughters of the American Revolution were tottering from the non-scandal attending Paul's own offspring, they were about to take an even bigger hit. And trust Kantner to save the best until last. For years Airplane had baited R.C.A. and Amerika with lyrics dealing, sometimes obliquely, others transparently, with sex and dope; now Paul turns to religion. With 'The Son of Jesus', the former Jesuit student delves into the murky regions that will one day reap millions for Dan Brown and others hypothesising a Nazarene family. Feathers were about to fly.

'This song was saying that if there had been a bastard son of Jesus, God would have loved him just as much as any other of his creatures,' Paul explained in 1984. 'The head of R.C.A. Records was an Italian Catholic afraid that his mother would hear the record.'

The founding of Grunt was supposed to inoculate Airplane from any attempts by an affronted record company to obstruct a release. Unfortunately, distributive heels were firmly dug in, R.C.A. only relenting when, unsurprisingly, they demanded excise of the song's original title, 'The Bastard Son of Jesus'; the removal from the lyrics of the 'B' word; and an alteration to one line: 'So you think young Jesus never balled a lady' became '...smiled a lady'; an absurdity, itself arguably psychotropic enough to have thrown up a red flag in R.C.A.'s boardroom back in 1967.

Relatively intact, the song was powerful and well written, suggesting Kantner had given his words more thought than usual during this period. Nothing could be done about the music, however, which trod the same lumbering path that had become axiomatic of the way Paul now framed most of his lyrics, from the blustering vocal to the chaotic over-arrangement. Paul later acknowledged that the controversial content had made waves, adding tellingly, 'which is sort of what I wanted to do anyway'.

'Easter?' 4.00 (Slick)

You wait years for an Airplane song about religion, then two come along at once. As if God-gate wasn't enough, Grace was going out of her way to let The Man know, in song, exactly what she thought of his doctrinal certainties. In 'Easter?' (original vetoed name: 'Pope Paul') she lets fly at Catholicism, 'stupid Christians' and an organised faith that presides over the death of one man of peace followed by a hundred wars:

> You keep murdering people in his Christian name
> I thought he said that was a sin.

With Grace clearly on the same page as her partner, once again it's a strong lyric, which she spits angrily over – once again – a determinedly dull arrangement. Her own piano comps ploddingly behind two lead instruments, Jorma's guitar and Papa John's violin, both of which make a lot of noise but say very little.

'Trial By Fire' 4.31 (Kaukonen)

Hot Tuna was now a proper band, constantly gigging with and without Airplane and boasting three album releases. The most recent, *Burgers,* definitively killed any idea that the group was a vanity project; that Jorma and Jack should leave the mothership to its own fading devices was only a matter of time.

A trio, with Tuna's regular drummer Sammy Piazza, 'Trial By Fire' is a blessed relief from *Long John Silver's* sonic porridge, featuring Jorma's double-tracked duet with himself. His switchblade electric lead hovers beautifully over his own country-fresh acoustic blues picking, as he delivers a typically reflective, existential lyric about living for the day and the inevitability of the end:

> Gonna move out on the highway, make this moment last
> Till it closes with the future, blending with the past
> Rollin' on and doin' fine, what do you think I see?
> That bony hand comes a'beckoning, saying buddy come go with me.

In the second verse, Jorma addresses someone whose preconceptions are clearly a caution:

> Don't try to tell me just who I am
> When you don't know yourself
> Spend half your time running out on the street

With your mind home on a shelf
Lookin' at me with your eyes full of fire
Like you'd rather be seein' me dead
Lying on the floor with a hole in my face
And a ten gauge shotgun at my head.

Although Jorma and Margareta Kaukonen would not divorce for several years, the union had long been turbulent. Was it fiery enough for the guitarist's combustible words here to be targeted at his wife? In Jorma's memoir *Been So Long,* he tells of a car-crash marriage that was crippled for years before ending in 1983, Margareta addicted to heroin, he a borderline alcoholic with smack on his horizon. For a man who, by his own admission, played marathon sets onstage in order to avoid his significant other, perhaps a temporary, nirvana-like solace was attainable through his music. By now, Jorma was an almost unfailingly excellent songwriter, fast outstripping Captain Kantner himself. As Jorma conceded in his memoir, 'Trial By Fire' is *Long John Silver's* most satisfying performance.

'Alexander The Medium' 6.38 (Kantner)
After the invigorating morning dew of 'Trial by Fire', 'Alexander The Medium' picks its torpid, glutinous way through the cyclopean exteriors that were now so exercising Paul's imaginings. Once again, it's a behemoth lurching from stanza to stanza, as Kantner continues his *Stargate-*stylee wanderings across time, space and weird dimensions, whistling up awkwardly disparate visions of sighing pyramids and 'priests of Karnak and Thebes [walking] through the ocean and the seas'. This is acid sci-fi, but with not a jot of the *frisson* that such an idea might promise.

'Eat Starch Mom' 4.34 (Kaukonen, Slick)
Bolinas had gained a reputation as a haven for reclusive devotees of natural foods and alternative lifestyles. On moving in, Grace couldn't miss the 'hairy armpit' hippies who were her and Paul's new neighbours and how they 'brushed their teeth with duck grease to avoid the preservatives in toothpaste'. The residents also persistently entreated the newcomers not to eat meat, despite Grace questioning why their prissy dietary regime should be given a pass when vegetables, she argued, were no less sentient than any fatted calf.

Unsurprisingly, this preachiness soon wore thin, and within barely two years the family was off back to San Francisco. Meanwhile, Paul erected an electronic gate to evade the neighbourly deliveries of banana bread, and Grace was moved to song. One, originally entitled 'Cannibal Soup', would be released on the Slick/Kantner album *Sunfighter* as 'Silver Spoon'. Another was 'Eat Starch Mom', a rowdy, metallic thumper co-penned, once more unusually, with Jorma, who delivers a crunchingly heavy riff and typically incisive wah-wah soloing.

And there's the rub: despite Grace's lyrics, expectorated with all the bilious contempt the singer can muster, 'Eat Starch Mom' is little more than the riff and the guitar solo seemingly stretched the length of the song. It's a mediocre, unprepossessing slog. With a couple of notable exceptions, sadly it sums up most of *Long John Silver.*

Go ride the music - Live Albums

The concert stage was Jefferson Airplane's natural habitat. It was where the destructive hostilities thrown up around the time of *Surrealistic Pillow* would be channelled into a tension that, on a good night, was as positive as it was creative, the resulting sugar-rush as vocalists and instrumentalists sparked off each other generating electric rock music of rare potency. If Airplane weren't exactly getting along offstage, Fillmore or Avalon audiences would be none the wiser. And if onstage the guitarist and the bassist, unconsciously or intentionally, were making life hard for the drummer, even if he was in bits at the end of every show, prior to 1970's departure Spencer Dryden gave every impression that he was able to take it, his gutsiness invaluable to so many intense and memorable group performances.

Airplane today boast a discography plump with live concert recordings. But despite the many bootlegs and copyright-lapsed radio broadcasts, no Airplane live album comes close to the seminal set from 1968 (released 1969 – appraised earlier) *Bless Its Pointed Little Head.* However, most of Airplane's portfolio of in-concert recordings appears sorely to misrepresent the band's onstage brilliance. Repeated listening reveals that, far from the performances of the singers and instrumentalists, it's often the properties of the live sound-mix prior to mastering that are up for debate.

It's worth noting that Airplane were in their live pomp several years before the 1970s' refinement of onstage monitor speakers. Singers fronting electric rock bands had a particularly raw deal, since they could only hear their vocals (initially amplified through a front-of-house public address system) as the sound reflected back to them from the audience and the hall's rear wall. Governed by the venue's acoustics, the attendant delay often hampered any vocalist trying to stay in tune and to sing rhythmically or harmonically with colleagues who were often – or always, in the case of Airplane – playing deafeningly amplified instruments. At a festival such as Woodstock, with only an exponentially larger congregation and the great outdoors to reverberate against, the problem intensified. Grace Slick, who underwent three procedures to remove nodes from vocal cords run ragged by the exigencies of live performance, lamented the frequent deficiency or absence of monitor speakers: 'With so many performances and my style of shouting out the lyrics as loudly as I could, my voice was suffering... I had to scream every night to hear what notes I was singing over the amplified guitars.'

Maintaining a consistently balanced onstage output was trebly difficult given the three lead singers. Unlike the perfectionists of the art – The Beach Boys, The Byrds, The Mamas & The Papas and Crosby, Stills, Nash & Young – Airplane rarely observed the conventions of vocal harmony. Instead, Kantner, Slick and Balin were more like jazz singers; ducking and diving and bobbing and weaving and leaving the obvious some way behind. While Paul's limited range consigned him mainly to stabilising the lower end, Grace and Marty were daring, unpredictable vocal gymnasts, each enticing the other into following then suddenly swerving away on a different tack altogether. The ad-libs varied wildly night after night, the duo's voices spitting back off each other like neutrons in a fission chain, causing havoc at the mixing desk and likely disappointment for purchasers of any subsequent bootleg. Soundboard recordings, of which 'boots' were many, were particularly prone to pushing the vocals too high up in the mix. Amid such potential for audial meltdown, it was unsurprising that Airplane's singers – and their sound engineers – found the shortfall in onstage monitoring particularly challenging.

An even muddier prospect than coping with the occasionally poor sound is establishing the provenance of all 'live' material claimed to be by Jefferson Airplane. Little publishing or retail control can be exerted over the content of a bootleg; unauthorised record releases have baited artists and industry alike since Dylan's *Great White Wonder* in 1969. And while a certain song, or an entire album, may be attributed in its accompanying publicity to Airplane, reality might prove this anomalous, with said material sometimes the work of a different artist altogether. The problem has intensified, due mainly to the relative ease with which the unscrupulous can push a mismatched and dubious product to a market that will devour anything apparently the work of a famous artist. In this, Jefferson Airplane and their fans have shouldered a heavy load.

The issue is further compounded by the decline of independent specialist collectors' record stores in the face of huge, impersonal online marketplaces. The traditional small dealer would know exactly what was for sale and would advise customers accordingly. Today, the sheer volume of product moved by mouse-click and algorithm makes the sharing of such surgically precise information impossible. Purchasers are therefore forced to take decisions based on peer reviews, which are often neither available nor intelligible. Failing that, it's down to pure gut instinct.

All of these issues must be factored in when discussing Jefferson Airplane's live inventory. The following is a digest of those concert releases the author considers the most interesting, together with track listings. Where practical (and it isn't always, as you'll see), the records are set out in chronological order of performance, beginning with early shows from 1965 featuring Signe Anderson. Individual songs are unpacked for discussion only where they're elsewhere unavailable or hard to find, or where the performance in question is especially noteworthy; a critical breakdown of every interpretation of 'Somebody To Love' would surely test to breaking point both the law of diminishing returns and the reader's patience.

Obviously everything's subjective. In shielding the consumer from the flotsam, digests such as the following can achieve little other than to remind you of the author's own predilections. And it's impossible to list every live compilation, particularly given the many released overseas under license (assuming the producers bothered to seek licensing permission in the first place – which in many cases they probably didn't). Establishing the source of live shows more than half-a-century on can be difficult, so other than basic info provided in album titles and sleeve notes (scarce resources when it comes to bootlegs), I've not dwelt too much on dates and places; it is, after all, the music that matters.

Where a listed album is generally of substandard quality but for one or more exceptional cuts, the caveat is clearly flagged in the review. Otherwise, when investigating live Airplane product, especially if you're buying online, listen to the short soundbites sometimes provided (or seek them on YouTube) and extrapolate accordingly. If this is impossible, keep an eye peeled for visual hints. If you're after, say, a *Live at Monterey* collection – and there are several around purportedly thus – beware of pursuing any CD whose sleeve depicts a big-shouldered, Starship-era Grace Slick montaged together with nondescript, line-conversion Dave Sparts who could be from different bands altogether.

Fly Translove Airways: 1965-1970 Broadcasts (Various)

This 2017 boxed collection comprises five CDs, each claiming to cover a single show or a mix of several. On sight of the cheap-looking, computer-generated box art, it's tempting to dismiss *Fly Translove Airways* as a disposable, unauthorised collection of live cuts hurriedly compiled and probably available elsewhere. A few certainly are; others might well be. Yet while these are sometimes poorly recorded bootlegs, the performances aren't all bad. And one, at least, is indispensable.

Disc 1: Fillmore Auditorium, 4 February 1967:

'Somebody To Love'/'Get Together'/'Let Me In'/'This Is My Love (And I Like It) [sic]'/'White Rabbit'/'Plastic Fantastic Lover'/'She Has Funny Cars'/'Jam'/'3-5 of a Mile In 10 Seconds'/'Fat Angel'.

Disc 2: Family Dog At The Great Highway, 13 June 1969 [sic]:

'The Other Side of This Life'/'Wooden Ships'/'Go Ride The Music'/'Crown of Creation'/'Greasy Heart'/'Good Shepherd'/'Fat Angel'/'Volunteers'/'The Ballad of You and Me and Pooneil'/'Eskimo Blue Day'/'The House at Pooneil Corners'/'Jam'.

Disc 3: Utica, New York, 24 November 1969:

'Somebody To Love'/'Uncle Sam Blues'/'Have You Seen The Saucers'/'Mexico'/'Wooden Ships'/'The Other Side of This Life'/'Nothing'/'Fat Angel'/'Won't You Try-Saturday Afternoon'/'Driftin' Around'/'Greasy Heart'/'The Ballad of You and Me and Pooneil'.

Disc 4: Winterland, San Francisco, 4 October 1970:

'Have You Seen The Saucers'/'Crown of Creation'/'Somebody To Love'/'Mexico'/'Up Or Down'/'Whatever The Old Man Does'/'Emergency'/'Wooden Ships'/'Bludgeon Of A Bluecoat'/'Greasy Heart'/'You Wear Your Dresses Too Short'/'We Can Be Together'/'Volunteers'.

Disc 5: Calliope Warehouse, 6 November 1965; various Fillmore performances broadcast 1966-67:

'It's No Secret'/'Tobacco Road'/'Running Around This World'/'3-5 of a Mile in 10 Seconds'/'Running Around This World'/'Somebody To Love'/'Today'/'Get Together'/'The Other Side of This Life'/'Fat Angel'/'Go to Her'/'She Has Funny Cars'/Interviews.

Disc 2 features the single cut that makes the purchase of this collection essential. The professed date is only partially correct. With Airplane having played and recorded a number of gigs promoted by Chet Helms' Family Dog collective, chronological veracity of each has long been debated. Most of the tracks on Disc 2 were indeed taped on 13 June 1969. However, two – 'The Ballad of You and Me and Pooneil' and 'Eskimo Blue Day' – were recorded the following year. Here the author defers to Craig Fenton and Ralph J Gleason: both have asserted that these renderings of 'Pooneil' and 'Eskimo' were taped on 4 February 1970.

This is important... why? Because the version of 'Pooneil', as captured in Gleason's video and again in the excellent authorised Airplane documentary DVD *Fly Jefferson Airplane*, is not only the final footage extant (at time of writing) of the band in its classic lineup – Spencer Dryden departed that very month – but it is also, in the author's opinion, Airplane's greatest single live performance on record. The old concert stalwart receives its most scorching reading of all, by a band soon to be unrecognisable yet for now absolutely smoking. The sheer firepower and excitement of the playing are jaw-dropping, notwithstanding Grace's and Paul's somewhat stoned dispositions. At 7.53, it's of average length – the band were known to stretch 'Pooneil' to eleven or fifteen minutes onstage – and it's just right, with a fine Casady bass solo and coruscating, perfectly-constructed closing statements from Kaukonen that launched a thousand air-guitar solos in my bedroom alone. At the traps, for a man already at the end of his tether and about to be dismissed anyway, Spencer is playing his heart out. If offstage Airplane were falling apart, the onstage evidence herein suggests the polar opposite.

Slightly re-ordered, with stated recording dates similarly wayward, Disc 2 is available elsewhere as *Family Dog At The Great Highway Sf–June 11th 1969* [sic] – a release notable only for the use on the sleeve of the *Life* magazine 'box' photo.

On Disc 3, Craig Fenton has declared that night's 'Fat Angel' to be among Airplane's finest versions of Donovan's song. Sadly whoever recorded it for this release (and possibly other live compilations) must have had the tape running too slowly, since Paul's voice has apparently sped up and leapt an octave or two. It's as if someone spirited away the band's stash of nitrous oxide and replaced it with a tank of helium. If you can get past the Chipmunks-style vocal, Craig's appraisal might be about right.

One day, post-Airplane, Joey Covington would hone his songwriting craft to some success. On the evidence of his 1970 product, not to mention his awkward, parentheses-strewn naming conventions, it's fair to say that he still had some way to go. Listening to 'Whatever The Old Man Does (Is Right)' and '(The Man) Bludgeon Of A Bluecoat', the clunkily-titled, Covington-penned tracks on Disc 4, it's tempting to fancy that Spencer Dryden's replacement arrived at the Big House with the music industry equivalent of a pre-nup; as if the price Joey levied for favouring the band's drum stool obliged Airplane to play his songs, irrespective of whether his mother ought to have allowed them out to play in the first place.

Proving that democracy isn't always what it's cracked up to be, Covington's execrable 'Thunk' was lurking with intent to besmirch the forthcoming *Bark*. Left off the same L.P., 'Whatever' and 'Bludgeon' were no better: lumpen evidence of the markedly different musical and personal style Covington brought to Airplane in Dryden's wake. The man-child of Grace's 'Lather', the Frank Zappa fan unafraid to introduce *musique concrète* to Airplane's generous palette, Spencer's approach to life was as laid-back as his percussive touch was deft and instinctive. In its turn, this was a perfect reflection of the 'classic' Airplane's own fluid, arrangement-lite anti-ethos. By contrast, Joey was all-action, no-nonsense, the pushy fratboy jock in the linebacker's shirt bashing his skins to a 4/4 talc. If Spencer epitomised mid-period Airplane at their most elegantly louche, Joey ably represented their later, cruder but undoubtedly effective hard-rock transformation.

He was clearly assertive enough to talk his new employers into performing his songs. He even got to sing on them. Delivered via a tuneless, faux-soulboy shout so painfully strained that Grace's polyps must have been queueing for timeshares, 'Whatever The Old Man Does (Is Right)' contains the most boorishly misogynist lyrics in Airplane's canon. The arrangement is instantly disposable, a listless, sub-soundcheck boogie that Status Quo wouldn't cross the road for, with soloing from Jorma so half-hearted he might have been auditioning for the Archies.

Joey's second donation to the set demonstrates a contrasting measure of political rectitude, even if titling concision still evades him. 'The Man (The Bludgeon Of A Bluecoat)' references the death of a Chicano civil rights activist, Rubén Salazar, following a tear-gas assault courtesy of the L.A. County Sheriff's Department. It's another bludgeoning rocker, if perhaps a little more Airplane-y in style than earlier, and not entirely unpleasant. However, whatever goodwill is banked by way of the right-on messaging and a properly fiery Kaukonen solo – the guitarist is in pretty good shape for most of this Winterland set – the account is immediately overdrawn by the hoarse, offkey croaking of Covington's dreadful lead vocal.

Another track shaved from *Bark* was Peter Kaukonen's 'Up Or Down', which is little more than a semi-funky vehicle for Marty's soulful testifying and an aggressive tour-de-tom-toms from a Keith Moon-channelling Covington. It's a mediocre if energetic slab of filler, not a million miles from Marty's R'n'B workout 'You Wear Your Dresses Too Short'. Disc 4 is available elsewhere as Disc 3 of the triple-CD set *Jefferson Airplane: Transmission Impossible*.

The first three tracks of Disc 5 were recorded at Bill Graham's earliest rock show: the appeal party for the San Francisco Mime Troupe at the Calliope Warehouse. They also form Airplane's first documented setlist. Marty Balin sounds powerful, his vocal moves already road-tested prior to founding Airplane, while the band exudes confidence and enthusiasm on a recording that's better than it ought to be. The interviews at the end of the disc are anachronisms: Bill Thompson, Paul and Grace patiently tick the boxes on a Dutch journalist's predictable interrogation at 1970's Kralingen Festival.

Live At The Fillmore Auditorium: Signe's Farewell (15 October 1966)

'Jam'/'3-5 of a Mile In 10 Seconds'/'Runnin' Around This World'/'Tobacco Road'/'Come Up The Years'/'Go To Her'/'Fat Angel'/'And I Like It'/'Midnight Hour'/Goodbye To Signe/'Chauffeur Blues'/'High Flyin' Bird'/Goodbye To Signe 2.

Live At The Fillmore Auditorium: Grace's Debut (16 October 1966)

'The Other Side of This Life'/'Let's Get Together'/'Let Me In'/'Don't Let Me Down'/'Run Around'/'It's No Secret'/'Tobacco Road'/'Kansas City'/'Bringing Me Down'/'And I Like It'/'High Flyin' Bird'/'Thing'/'3-5 of a Mile In 10 Seconds'.

Live At The Fillmore Auditorium: We Have Ignition (25-27 November 1966)

Disc 1: 'Plastic Fantastic Lover'/'High Flyin' Bird'/'Bringing Me Down'/'D.C.B.A.-25'/'Go To Her'/'My Best Friend'/'White Rabbit'/'It's No Secret'/'She Has Funny Cars'/'3-5 of a Mile In 10 Seconds'/'The Other Side of This Life'
Disc 2: 'Tobacco Road'/'J. P. P. Mc Step B. Blues'/'She Has Funny Cars'/'Fat Angel'/'Plastic Fantastic Lover'/'In The Morning'/'3-5 of a Mile In 10 Seconds'/'White Rabbit'/'Plastic Fantastic Lover'/'In The Morning'/'Let Me In'/'High Flyin' Bird'/'She Has Funny Cars'/'Today'/'It's No Secret'/'My Grandfather's Clock'/'The Other Side of This Life'.

Return To The Matrix (01 February 1968)

Disc 1: 'Somebody To Love'/'Young Girl Sunday Blues'/'She Has Funny Cars'/'Two Heads'/'Martha'/'Kansas City'/'The Other Side of This Life'/'Today'/'Won't You Try-Saturday Afternoon'/'It's No Secret'/'Blues From An Airplane'
Disc 2: 'Watch Her Ride'/'Plastic Fantastic Lover'/'White Rabbit'/'3-5 of a Mile In 10 Seconds'/'Share A Little Joke'/'Ice Cream Phoenix'/'Fat Angel'/'The Ballad of You and Me and Pooneil'.

In 2010 a Sony subsidiary, Collectors' Choice Music, released a handsome quartet of early-ish live Airplane material. Containing mostly excellent, well-recorded performances curated by Gordon Anderson, Craig Fenton, Dave Tamarkin and Richie Unterberger, beautifully packaged and each illuminated by Fenton's scholarly sleevenotes, the full set shows the distinct progressions the band made from Signe Anderson's departure, through Grace Slick's arrival and on to early 1968, when Airplane really began to hit their stride.

The first CD marks Signe's final concert. Following Bill Graham's arch announcement ('Candidates for the sexual freedom league... Jefferson Airplane!') the band pitches straight into the obligatory extended jam, a lengthy improvised set-piece usually reserved for later in the show when the musicians are nicely warmed up. As with most S.F. bands of the period, Airplane's onstage song sequencing was tentative at best; Paul's pre-show setlist was always subject to instant reshuffling depending on the ever-shifting variables of live performance.

For most of Grace Slick's maiden performance, captured on the second CD, she's the wide-eyed newcomer anxious not to rock the boat. By the end, no one can doubt that Grace doesn't just replace Signe Anderson, she's steering Airplane along another path altogether. She generates energy and tone the equal of her predecessor, but while both vocalists boast pipes of a similarly high wattage, Grace's singing is by far the less mannered, unburdened with the heavy vibrato which characterised Signe's more knowing style of crying the blues.

Listen to their respective readings of 'High Flyin' Bird', especially its third verse: Signe takes hers with a growly ululation which, though indisputably powerful, sounds contrived, a white woman consciously singing black music and in the process overcooking it. By contrast, Grace, having kept her powder dry for most of her Airplane debut, suddenly lets rip with an unrestrained shriek that rockets into the Fillmore's rafters, ineluctably punching her identity into Airplane's front line with the force of a Minuteman. Within a few daring bars of potent musicality, she's assuring her new colleagues, just before the end of her first show, that yes, I can help you with the same old stuff if you want; but, trust me, together we can do so much more.

Grace had been with the band for just a month when *We Have Ignition* was recorded at the Fillmore. By now, the rocketry is having its effect; the musicians and singers are gelling beautifully, each indispensable member of the classic sextet playing his or her part in propelling Airplane into regions little explored by other groups. The third CD is noteworthy for including the only known concert performance of Paul's exquisite 'D.C.B.A.-25' and for one of only a few readings of the Skip Spence gem inexplicably dropped from *Surrealistic Pillow*, 'J. B. B. Mc Step B. Blues'.

By 1 February 1968 and the fourth CD, Marty has sold his share of the Matrix. And after months of annealing in the furnaces of the Fillmore, the Avalon and Winterland, Airplane have already outgrown their old alma mater.

The performance is superb, as if they're trapped in a pressure cooker, the relatively small space struggling to contain the band's bulging, percussive tsunami of sound. Of special note are the first and only documented live readings of 'Blues From An Airplane', 'Share A Little Joke' and 'Ice Cream Phoenix' – the latter the launchpad for a superb ten-minute jam – and Grace and Marty cuddling up in an intimate version of 'Today' that comes closer than any in spirit and uplift to the sublime studio original. With the best in this fine quartet of CDs saved for last, *Return to the Matrix* showcases as well as any other live album where the Airplane had come from, and where they were bound.

Disc 1 of *We Have Ignition* is available elsewhere as Disc 1 of the triple-CD set *Jefferson Airplane: Transmission Impossible (Eat To The Beat ETTB109)* and as titled *Live at the Fillmore – November 25th 1966 (Keyhole KHCD9017)*.

Live in San Francisco 1966
'It's No Secret'/'White Rabbit'/'Don't Let Me Down'/'Somebody To Love'/'The Other Side of This Life'/'And I Like It [This Is My Life]'/'Don't Slip Away'/'Let's Get Together'/'Tobacco Road'/'3-5 of a Mile In 10 Seconds'/'My Best Friend'/'Come Back Baby (Jorma's Blues)'/'She Has Funny Cars'/'Bringing Me Down'/'Today'/'Runnin' 'Round This World'/'Thing'/'Plastic Fantastic Lover'/'High Flyin' Bird'.

Inexpensive at time of writing, this is a bootleg CD with no information other than a tracklist and, unforgivably, two anomalous pics of Jefferson Starship on the inner sleeve. Otherwise, this is an excellent and transformative set, despite occasional gremlins and mysterious fade-outs. There are too many of the latter to convince as a credible playing sequence, although the sonic quality and the band's enthusiasm are uniform throughout. Airplane played at least three dates at the Fillmore at the end of November 1966, so perhaps this is a meaty compendium from all five shows (the pre-recorded 'take-off' SFX intro appears twice). Particularly thrilling versions of 'It's No Secret', 'The Other Side of This Life' and 'Somebody To Love', with Marty Balin in pugnaciously call-&-response mood, amply demonstrate how Airplane, Grace's feet barely under the table and *Surrealistic Pillow* completed only days before, was fast escaping its polite folk-rock roots for intelligent, assertive, kick-ass rock'n'roll.

Cleared for Take Off (Winterland 10-12 March 1967)
'3-5 of a Mile In 10 Seconds'/'Don't Let Me Down'/'Don't Slip Away'/'She Has Funny Cars'/'Get Together'/'High Flying Bird'/'It's No Secret'/'Jorma's Blues (Come Back Baby)'/'Plastic Fantastic Lover'/'Running 'Round The World'/'Somebody To Love – Leave You Alone'/'The Other Side of This Life'/'Thing'/'Tobacco Road'/'Today'/'White Rabbit'/'You're Bringing Me Down'/'My Best Friend'.

127

Don't be put off by the insert's ridiculous 'Live in 1961' claim or some inconsistencies in track listings. Taped over three consecutive March 1967 nights three months before Monterey and despite variable audio quality, the band is on fire, whacking out performances that in places are superior to those of the great festival itself. Especially noteworthy are 'The Other Side of This Life' and a steamrolling 'Somebody To Love', here extended with Marty's splenetic soul shouter 'Leave Me Alone'. Though uniformly good, the selections are randomly chosen across the three nights, with the CD's final cut 'My Best Friend' mistakenly entitled 'You're My Best Friend', presumably to excite Queen fans. Few Airplane tunes were less suited to a dizbusting finale than Skip Spence's gossamer pop song from *Surrealistic Pillow* – and on the night it wasn't – but the last date of that Winterland run was the final time the band played 'My Best Friend' onstage.

Live at the Monterey Festival (17 June 1967)

'Somebody To Love'/'The Other Side of This Life'/'White Rabbit'/'High Flying Bird'/'Today'/'She Has Funny Cars'/'Young Girl Sunday Blues'/'The Ballad of You and Me and Pooneil'.

When John Phillips and his L.A. set came talent-scouting around the Bay Area for the Monterey International Pop Festival, naturally Airplane was first on their list. With 'Somebody To Love', 'White Rabbit' and *Surrealistic Pillow* already substantial hits, the first of the 1960s triumvirate of major American outdoor rock events, later immortalised on film by D. A. Pennebaker for multinational consumption as *Monterey Pop,* allowed Airplane to set out its onstage stall to its biggest audience yet.

For students of West Coast acid rock, *Live at the Monterey Festival* is a seminal release and an indispensable addition to any Airplane archive. 'A perfect example of what the world is coming to' – you can see the twinkle in Jerry Garcia's eye as he wryly introduces his friends to the stage – the band is generally in fine form, submitting a truncated set of five songs from the first two albums and two to be unveiled on the forthcoming *After Bathing At Baxter's.* The sole non-album piece is a great version of 'The Other Side of This Life', featuring brilliant bass and lead guitar. The finale, an eleven-minute 'The Ballad of You and Me and Pooneil', is barely a month old and is tentative at first, betraying the song's youth. After Jack's solo bridge slips into an insistent walking bassline, however, the band hit a splendid groove, Jorma's solos quoting from Willie Dixon's 'Spoonful' – a song that was becoming a vehicle for extended live jamming by the guitarist's heroes, Cream – and pre-empting licks Kaukonen would later dig out for 'Fat Angel'.

On the release of *Monterey Pop* in December 1968, the media-fabricated Cult of Slick became farcical. In the final cut, footage of Airplane's performance of 'Today' was reduced to a single moody closeup... of the wrong vocalist. *De facto* lead singer Marty is never seen; instead the camera lingers lovingly on Grace, even though her lip movements – she's actually singing backup – suggest a bad mime from an old episode of *Thank Your Lucky Stars*. Given the wide exposure afforded by the movie, Marty was miffed, and rightly so. Pennebaker's later excuse was that no one onstage but Grace was lit during the song, effectively shifting the blame to the festival's organisers, if not Airplane's own lighting crew. But it's vanishingly difficult to believe that no spotlight, still less one manned by Team Airplane, was shone on Marty while he so obviously took the lead throughout. Even if no one from Airplane's road crew could be held accountable, the incident was just another reason for Marty feeling cold-shouldered by his own creation. Viewed today, the blunder is unforgivable, and it's sad to think that it contributed to the bad blood that eventually killed off the band.

Incidentally, this CD release on the Thunderbolt label features a bland sleeve pic of Airplane onstage. It's an outdoor gig, but nowhere near Monterey; the same shot is used in the booklet for *At Golden Gate Park*, reviewed below. Don't be put off; despite the anomalous cover, the music within is the real McCoy. As Craig Fenton wrote, this Thunderbolt release is 'the only version [of Monterey] that every fan should own'.

Feed Your Head Live '67 – '69 (various dates)

'The Other Side of This Life'/'Somebody To Love'/'Plastic Fantastic Lover'/'White Rabbit'/'3-5 of a Mile In 10 Seconds'/'She Has Funny Cars'/'High Flyin' Bird'/'It's No Secret'/'Today'/'My Best Friend'/'Don't Slip Away'/'This Is My Life and I Like It' [sic].

Somebody To Love (various dates)

'White Rabbit'/'Somebody To Love'/'Plastic Fantastic Lover'/'She Has Funny Cars'/'It's No Secret'/'My Best Friend'/'Don't Slip Away'/'The Other Side of This Life'/'High Flyin' Bird'/'3-5 Of A Mile in 10 Seconds'/'You're So Loose'/'What You're Askin''/'Would You Love Me'/'Ride'/'This Is My Life [sic]'/'What Do You Want With Me' [sic – She Has Funny Cars]/'Get Together'/'Today'.

Jefferson Airplane (various dates)

'White Rabbit'/'Somebody To Love'/'She Has Funny Cars'/'Ride'/'High Flyin' Bird'/'Would You Love Me'/'My Best Friend'/'Plastic Fantastic Lover'/'Don't Slip Away'/'3-5 of a Mile In 10 Seconds'/'It's No Secret'/'The Other Side of This Life'/'Today'/'What You're Askin''/'You're So Loose'/'This Is My Life [sic]'.

Examples of cheaply produced compilation CDs. They're effectively bootlegs, although this classification would apply to many of the Airplane records listed in this chapter, and plenty more whose inclusion herein is thwarted by word count limitations, readers' patience and the amount of product pushed, often with undue haste, out to market. They turn up in unlikely places, such as street-market video stalls and old-fashioned bric-a-brac stores (not to mention the murkier reaches of the internet) and rarely contain any sleeve information other than a retrodden press release if you're lucky. Some tracks aren't even by Airplane.

Distributed by Prism Leisure PLC (which seems no longer to exist) *Feed Your Head* is mainly to be avoided, as nearly everything's available elsewhere and isn't always even 'live' to begin with – it's merely a multi-source mashup from *Monterey, Bless Its Pointed Little Head, Jefferson Airplane Takes Off* and *Surrealistic Pillow*. The one uncertainty is 'And I Like it' (erroneously titled 'This Is My Life'): it's definitely live, possibly taped at Winterland on 3 March 1967, and it's one of the better versions of an admittedly mediocre song. (A Wikipedia entry states that it's the studio version of the track from *JATO*, but this idea is discredited by Marty's stylised vocal and a brief closing moment of distant applause that probably didn't originate on the studio mixing desk). The CD is really for completists-stroke-obsessives only. Try to find this version of 'And I Like it' as a download, then save your money and get the proper stuff listed above.

Live at the Fillmore East (3-4 May 1968)
'The Ballad of You and Me and Pooneil'/'She Has Funny Cars'/'It's No Secret'/'Won't You Try-Saturday Afternoon'/'Greasy Heart'/'Star Track'/'Wild Tyme'/'White Rabbit'/'Thing'/'Today'/'The Other Side of This Life'/'Fat Angel'/'Watch Her Ride'/Closing comments/'Somebody To Love'.

This inconsistent set was taped from Airplane's first weekend of shows at what would become one of the band's favourite venues. The big set-piece jam, called 'Thing' for the final time, is based on the same four ascending notes which will fuel 'Bear Melt', to be recorded at the same ballroom that November. Unlike the latter, this 'Thing' is all-instrumental, and it cooks. 'The Other Side of This Life' gets a radical overhaul, the band exploring the funk possibilities of Fred Neil's song. For once, it doesn't come off, the abrupt climax suggesting the band feel the same way, but fair play to them for trying. They make up for it with excellent versions of 'Fat Angel' and 'It's No Secret'.

Nothing In Particular: The Lost 1968 Dutch Broadcast (Concertgebouw, Amsterdam, 15 September 1968, plus various other dates)
'Won't You Try-Saturday Afternoon'/'Rock Me Baby'/'(If You Feel) Like China Breaking'/'Crown of Creation'/'Today'/'Somebody To Love'/'Plastic Fantastic Lover'/'Nothing in Particular Jam'/'In Time'/'The Ballad of You and Me and Pooneil'/ 'White Rabbit'/'Somebody To Love'/'Crown of Creation'.

Nothing in Particular has more interest value than listener appeal. At the time of writing, the sole available live document from Airplane's autumn 1968

European tour with The Doors, it hints at what was missed by young Brits such as the author, forbidden by parental fiat from attending the previous weekend's Roundhouse shows. While the Concertgebouw performance is generally good, it's badly compromised by the recording, taped from the audience and probably from the rear of the auditorium. The sonic effect is that of hearing an Airplane tribute band playing very loudly in a cavernous hall from three streets away.

The obligatory jam is the album's title track. Prefaced by two seconds of Jack strumming an audience-requested 'Louie Louie', it meanders along for ten minutes with similar passages to, but lacking the uncannily coherent structure of, its *Bless Its Pointed Little Head* counterpart, 'Bear Melt'. Sadly there's no aural evidence of Jim Morrison dancing onstage during 'Plastic Fantastic Lover', although Marty Balin helpfully alludes to the blitzed Doors' singer's infamous 'pinwheel' moves from the earlier show. A decent 'The Ballad of You and Me and Pooneil' is carelessly faded off at the end, and the Dutch concert set is incongruously topped off with three recordings from the Smothers Brothers' TV show, including the 'Crown of Creation' in which Grace performed in blackface.

This album is available elsewhere as Disc 2 of the triple-CD set *Jefferson Airplane: Transmission Impossible.*

More Head (various dates)

'Fat Angel'/'Rock Me Baby'/'White Rabbit'/'Somebody To Love'/'The Ballad of You and Me and Pooneil'/'The House at Pooneil Corners'.

The BMG-Heritage CD reissue of *Bless Its Pointed Little Head* in 2004 included three tracks left off the 1969 vinyl: 'Today', 'Watch Her Ride' and 'Won't You Try'. Given the length of the average Airplane show of the time, the question's begged: what happened to everything else? This charmlessly titled, vinyl-only 2013 boot redresses the balance a little more. All tracks were taped at Fillmore West on 26 October 1968, of which just one is identical to that on *BIPLH*. Here Jorma's reading of 'Rock Me Baby', edited for the earlier album, receives its full eight minutes 49 seconds. Unsurprisingly given its *Pointed Head* provenance, it's this bootleg's best quality cut; the crispness and clarity of B. B. King's old blues standard are particularly impressive.

Speaking of editing, as 'Somebody To Love' finishes, Grace announces no less than a 45-minute version of the two Pooneils. Unusually, Airplane adjoin 'Ballad' with its evil twin, 'Corners'. (The marriage should have been obvious, but for some reason, the two songs were infrequently performed together). With the whole thing running a bit over fifteen minutes, either Grace misread her instrumentalists' stamina that night, or the rest of the music is on a studio floor somewhere. A word on the sleeve: it's the *BIPLH* cover, crudely despoiled with a thought bubble containing the childlike figures from the poster that accompanied the original vinyl L.P.'s U.S. edition. Presumably the images here

131

represent whatever blobby lifeforms were inhabiting Jack Casady's comatose dreams. It's the nastiest bowdlerisation of somebody else's art since Marcel Duchamp daubed a moustache on the Mona Lisa, and nowhere near as funny.

At Golden Gate Park (7 May 1969)
'The Other Side of This Life'/'Somebody To Love'/'The Farm'/'Greasy Heart'/'Good Shepherd'/'Plastic Fantastic Lover'/'Uncle Sam Blues'/'Volunteers'/'White Rabbit'/'Won't You Try'/'Saturday Afternoon'/'Jam'/'We Can Be Together'/'3-5 Of A Mile in 10 Seconds'.

The occasional concert at Golden Gate Park's Polo Field – site of the famous Be-in of January 1967 – was a popular way for the Airplane and other S.F. bands to get down among the kids and play real good for free. On this evidence the performance feels slightly bloodless, until you factor in the great outdoors and the attendant problems of electric audio waves dispersing to the four winds like spores from a puffball. If the sound could be better, this long-bootlegged set is evidence of a decent workout for the Airplane ahead of the Big One. Much as Chip Monck will three months later up in Woodstock, a well-refreshed Grace takes good-humoured M.C. duties, and the band seem to be enjoying themselves.

Pay no mind to the track-listing on the sleeve of the 2006 Charly CD release; the set finale is actually a ripping '3-5 of a Mile In 10 Seconds'. At the end of 'We Can Be Together', the band plainly encountering sound problems, Paul announces 'Mexico', but the 1970 single never appears. If the band had played it – and the onstage confusion makes it impossible to tell what might have been deleted – this would have been 'Mexico's first performance.

The Woodstock Experience (17 August 1969)
'Intro'/'The Other Side of This Life'/'Somebody To Love'/'3-5 of a Mile In 10 Seconds'/'Won't Try-Saturday Afternoon'/'Eskimo Blue Day'/'Plastic Fantastic Lover'/'Wooden Ships'/'Uncle Sam Blues'/'Volunteers'/'The Ballad of You and Me and Pooneil'/'Come Back Baby'/'White Rabbit'/'The House at Pooneil Corners'.

The complete *The Woodstock Experience* is a 10-CD box set of live recordings, all available individually, from 1969's Woodstock Music & Arts Fair. The box encompasses some of the festival's more visible acts, featuring complete sets by Airplane, Janis Joplin, Santana, Johnny Winter and Sly & The Family Stone (but not Jimi Hendrix, whose part-routine, part-extraordinary performance is already captured in full on a separate CD). An unusual feature, at least for a live collection, are the additions of the respective artists' concurrent studio albums, providing a useful opportunity to compare the equivalent Woodstock performances. In Airplane's case, the studio set was *Volunteers,* whose completion, though not release, almost coincided with the festival.

The band had mixed feelings about Woodstock. Paul was unimpressed; he tried hard, not entirely successfully, to have Airplane expunged from the documentary movie. Jack told Jeff Tamarkin: 'It's not my favourite performance... Everybody's dog tired, out of tune and had been awake for about 24 hours... I guess we played OK.' Marty took the broad view, beyond Woodstock's immediate shortcomings: 'It was a mess for our performance, but it was the beginning of what music can do politically and as a force.' Grace, who admits to having a bladder 'the size of a dime', lamented the washroom facilities. If in the movie footage the singer looks uncharacteristically washed out, it's hardly surprising: booked to appear at 9pm on festival Saturday, Airplane were only able to take the stage at 7.30 the following morning. The band had been obliged to muddle through the night on rations of fresh fruit, cheese, wine, weed and, courtesy of the ubiquitous Owsley, the finest giveaway acid. Despite the uncertain bathroom arrangements, in her memoir, Grace would praise Woodstock as 'a magnificent symbol of an era... the spirit was so powerful it overrode all technical considerations'.

Critical response to Airplane's Woodstock set has been just as varied. To these ears, they're okay, if far from their best; a reasonable exposition of Airplane's famed live 'sheets of sound'. Augmented by Nicky Hopkins' unobtrusive yet crucially important piano, the band is undoubtedly powerful and tight as a nut, without being so tensely strung that the usual free flow of ideas is impeded. There's a decent twenty-minute 'Wooden Ships'; clearly, the previous night's *al fresco f*east had put the band in the mood to blow. Although Spencer professed to share Grace's early reservations, the drummer is nonetheless muscular and crisp; on the Jorma-arranged blues standard 'Come Back Baby', his thunderous intro sounds ironically like Joey Covington, who had already played onstage with Airplane and would be granted permanent residence of the band's drum stool within the year.

At the Family Dog Ballroom (September 1969)
'The Ballad of You and Me and Pooneil'/'Good Shepherd'/'We Can Be Together'/'Somebody To Love'/'The Farm'/'Crown of Creation'/'Come Back Baby'/'Wooden Ships'/'Volunteers'/'Jam' (featuring Jerry Garcia).

A generally decent performance by the classic lineup, plus an appearance in the closing 26-minute jam by Jerry Garcia moonlighting from The Grateful Dead. Improvs of that length don't always come off, especially when a regular band who know each other inside-out are augmented from outside. Happily, Jerry was virtually an Airplane insider, his rapport with Jorma going back to the guitarslingers' coffee-bar days. The musical understanding realises an extended piece that works, despite an amalgam of licks we've heard elsewhere; in places, Jerry's twinkling co-lead seems to want to head out to 'Dark Star' territory, while Jorma and Paul pull in passages familiar from some of Airplane's longer readings of 'The Ballad of You and Me and Pooneil'. No matter: it's a largely enjoyable romp; following a brief drum solo at 23:00, it all finishes with everyone channelling Chuck Berry anyway.

Nb: a Gleason family DVD, *A Night at the Family Dog,* includes a lengthy closing jam which also features Jerry Garcia (alongside Carlos Santana and a couple of Carlos' percussionists). It's also pretty good, but it's from a later gig.

Sweeping Up the Spotlight: Live at the Fillmore East 1969 (28-29 November 1969)
'Volunteers'/'Good Shepherd'/'Plastic Fantastic Lover'/'Uncle Sam Blues'/'3-5 of a Mile In 10 Seconds'/'You Wear Your Dresses Too Short'/'Come Back Baby'/'Won't You Try'/'Saturday Afternoon'/'The Ballad of You and Me and Pooneil'/'White Rabbit'/'Crown of Creation'/'The Other Side of This Life'.

As an onstage testament of time and place, *Sweeping Up the Spotlight,* taped just one month before Altamont, is probably only surpassed by *Bless Its Pointed Little Head.* This Fillmore East set lacks the silky tactility of Airplane's greatest concert record, but for sheer intensity, passion and verve there's little else among mid-to-late-period, classic-lineup Airplane live albums to touch it.

'Volunteers' sets a benzedrine-fuelled pace, Grace and Marty tossing the vocalising back and forth like a pair of quarterbacks with the nuclear football. If by this time Jorma and Jack really were ganging up on Spencer onstage, the drummer acquits himself remarkably well, responding in kind to the furious patterns laid down by his associates. By the end, a banging 'Other Side', the rhythm section's eating through the Fillmore stage, while Jorma's soloing stings like a hornets' nest in a blizzard of cocaine.

It's a shame that whoever chose the sleeve pics for this BMG-Legacy CD couldn't identify Spencer Dryden from Joey Covington. When *Sweeping* was released in 2007, most of its material was unavailable elsewhere; 'Good Shepherd' and 'Plastic Fantastic Lover' were already included on BMG-Heritage's CD reissue of *Volunteers.*

Up Against the Wall... (various dates)
'We Can Be Together'/'Volunteers'/'Eskimo Blue Day'/'Mexico'/'Somebody To Love'/'Wooden Ships'/'Plastic Fantastic Lover'/'Emergency'/'The Ballad of You and Me and Pooneil'.

I found this 12-inch vinyl 'boot' in a north London record store in 1971. The album came with zero information other than track titles, although forensic digging has since revealed that its nine cuts were recorded over two PBS TV specials: *A Night at Family Dog* ('Ballad' and 'Eskimo') and *Go Ride the Music* (all else taped at Pacific High in San Francisco). The latter recordings are enjoyably punchy, while the Family Dog material, as described above, is essential. As usual in the feverish wild-west world of the archive, everything here is available elsewhere. Both sets can also be found on a Gleason-family

DVD, *Go Ride the Music.* The two Family Dog cuts feature Spencer Dryden shortly before he quit Airplane; by contrast, Joey Covington drums on everything else. Despite the Pacific High material dating from before Spencer left, this may have been Joey's first time playing with the band. The set also includes one of the Airplane's earliest readings of Balin's R'n'B workout, 'Emergency', a funky, gutsily-sung throwaway in which Marty, with babe-magnet *braggadocio,* casts himself as the love doctor:

> Tell me where it hurts, girl
> and I'll make it go away...

Stoney Brook 1970 (Stoney Brook University, NY, 1 March 1970)

'Volunteers'/'Somebody To Love'/'The Other Side of This Life'/'Mexico'/'Come Back Baby'/'White Rabbit'/'3-5 of a Mile In 10 Seconds'/'Crown of Creation'/'Good Shepherd'/'Jam'/'Have You Seen the Saucers'/'We Can Be Together'/'Volunteers'/'The Ballad of You and Me and Pooneil'.

Hyped as a return to form following Altamont and Spencer's exit, this double CD suffers badly from poor or non-existent onstage monitoring, the vocalists pulled too far up in the mix. Apparently, the band were having sound problems on the night. Underneath it all, the instrumental performance on *Stoney Brook* is decent enough, but with bad audio and no surprises, it's inessential.

Thirty Seconds Over Winterland (Auditorium Theatre, Chicago, 24-25 August 1972; Winterland Ballroom, San Francisco, 21-22 September 1972)

'Have You Seen The Saucers'/'Feel So Good'/'Crown of Creation'/'When The Earth Moves Again'/'Milk Train'/'Trial by Fire'/'Twilight Double Leader'.

Last Flight: The Winterland Arena (22 September 1972)

Introduction by Bill Graham/'Somebody To Love'/'Twilight Double Leader'/'Wooden Ships'/'Milk Train'/'Blind John'/'Come Back Baby'/'The Son of Jesus'/'Long John Silver'/'When the Earth Moves Again'/'Papa John's Down Home Blues'/'Eat Starch Mom'/'John's Other'/'Trial by Fire'/'Law Man'/'Have You Seen The Saucers'/'Aerie (Gang of Eagles)'/'Feel So Good'/'Crown of Creation'/'Walking the Tou Tou'/'Medley: Diana/Volunteers'.

1973's *Thirty Seconds Over Winterland,* officially the final Airplane release before the 1989 reunion, is no *Bless Its Pointed Little Head,* but it does showcase a live unit that's undoubtedly tight and powerful. It's a perfectly decent live album and, in places ('Feel So Good', in particular) quite thrilling. Since *Last Flight's* release in 2007, received wisdom has it that the double CD contains the same performances, and more, as the vinyl original. If only it were that simple; the earlier *Thirty Seconds* L.P. mixed'n'matched recordings from the Chicago Auditorium in August 1972 and the Winterland Ballroom a month later. By contrast, the CD was extended to cover the whole of the San Francisco concert only, inexplicably losing the encore: Grace's peculiar 'Dress Rap' segueing into Marty's sock-it-to-me soul shouter 'You Wear Your Dresses Too Short'. The latter is available on the boxed collection, *Jefferson Airplane Loves You*, reviewed below. The original *Thirty Seconds* is much the better recording.

Marty had been an unscheduled guest at Winterland, the first time he'd performed with his old bandmates-cum-nemeses since Thanksgiving 1970. Whether the brief non-aggression pact suggested a broader thaw in the relationship is unlikely, but given what was to come, the poignancy of Marty's return was intensified by degrees. Could he, or anybody on that famous San Francisco stage on 22 September 1972, have foreseen that this would effectively be Jefferson Airplane's swansong, with no more activity under that name until the reunion 17 years later? Perhaps Marty's inner voices were telling him something.

In 1994, the legal entity still known as Jefferson Airplane sued Berkeley Systems, the firm behind the big-selling 'After Dark' screensaver. The claimants accused the software developer of lifting the 'Flying Clock-Toasters' illustration from the sleeve of *Thirty Seconds Over Winterland* for its 1989 product. The case looked cut and dried, despite Berkeley pleading ignorance of the original cover imagery. The firm's apparent deceit finally held, while the Airplane's case evaporated, on discovery that the band had never trademarked the album's artwork. It was a rare instance of Bill Thompson taking his eye off the ball.

We Can Be Together - Compilations

Like most successful artists of the 1960s, Jefferson Airplane have been ill-served by the sheer weight of vinyl and CD releases purporting to represent the band's best moments. In an era in which anyone with a superfast optical burner and a decent colour printer can churn out bootleg or otherwise illegal 'greatest hits' CDs, which then find their way to market stalls and shops (be they bricks or clicks) whose main stock-in-trade is similarly pirated DVDs and skin mags, most are to be avoided. The same caveats apply as the warnings above for live albums.

Some compilations demand extra care when considered for purchase. 'There have been many complaints about hybrids,' Craig Fenton told me. 'Unauthorised recordings have existed since the arrival of CDs, particularly in the U.S.A., the U.K. and Italy. One trick to suck in unwary collectors is to edit regular Airplane tracks – chop out a few seconds, add echo to Grace's original vocal, lower the pitch of Jorma's guitar, perhaps even overlay another solo altogether, and so on.' This explains those songs on cowboy *Best Ofs* that sound distantly like Airplane but aren't. 'Don't Slip Away', '3/5 of a Mile' and 'It's No Secret' are just three to have been subject to this egregious tinkering.

Again, seasoned Airplane fans will spot the bogus stuff with relative ease, from the cheapo sleeve art to the frequently and obviously incorrect credits. But if you're new to the Airplane and you're not yet ready to take the completist's plunge and devour every last release, best stick with one or more of the following.

The Worst Of Jefferson Airplane (1970)

'It's No Secret'/'Blues From an Airplane'/'Somebody To Love'/'Today'/'White Rabbit'/'Embryonic Journey'/'Martha'/'The Ballad of You and Me and Pooneil'/'Crown of Creation'/'Chushingura'/'Lather'/'Plastic Fantastic Lover'/'Good Shepherd'/'We Can Be Together'/'Volunteers'.

A workmanlike *Best Of* culled from the first six albums, giving a good all-round overview, within the time limitations of an original vinyl L.P., of what Jefferson Airplane was about between 1966 and 1969. *The Worst of Jefferson Airplane* was taken to market late in 1970 by a record company forced to accept that no new Airplane product was arriving anytime soon, despite a gap of more than a year since *Volunteers*. R.C.A. needn't have worried; the collection hit #12 on the *Billboard* chart and would be among Airplane's biggest-selling albums. At least someone in the band had the final say in the mischievous title, although whether this was Paul Kantner, Marty Balin or Bill Thompson – all claimed honour – is unknown.

Early Flight (1974)

'High Flyin' Bird'/'Runnin' 'Round This World'/'It's Alright'/'In the Morning'/'J. P. P. Mc Step B. Blues'/'Go to Her'/'Up or Down'/'Mexico'/'Have You Seen The Saucers'.

As Thompson confirmed in his original sleeve notes, *Early Flight* provided a platform for nine tracks never before included on any Airplane album. Of most interest is 'Runnin' 'Round This World', jettisoned, on R.C.A.'s instruction, from *Jefferson Airplane Takes Off* for its alleged sex and drug references. The subsequent CD release of Airplane's remastered back catalogue, as well as 1992's three-CD box-set, *Jefferson Airplane Loves You* – all bulked out with the usual plethora of unreleased material – has rendered *Early Flight* largely inessential, although the convenience of a single CD makes it a most agreeable travelling companion on a long car journey.

2400 Fulton Street (1987)

Beginnings: 'It's No Secret'/'Come Up the Years'/'My Best Friend'/'Somebody To Love'/'Comin' Back to Me'/'Embryonic Journey'/'She Has Funny Cars'/'Let's Get Together'/'Blues From an Airplane'/'J. P. P. Mc Step B. Blues'.
Psychedelia: 'Plastic Fantastic Lover'/'Wild Tyme'/'The Ballad of You and Me and Pooneil'/'A Small Package of Value Will Come to You, Shortly'/'White Rabbit'/'Won't You Try-Saturday Afternoon'/'Lather'/'Fat Angel'/'The Last Wall of the Castle'/'Greasy Heart'.
Revolution: 'We Can Be Together'/'Crown of Creation'/'Mexico'/'Wooden Ships'/'rejoyce'/'Volunteers'/'Have You Seen the Saucers'/'Eat Starch Mom'.
Airplane Parts: 'Pretty as You Feel'/'Martha'/'Today'/'Triad'/'Third Week in the Chelsea'/'Good Shepherd'/'Eskimo Blue Day'/The Levi Commercials.

Each of *2400 Fulton Street's* original four sides of vinyl is endowed with a theme, under which the compilers list the songs they clearly believe slot into that particular pigeonhole. This attempt to collate and categorise the work of one of rock's most unclassifiable groups is as mystifying as it is inept, serving only to realise a track sequence that defies chronology, musical feel and basic logic. Who would deny the psychedelic content of 'She Has Funny Cars'? Where is the revolution in 'rejoyce'? And who dismissed at least five of the band's greatest songs as little other than spare parts?

But, as they say, it is what it is. If you can get past the chaotic programming, it's a decent enough collection, even if magical songs such as 'D.C.B.A.-25' and 'In Time' have been overlooked and all the songs are (and were, at time of L.P. release) available elsewhere. The exceptions date from spring 1967, Airplane by now accorded the status of what would today be called 'influencers', when they risked their countercultural credentials by agreeing to an advertising campaign for Levi jeans. Allowed studio carte-blanche provided the branding was clear, the group dashed off a self-consciously 'psychedelic' quartet of radio spots, pitched at a young demographic, allegedly as eager to purchase White Levi's as 'White Rabbit'. Predictably – although Airplane seemed not to see it coming – the exercise incurred the wrath of the commentariat, among them political activist Abbie Hoffman. The Yippie provocateur saw Airplane's heresy as confirmation of the doubts he and others held at the time over the real objectives of hippiedom's heads of state. Hoffman's barbs hit the mark; the Airplane never made another commercial. Included here, they're predictably awful.

Jefferson Airplane Loves You (1992)

'I Specialize in Love'/'Go to Her'/'Bringing Me Down'/'Let Me In'/'Chauffeur Blues'/'Free Advice'/'Somebody To Love'/'Today'/'Embryonic Journey'/'White Rabbit'/'Come Back Baby'/'The Other Side of This Life'/'Runnin' 'Round This World'/'She Has Funny Cars'/'High Flying Bird'/'Tobacco Road'/'Let's Get Together'/'White Rabbit'/'Comin' Back to Me'/'Won't You Try-Saturday Afternoon'/'The Ballad of You and Me and Pooneil'/'Things Are Better In The East'/'Watch Her Ride'/'Two Heads'/'Martha'/'Don't Let Me Down'/'Crown of Creation'/'Lather'/'In Time'/'House at Pooneil Corners'/'Ribump Ba Bap Dum Dum'/'Would You Like A Snack'/'3-5 of a Mile in 10 Seconds'/'It's No Secret'/'Plastic Fantastic Lover'/'Uncle Sam Blues'/'Wooden Ships'/'Volunteers'/'We Can Be Together'/'Turn My Life Down'/'Good Shepherd'/'Hey Frederick'/'Emergency'/'When The Earth Moves Again'/'Pretty as You Feel'/'Law Man'/'Feel So Good'/'Twilight Double Leader'/'Aerie (Gang of Eagles)'/'Trial by Fire'/'Dress Rap-You Wear Your Dresses Too Short'.

This is better: a three-CD collection with a sense of chronology, whose compilers knew the value of alternative studio takes and previously unreleased concert performances. For this reason, this lavish set (in an oversized box better suited to a shelf of cookery books than CDs) should be seen as a companion to a regular inventory of Airplane records rather than a pared-back digest. The package includes a booklet containing track information, Bill Thompson's introduction and an essay by Jeff Tamarkin: effectively a distillation of the same author's biography, *Got a Revolution!*. Unfortunately, the designers couldn't quell the urge to make every glossy page look as garishly 'psychedelic' as they could; the design does scant justice to Tamarkin's lengthy and excellent piece, its densely overprinted, small-font serif text about as readable as a page from Oz magazine c1968.

Though fairly comprehensive, the collection is not without its longueurs. Mainly these are the stoned sound collages left over from the *Crown of Creation* sessions, whose inclusions as extras in the BMG-Heritage remasters series render them still more redundant here. Personally, I cannot forgive the absence, once again, of 'D.C.B.A.-25'; that one of Paul Kantner's finest songs should give ground to the likes of 'Ribump Ba Bap Dum Dum' is criminal. But if there's any reason for shelling out whatever algorithm-generated price Amazon is quoting this week, it's the full nine minutes of Jorma's superb blues jam 'Feel So Good', from which the version on *Bark* was slimmed down.

The Best of Jefferson Airplane (2001)

'Embryonic Journey'/'High Flying Bird'/'It's No Secret'/'Come Up the Years'/'Somebody To Love'/'Blues From an Airplane'/'White Rabbit'/'Plastic

Fantastic Lover'/'Aerie (Gang of Eagles)'/'The Ballad of You and Me and Pooneil'/'Crown of Creation'/'Lather'/'The Last Wall of the Castle'/'Greasy Heart'/'Volunteers'/'When the Earth Moves Again'/'Triad'/'We Can Be Together'/'Wooden Ships'/'Milk Train' (Live)/'Have You Seen the Saucers' (Live).

Another remastered journeyman collection and another cockeyed chronology. Perfectly decent, even if the single CD-length again means losing some of Airplane's best tracks.

I still believe in all the music - Jefferson Airplane (1989)

Marty Balin: vocals
Grace Slick: vocals, keyboards
Paul Kantner: rhythm guitar, vocals
Jack Casady: bass
Jorma Kaukonen: vocals, guitars
Guests:
Kenny Aronoff: drums, percussion
David Paich: keyboards
Michael Landau: guitars
Nicky Hopkins: keyboards
Flo & Eddie (Mark Volman, Howard Kaylan): backing vocals
Charles Judge: keyboards
Efrain Toro: percussion
Peter Kaukonen: guitars
Mike Porcaro: bass
Steve Porcaro: keyboard programming
Produced at The Record Plant, Los Angeles, by Ron Nevison, Greg Edward and Jefferson Airplane
Released: August 1989
Highest chart place: U.S. *Billboard* 200: 85

The world wasn't exactly hankering after the reunion in 1989. Even Jack Casady was unsure. After enabling the reintegration of musicians who'd lately raised apparently insurmountable barriers between each other, the bassist likened the event to 'getting together with all of your ex-wives in one room and having to create.' As Jeff Tamarkin remarked, 'It was a major accomplishment that they were all standing in the same room without pulling out weapons.'

Truth to tell, the restructured Airplane had a target on its back. 'Few big names from the late 60s have dated worse than Jefferson Airplane,' sniffed the former *Sounds* journo Jon Savage. *Rolling Stone* was also unimpressed, the magazine voting Airplane's eponymous reunion album that year's 'most unwelcome comeback'.

It all started in March 1988, after Paul Kantner and Grace Slick guested with Hot Tuna at the reopened Fillmore Auditorium. Someone came up with the bright idea of re-forming Airplane's classic lineup – more or less, for Spencer Dryden would be sidelined. Old wounds still hurt; insisting, barely diplomatically, that the band needed a younger, stronger drummer, Paul still hadn't forgiven Spencer for siding against Bill Graham when the former manager was ousted in 1968. For the album and subsequent tour, in came the undeniably excellent sessions thumper Kenny Aronoff, recommended by new producer and stalwart 1980s hitmaker – not least with Jefferson Starship

– Ron Nevison. Although Bill Thompson was first choice for managerial duties, Airplane's veteran consigliere decided to stick with Starship. The band instead appointed Trudy Green, an L.A. power-player with an MTV-friendly C.V. from successes with Heart and Janet Jackson, who was able quickly to close a reunion album deal with Epic Records. As Grace waspishly wrote in her memoir, 'I was delighted with both [Green's] easy manner and [her] sharklike business sensitivities.'

One thing was clear from the outset: Airplane could never again be what they were. After a few decent songs during a transitionary 1970s, in which traces could still be detected of the mothership's sound, image and sybaritic character, by the mid-80s Jefferson Starship were airbrushed to artifice. Whoever was left among those questing musicians had finally located that elusive arrangement, alighting on an undemanding formula of routine but stadium-filling hard rock. Light years from Airplane's slapdash, suck-it-and-see impudence, populist hits were tailored to the Reaganite 1980s and the growing MTV market. This was shiny A.O.R. with big shoulders, bigger hair and a huge bank balance. As the last links were severed with the old band – Starship sheared off the 'Jefferson' in 1985 following legal action by Kantner – the path was cleared for the histrionics of endless megadrome shows, platinum-selling albums and massive hit singles such as 'We Built This City' (1985) and 'Nothing's Gonna Stop Us Now' (1987).

If nothing was stopping the world from taking Starship to huge success, the chattering classes were having none of it. Few among the critical cognoscenti would say anything good about a reanimated Airplane: a band whose original music was now perceived by too many as anachronistic, and who'd since generated little of interest other than toxic hostility towards one another. As the 1990s dawned, San Francisco's finest were dismissed as mere footnotes in rock history.

While industry stakeholders hoped everyone had kissed and made up, familiar animosities were soon reawakened. Jorma Kaukonen was short of money and busy fighting his heroin addiction. His and Jack's kinship had needed rebuilding after 1978, when the guitarist walked temporarily away from Hot Tuna. Grace and Paul were in and out of court, mainly over rights to the Starship name and assets accrued from their six-year romance, which ended in 1976. Between the squabbling factions it was left to Jack to mediate, assuming he could wrap diplomacy around his bouts of heavy drinking. Tentatively remade, the pals finally enticed Marty Balin, newly engaged to marry and in a better place than his old co-workers, back into the fold.

Expectations had to be managed, though. Jealousies and excess never stopped Airplane from producing their greatest work, which lyrically, musically, emotionally and spiritually was solely a product of its time. Two decades on, the antipathy would still be there by the shovelful, but not a single new song was likely to exhibit a fraction of the brilliance of 'In Time', or 'Greasy Heart', or 'Today', or 'White Rabbit'. Did it actually matter that present tensions and the passage of years militated against great music-making? Probably not, but only on the strict understanding that, despite the title and the reunion hype, this was avowedly *not* a Jefferson Airplane album. According to Craig Fenton, Marty, from the start, wanted the record to sound as if it had been fashioned in the 1960s or 70s. 'He did his own mix of the reunion sessions, hoping that it would be used for this release in his original mix, or down the line as part of a reissue or compilation programme for the benefit of older fans,' Craig told me. 'Unfortunately, the record company overruled.'

Marty's mix might have proved interesting, but for the 1989 reunion, the suits probably made the right decision. Any attempt to ape past glories could invite comparisons with the derivative 'psychedelic' pop that would typify 1990's imminent and much-publicised 'second Summer of Love'. The album could prove to be a sad falsehood, like parents awkwardly getting down with the kids at a 21st birthday party. So even if Airplane risked coming across as graduates of the Diane Warren school of adult-oriented power balladry, better that they give a relatively honest account of where their heads lay – insomuch as they were permitted to by an unashamedly hit-seeking producer – than risk sounding like their own tribute band.

This said, no-one on *Jefferson Airplane* sounds much like Jefferson Airplane. For some reason, Jorma is outranked by the producer's army of session guitarists. And Nevison effectively neuters Jack Casady; once a first among equals, the bassist is sternly reigned in, the extraordinary flights of fancy and Airplane-defining dogfights with Jorma grounded in the service of the most commercial record possible. Arrangements are all very arousal-by-numbers, too many tracks elevated equally to quasi-hymnal, even sententious importance. There's little left at the end to wave cigarette lighters to.

Yet even if a formulaic sense of safety had permeated the music and the guest list reads like a Toto album, there's oddly still much to enjoy. Indeed, the best way to appreciate *Jefferson Airplane* is to pretend it's not an Airplane set at all, but a well-produced, beautifully-played record of sometimes sugary but often highly pleasurable mainstream rock with 'M.T.V. promo videos' written all the way through. Not so far removed from a Toto album, then; Steve Porcaro and David Paich even contribute one of the songs. (Call me a conspiracy theorist, but did *Jefferson Airplane*'s critics toll its death-knell largely because of this pair's presence? Throughout the 80s and beyond, the criminally-maligned L.A. band was rarely far from the gunsights of those fashionable pundits for whom quality too often meant sterility). If nothing else, the album has the virtue of avoiding the guitar-heavy gurning of Starship at its most bombastic. Instead, this Airplane-redux concentrates on decent musicianship and arrangements and a clutch of reasonably good songs, at least two each composed respectively by Grace and Jorma. And, frankly, it's a better album than *Long John Silver.*

But anyone expecting the worst must have loved the cover, a mono photo of a slovenly posse who could be your kid brother's mates arriving late for his wedding. A JEFFERSON AIRPLANE banner of red type out of a black box sits above Jack grimacing in shades and a big quiff, Jorma apparently whispering sweet nothings in Jack's ear, a bleach-blond, gym-tuned Marty leerily embracing a nervously-smiling Grace, who'd clearly sooner be anywhere else than on a blind date with this man. On Grace's shoulder snoozes Paul, oblivious. Hired-hand Aronoff is nowhere to be seen. The hacks from *Rolling Stone* must have dined out on the schadenfreude.

Singles from *Jefferson Airplane*:
'Summer of Love'/'Panda' (7-inch '45; *Billboard* Adult Contemporary: 15)
'Planes' (1-track CD; *Billboard* Mainstream Rock: 24)
'True Love' (1-track CD; did not chart)

'Planes (Experimental Aircraft)' 4.26 (Kantner)

Paul Kantner opens his reunion account with a stirring reminder of a childhood love that informed a lifelong career. Listening to 'Planes', it's easy to imagine a 10-year-old Paul in his bedroom in 1951, dreaming of life as a folk-singer as he glues together a Revell Superfortress. Following a dramatic intro, with sonic echoes of the 'take-off' SFX that opened early Airplane shows, Paul slips into the familiar theatrical vocal style he'd carried from Airplane through the Jefferson Starship years. Gone, however, is the sense from *Long John Silver* that the musicians had given up on the search for that ever-elusive arrangement in favour of simply blowing each other out of Wally Heider's studio. On 'Planes' and on the rest of the album, a firm pair of hands is working the faders, the setting tight and confident, less scattergun than the overegged melodrama of the previous Airplane release.

'Planes' still feels jam-packed, however, if only because of the mysterious addition of so many extra-Airplane sidemen. Producer Nevison wanted a hit record, and had tactlessly opined that Airplane technically 'was never a great band'. Such a breezy, nonsensical dismissal of his current clients should have come as no surprise; Nevison was the veteran enabler to musically-proficient but bland, antiseptic acts such as Kiss, Heart and late-period Chicago. Jorma later wondered why such a 'massive melange of musical talent' was necessary to make an album, but conceded that Nevison sought 'a crew that he was comfortable with'. Indeed, Jorma's guitar is largely subsumed; at 3.48, he sounds as if he's starting a solo, but he's quickly elbowed aside by one of the hired guns, possibly his brother Peter, further up in the mix.

Lyrically, 'Planes' is naïvete itself. Paul begins the third verse as if reciting a school primer on the birds and bees:

And the little little boy is still like a little boy
And he met another little girl and they made another little boy
And the new little guy still loves planes and flying things
And both his mother and father love him and
Hold him and hug him whenever he needs it…

...and so on. But such is its charm it seems almost churlish to criticise 'Planes'. Where the later Airplane with all their bells and whistles could sometimes sound like a barroom brawl on crystal-meth, the comeback here suggests everyone knows his or her place, kettled for security by gangmaster Nevison. It's a careful start but by no means an unpleasant one.

Incidentally, the hilarious video that accompanied the 'Planes' single, complete with aircraft montages, a Howard Hughes lookalike and Jorma gliding incongruously through on his Harley, proved that M.T.V. promos never really moved on from their equivalents of 20 years' before. The special effects just got better. But only just.

'Freedom' 4.54 (Slick)

'Freedom' is a stunning piece, a gorgeous arrangement that juxtaposes Grace's love of Spanish music with the feel of jazzy, urbane late-night clubland. A minor-key electric piano intro, reminiscent of Kiki Dee's 'Amoureuse', counts in Grace's clear and expressive vocal. It's as if seventeen years have melted away. Much of Grace's music, in and out of Airplane, has featured flamenco-style guitar, and it dovetails beautifully here. In the third verse, the mood momentarily switches to a cabaret piece, due mainly to a clever change and the subtle inflections of the singer's still peerless voice, along with gloriously tinkling piano (probably Hopkins) and gentle organ colouration behind. The guitar becomes heavier and Grace's voice soars, but the dynamic and open arrangement ensures no descent into histrionics. Spain remains a flavouring that never overwhelms the whole dish; towards the end, there's even a side-order of castanets.

Lyrically Grace ruminates once more on, yes, freedom, recalling an era when the concept of 'being free' floated around the counterculture like balloons at a Be-in. Freedom was a badge of office, a complacent measure of distance from the mere mortals of Amerika. Freedom was given away with every dollar deal, every tab or wrap, every Jefferson Airplane album. 'Please someone tell me what do I do while I'm waiting to be so cool,' asks Grace, as the writer's keen intelligence, married to the hindsight of two decades, prompts her to ponder the real meaning of 'freedom', the actions and attitudes that deliver it, and whether it's even attainable in the first place. By some miles, 'Freedom' is the best track on this record.

'Solidarity' 5.08 (B Brecht, Balin, M Cummings)

The 'Solidaritätslied' ('Solidarity Song') was written as a proletarian polemic between 1929 and 1931 by the intellectual left's pin-up poet, Bertolt Brecht. Today it's hard to divorce the concept of 'solidarity' from resistance politics; famously the term was co-opted by the union movement that was busy saving Poland from the Soviets, even as Marty Balin was absorbing H. R. Hays' Brecht translation with a view to a new interpretation.

Two decades from the days when Airplane were considered San Francisco's pre-eminent politicos, Marty proves the flame of righteous communitarianism

145

still burns strong and bright. 'Solidarity' is an animating canticle featuring florid piano arpeggios from Hopkins, Aronoff's heavy, 1980s-style drum pattern and a thorough dousing of synth programming, all enveloping Marty's impassioned lead vocal like a warm bath. Critics will hear only sermonising, but 'Solidarity' still produces the tingle of the spine that only Marty and the massed Airplane chorale can inspire.

'Madeleine Street' 4.15 (Kantner, Balin)

By 1989, Paul Kantner had lowered his horizons. Dreams of provoking a mass interstellar breakout were now history as he committed himself to a more Earthbound cause: the Nicaraguan Sandanista government, which between 1981 and 1989 fought off U.S.-backed Contra rebels. Following Uncle Sam's meddling, yet again, in the affairs of someone else's country, the Sandanistas became poster-children for western rock'n'rollers as Paul, ever the early adopter, joined The Clash, U2 and other worthies waving their fists for the Junta. His contribution to the struggle was 'Nicaragua Trilogy', comprising 'Mariel', which he'd recorded with the Kantner-Balin-Casady pre-reunion band KBC, and two songs from the new album.

Superficially, 'Madeleine Street' suggests a funky jazz boulevard in the Lower 9th, Paul gleefully lobbing into the pot knowing New Orleans/Tennessee Williams references. Hopkins' trickling piano accompanies an ambient saloon hubbub, evoking a smoky bodega that's just copacetic for hatching the revolution – or simply watching it go by with a typically Latin sense of *manana*. As Craig Fenton confirmed, no 'Madeleine Street' exists in either New Orleans or Managua. 'Paul visited Nicaragua and met revolutionary leaders,' Craig told me. 'He recognised their love for art and the prominence, even under fire, of theatre, poetry, music and dancing.' For the Sandanistas, these were life-affirming joys that could ease a beleaguered society through the most violent of civil conflicts. 'He invents Madeleine Street to sidestep the Nicaraguan convention of numbered streets and prosaically identifying neighbours by location, thereby depicting a friendly, spirited community that's New Orleans-like in its vibrancy.'

To Paul's credit, he avoids the posturing to which many frequently descend when waving another's revolutionary flag. Instead, 'Madeleine Street' is political commentary that celebrates life, steers clear of proselytising and remains enjoyably bluster-free, a virtue lost on many critics of the better new Airplane songs of this reunion.

'Ice Age' 4.15 (Kaukonen)

Jorma brought 'Ice Age' to the Airplane from his 1985 acoustic solo album *Too Hot To Handle,* of which three songs were co-written by the guitarist and his by-then estranged wife. Channelling mid/late-period Dylan in vocal style if not sentiment, Jorma predicts a coming darkness:

146

This time next year I'll build my coffin
Made out of lead so X-rays cannot see.

Although his marriage breakdown is surely on his mind, more broadly, the singer is scornful of complacent politicians who know their time is up, the eternal iciness they're about to visit upon their grandchildren no longer an issue. Unconcerned for what will really happen in the future, they're selective about the past, ensuring a bogus but palatable legacy by papering over wherever it is they went wrong.

A gloomy meditation on the cynicism of an older generation, 'Ice Age' had been a regular on Hot Tuna's setlist. Usually lengthier onstage, its brooding flavour of resignation and the inevitability of the end doesn't quite catch fire on the album, Jorma's starkly personal reflections enveloped, like most tracks, in the glossy 1980s production. At least he gets to play a solo on his own song, but it would have been impolite indeed if one of the journeymen had received the call.

'Summer of Love' 4.16 (Balin)

Only the King of Yearn could hanker after Jefferson Airplane's salad days with an arrangement Jorma and Jack would once have chased out of the studio with an M16. Washed in electric piano and C.M.I. programming and a very far cry from anything else in Airplane's playbook, 'Summer of Love' is possibly the most unabashedly sentimental song the band's founder ever wrote, its very un-Airplane-ness a massive exercise in paradox.

As with Grace Slick's contributions to *Jefferson Airplane,* this sounds like a solo effort; the song would have comfortably sat with Marty's 1981 A.O.R. hit 'Hearts'. Through dewey eyes, the singer gazes winsomely back: Marty concentrates on the mindset which, ironically, prevailed around eighteen months earlier than what was actually sold to the world as the eponymous summer. For anyone who partook of the sunny optimism of San Francisco in 1965-66 before the DayGlo turned grey, it must be hard to hear this and not join Marty, the psychedelic Johnny Ray, in shedding copious tears.

'The Wheel (For Nora and Nicaragua)' 6.08 (Kantner, transl Margaret Randall)

In his second of the album's brace of tributes to Nicaragua, Paul salutes Nora Astorga, who before her death in 1988 was the Sandanistas' ambassador to the United Nations, having already been refused White House credentials as her country's Woman in Washington. Paul celebrates Nora and the Junta with a suitably rousing and hugely optimistic rallying cry that stops just short of preaching. It's as amiably righteous as anything he created for late-period Airplane and beyond, essaying the standard hippie call for a better world without even the tiniest hint of how that might be achieved. That 'The Wheel' is entirely naïve is beyond question, but once again, there's no doubting Paul's motives or sincerity. And although the song falls into the album-wide trap of anthemising, it's stirring enough to get the juices flowing without having to think too much.

'Common Market Madrigal' 2.46 (Slick)

Years after its massive success, Grace Slick was belatedly critical of 'We Built This City' and its post-Airplane hitmakers: 'Starship I hated,' she assured *Vanity Fair.* 'Our big hit single was awful.'

Perhaps hindsight will one day permit her a similar evaluation here, as Grace continues the positive mood of the two previous tracks with a love song wrapped in another anthemic plea for universal togetherness. It's all very rousing; such are the writer's good intentions that to criticise 'Common Market Madrigal' feels like breaking wind in church. But, frankly, Grace's vocal, the words she sings and the arrangement in which everything is embalmed are cornily overwrought. In one verse, a short, annotated trumpet fanfare and a briefly trilled keyboard arpeggio embellish sentiments so purple they're desperate for a cold compress:

> Wooden shoes and tulips in Holland
> English guards with medieval swords
> Conquistadors and Spanish galleons
> Vikings sailing the mountain fjords.

...which must win the Roger Miller Bobbies-on-Bicycles Award for clichéd international racial profiling. With the overall sensation one of having a box of excessively gooey chocolates stuffed in your ear, it's hard to imagine the Grace Slick of 1968 tolerating this mush, let alone writing it.

'True Love' 3.43 (S Porcaro, D Paich)

You can almost hear Bobby Kimball singing, such is the resemblance of 'True Love' to the work of its writers' band, Toto. It's a perfectly decent helping of glossy, mainstream power-pop, its arrangement and musicianship unimpeachable, its lyrics all about nothing at all.

Most noteworthy, for all the wrong reasons, is the accompanying promo video, which is even more enjoyably trashy than 'Planes'. A sound-stage, garishly reminiscent of a confetti-strewn, late-1980s *Top of the Pops* set, is a circus bedlam, in the midst of which Airplane and hired dwarves, clowns, jugglers and trapeze-artists all seem to bumble around inconsequentially, as if playing blindman's buff without the blindfolds. Top-hatted M.C. Marty mimes a powerful lead vocal while Jorma, a wasted biker lost in a Studio 54 campfest, play-acts a solo on his Telecaster that sounds nothing like him; perhaps it's either his brother Peter or Michael Landau on the actual recording. Keys are taken by Tim Gorman, while Aronoff, all mullet and tough-guy white vest, makes a convincing charade of knocking lumps out of his drumkit. Wearing a wig like a tinsel mop an especially porcine clown, who may or may not be the sylphlike Mark Volman, looks as if he's flashing at Grace Slick. Another plays Paul's guitar with his teeth. Dressed – again – as the world's sexiest nun, Grace's expression near the beginning of the video says it all.

'Upfront Blues' 2.02 (Kaukonen)

An almost throwaway instrumental jam by Kaukonen, Casady and Aronoff – although Kantner might also be lurking in the mix – 'Upfront Blues' is the kind of thing the guitarist can pick in his sleep; a reminder of where the guitarist came from and to where he'll return. Over the relaxed shuffle beat at the end, Jorma's steel guitar almost sounds like someone whistling, adding to the casual flavour. It's as if Nevison had fallen asleep and left the homies to knock out an easygoing antidote to what Jorma subsequently derided as 'the modular, sequenced L.A. way of recording… well done but not very passionate'. The feeling is one of carefree fun while the grown-ups get on with the more grandiose fare of the rest of the album.

'Now Is the Time' 4.53 (Slick)

A cynic might say 'Now Is the Time' merely inflates further the already tumescent 'Common Market Madrigal' following the two relatively self-effacing tracks that separate them. But if anything, this is even more pompous than its cousin. The words of the earlier song, often cheesy, at least had the virtue of serious intent behind the loquacity; that if Grace was going to write a torch song, she was going to put her heart and soul into it, and hang the expense. In 'Now Is the Time', such lyrical commitment is absent. Instead, she and Marty stridently declaim glutinous high-school doggerel which the writer of 'rejoyce' and 'Greasy Heart' could have transcribed on autopilot after a couple of bottles of Bailey's – if she was going to bother at all. Whether sung or read from the page, the lyrics have little resonance beyond investing the simple desire of two people to get it on with slightly comical mawkishness. And because the song essentially means nothing – remembering that, unlike the band's earnest remit of 1989, the occasional pointlessness of Airplane product c1968 was often its own virtue – the vocal attack and bloated arrangement just sound like ersatz over-emoting, a lot of sound and fury to no real end.

'Too Many Years' 4.10 (Kaukonen)

'Too Many Years' has similar changes to P. F. Sloan's 'Eve of Destruction' (which Hot Tuna would cover on their 1990 comeback record *Pair a Dice Found)*. But here, the resemblance ends. This is a lovely, typically self-effacing ballad about Jorma Kaukonen's difficult first marriage. By his own candid admission, Jorma's relationship with Margareta filtered through to many of his songs, but there's something valedictory about 'Too Many Years' that's far more than the griping of a wronged rock-star husband. Accepting the marriage cannot be salvaged – it's likely he wrote the song prior to the 1983 breakup – Jorma pleas with his wife for dialogue, rather than sudden termination. While many accounts of the Kaukonens' marriage imply that it foundered on Margareta's perceived weaknesses, it's to Jorma's endless credit that his songcraft continually sidesteps the judgemental carping of the partner scorned. Indeed, he's almost painfully even-handed, his humility tipping over into savage self-analysis:

In an unwritten time I thought that life was for sharing;
And living together was simply a matter of caring;
But things did not work out like I planned;
And alienation has left me here damned.

Another song originally from *Too Hot To Handle,* 'Too Many Years' outlived Jefferson Airplane's reunion, lending its title to another solo album in 1998 and, like 'Ice Age', becoming a regular feature of the guitarist's live sets. Featuring Jorma's echoey 12-string with a rhythm guitar, bass, drums and organ, it's another gentle corrective to *Jefferson Airplane's* electronic blanket of synths and systems. This said, 'Too Many Years' is best heard in its live solo form: a stunning example of one man and an acoustic guitar making intimate, contemplative music of a rare warmth and beauty.

'Panda' 3.37 (Slick)
Years after watching TV footage of a frightened baby panda in a Japanese zoo surrounded by a baying media crowd, Grace Slick wrote in her autobiography: 'I hadn't cared one way or the other about animals before. I'd always thought they were just part of the scenery.' It's possible that Grace was once again being disingenuous for effect, the *faux-naïf* shrouding her fierce intelligence lest it be mistaken for pomposity. For it's unlikely the writer of such epics of ecological awareness as 'Eskimo Blue Day', 'Aerie' and even – should you interpret its words thus – 'Bear Melt', would really be so indifferent.

Whatever she was thinking about before, by 1989, there could be no mistaking the honesty of 'Panda'. Happily, Grace puts behind her the overkill of her two mid-album songs, with a plea so heart-rending that, by the end, you're needing not so much Kleenex as defibrillator paddles. With motivating, piano-led music and words that stay just on the right side of syrupy, the singer excoriates those who profit from poaching and the destruction of natural habitats:

He can feel the night, the last sunset is in his eyes
They will carry him away, take his beauty for their prize
Ah, but hunger would have come when the bamboo forest died
Oh Panda Bear, you can't seem to win
No matter how hard you try
Oh Panda Bear, my gentle friend
I don't want to say goodbye.

By the end, we're in no doubt of Grace's sincerity and affection. After 1989 she would frequently convert her convictions into positive action on behalf of animal rights. While 'Panda' conforms to *Jefferson Airplane's* habit of turning every other song into its own scarf-waving finale, at least this time it's the album itself that's closed off. And right at the end, Grace does this in the most touching way imaginable, dangling the song's single-word title with an ambiguous inflection that could convey optimism, or hope, or despair: *Panda.*

Final Concerts

While most of the world dozed over *Jefferson Airplane,* the accompanying live gigs, including a set by Hot Tuna, were generally well-received. This was due mainly to the liberal salting of classic Airplane tunes; it was always obvious that songs like 'She Has Funny Cars', 'Today', 'Lather', 'Somebody To Love' and 'White Rabbit' would lay bare the relative shortcomings of the reunion material. With Aronoff in the drum stool alongside other hired help, Tim Gorman (keys, formerly with KBC), Randy Jackson (guitar, keys and vocals) and Peter Kaukonen (guitar), the 24-show U.S.-only tour – a subsequent Japanese trip was cancelled – began in Wisconsin on 18 August 1989 and officially finished in Golden Gate Park on 30 September.

One week later, Jefferson Airplane appeared at the March for the Homeless in Washington D.C. They were introduced by Bill Graham. They played five songs. None was from the reunion album.

And that was that.

Postscript: What Came Next

Marty Balin (b. Martyn Jerel Buchwald, Cincinnati, Ohio, 30 January 1942) toggled Jefferson Starship with other bands and a solo career. To mark Airplane's 50th anniversary in 2015, Marty re-recorded a tranche of Airplane and Jefferson Starship songs for a double CD, *Good Memories*. Following open-heart surgery in 2016, Marty died on 27 September 2018.

Grace Slick (b. Grace Barnett Wing, Highland Park, Chicago, Illinois, 30 October 1939) made four solo albums and worked with Jefferson Starship and Starship. An accomplished fine artist, Grace lives in Malibu, California. She still occasionally contributes to radio and TV chat shows and professes boredom with the 1960s.

Paul Kantner (b. Paul Lorin Kantner, San Francisco, 17 March 1941) gamely continued as the single constant with Jefferson Starship. Seizing legal control over 'Jefferson' as intellectual property, Paul reconvened Jefferson Starship: The Next Generation. Returning to his folk/protest roots, he worked with a number of other post-Airplane groups and on several albums. To the end a flagbearer for the ideals of the Summer of Love, Paul died from multiple organ failure following a second heart attack on 28 January 2016. His passing coincided, to the day, with that of Signe Anderson.

Jorma Kaukonen (b Jorma Ludwik Kaukonen, Washington D.C., 23 December 1940) focused his post-Airplane energies on Hot Tuna. After hiatus in 1978, Jorma led several post-punk outfits before returning as a solo. Today he lives at and runs a guitarists' retreat, the Fur Peace Ranch, in the Ohio Appalachians. Jorma continues to tour with Jack Casady and other friends as Hot Tuna.

Jack Casady (b. John William Casady, Washington D.C., 13 April 1944) worked with Hot Tuna until the 1978 furlough, then with SVT, KBC and with Paul in a remodelled Jefferson Starship. In 2003 he produced his first solo album, *Dream Factor*. As well as gigging with Hot Tuna, today Jack hosts regular bass workshops at Jorma's Fur Peace Ranch. He lives in Jersey and Los Angeles.

Spencer Dryden (b. Spencer Charles Dryden, New York City, 7 April 1938) joined Grateful Dead offshoots The New Riders of the Purple Sage, becoming the group's manager in 1977. In 1982, alongside other 1960s San Francisco luminaries, Spencer joined The Dinosaurs. In 2004 he played in public for the last time, with Airplane bandmates, at a launch party for the *Fly Jefferson Airplane* DVD. Spencer died from metastasised colon cancer on 11 January 2005.

In 1996, The Grateful Dead's Phil Lesh and Mickey Hart inducted Jefferson Airplane's classic 1966-70 sextet into the Rock and Roll Hall of Fame. Marty, Paul, Jorma, Jack and Spencer all attended, but not Grace, who sent her apologies, citing medical reasons. The band performed 'Volunteers' and 'Crown of Creation', and Jorma played his solo 'Embryonic Journey'.

In 2016, Marty accepted the Grammy Honorable Lifetime Achievement

Award in absentia on behalf of Jefferson Airplane. And in 2020, perhaps the ultimate accolade for a group of musicians too smart, sexy, intemperate, unpredictable and downright stubborn to be classified as anything at all, the hippies' ultimate house band were awarded their very own Star on the Hollywood Walk of Fame.

Joni Mitchell - *on track*
every album, every song

Peter Kearns
Paperback
160 pages
35 colour photographs
978-178-952-081-1
£14.99
USD 21.95

**Every track recorded
by this Canadian
singer-songwriting
legend.**

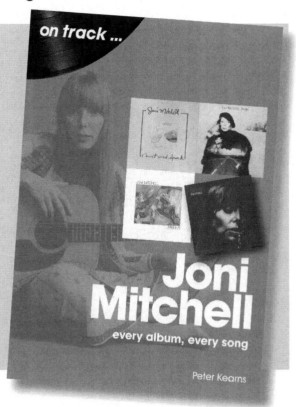

on track ...

**Joni
Mitchell**

every album, every song

Peter Kearns

In her long career, Canadian songstress Joni Mitchell has been hailed as everything from a 1960s folk icon to 20th-century cultural figure, artistic iconoclast to musical heroine, extreme romantic confessor to both outspoken commentator and lyrical painter. Eschewing commercial considerations, she simply viewed her trajectory as that of any artist serious about the integrity of their work. But whatever musical position she took, she was always one step ahead of the game, making eclectic and innovative music. Albums like *The Ladies Of The Canyon*, *Blue*, *Hejira* and *Mingus* helped define each era of the 1970s,

as she moved from exquisitely pitched singer-songwriter material towards jazz. By the 1980s, her influence was really beginning to show via a host of imitators, many of them big names in their own right. Her profound influence continues in popular music to this day.

This book revisits her studio albums in detail from 1968's *Song to a Seagull* to 2007's *Shine*, providing anecdote and insight into the recording sessions. It also includes an in-depth analysis both of her lyrics and the way her music developed stylistically over such a lengthy career, making this the most comprehensive book on this remarkable artist yet written.

Iggy & The Stooges
On Stage 1967-1974

Per Nilsen
Paperback
160 pages
44 colour photographs
978-178-952-101-6
£16.99
USD 24.95

**An in depth
exploration of every
live concert played by
this iconic rock band.**

The Stooges were formed in 1967 in Ann Arbor, outside Detroit. They created three classic albums between 1969 and 1973, *The Stooges*, *Fun House* and *Raw Power*. Despite a lack of commercial success, the band attracted a small, devoted following and laid a musical foundation that would influence generations of artists. The Stooges' music was raw, primal, exciting, and the unique and compelling stage presence of the band's singer, Iggy, made them legendary. The Stooges' performances were unpredictable, with Iggy inciting audiences to react and making it impossible for them to remain complacent. Iggy was passionate, fearless and, at times, expressed himself in genuinely frightening ways, performing self-mutilation, stage dives, crowd surfing and rushing into crowds to confront hecklers or spontaneously interacting with audience members who struck his fancy. Iggy tore down the barriers that traditionally existed between audience and performer, forcing the audience to become part of the overall performance. By 1974, Iggy was locked into an orbit of self-annihilation and drug abuse that ultimately led to the demise of the band in February 1974. This book explores in depth all the concerts the Stooges played from 1967 to 1974, bringing the live experience to life through eyewitness accounts, press reports and other source materials to present an unprecedented account of the Stooges' performances during this period.

On Track series

Tori Amos – Lisa Torem 978-1-78952-142-9
Asia – Peter Braidis 978-1-78952-099-6
Barclay James Harvest – Keith and Monica Domone 978-1-78952-067-5
The Beatles – Andrew Wild 978-1-78952-009-5
The Beatles Solo 1969-1980 – Andrew Wild 978-1-78952-030-9
Blue Oyster Cult – Jacob Holm-Lupo 978-1-78952-007-1
Marc Bolan and T.Rex – Peter Gallagher 978-1-78952-124-5
Kate Bush – Bill Thomas 978-1-78952-097-2
Camel – Hamish Kuzminski 978-1-78952-040-8
Caravan – Andy Boot 978-1-78952-127-6
Eric Clapton Solo – Andrew Wild 978-1-78952-141-2
The Clash – Nick Assirati 978-1-78952-077-4
Crosby, Stills and Nash – Andrew Wild 978-1-78952-039-2
The Damned – Morgan Brown 978-1-78952-136-8
Deep Purple and Rainbow 1968-79 – Steve Pilkington 978-1-78952-002-6
Dire Straits – Andrew Wild 978-1-78952-044-6
The Doors – Tony Thompson 978-1-78952-137-5
Dream Theater – Jordan Blum 978-1-78952-050-7
Elvis Costello and The Attractions – Georg Purvis 978-1-78952-129-0
Emerson Lake and Palmer – Mike Goode 978-1-78952-000-2
Fairport Convention – Kevan Furbank 978-1-78952-051-4
Peter Gabriel – Graeme Scarfe 978-1-78952-138-2
Genesis – Stuart MacFarlane 978-1-78952-005-7
Gentle Giant – Gary Steel 978-1-78952-058-3
Gong – Kevan Furbank 978-1-78952-082-8
Hawkwind – Duncan Harris 978-1-78952-052-1
Roy Harper – Opher Goodwin 978-1-78952-130-6
Iron Maiden – Steve Pilkington 978-1-78952-061-3
Jethro Tull – Jordan Blum 978-1-78952-016-3
Elton John in the 1970s – Peter Kearns 978-1-78952-034-7
Gong – Kevan Furbank 978-1-78952-082-8
The Incredible String Band – Tim Moon 978-1-78952-107-8
Iron Maiden – Steve Pilkington 978-1-78952-061-3
Judas Priest – John Tucker 978-1-78952-018-7
Kansas – Kevin Cummings 978-1-78952-057-6
Level 42 – Matt Philips 978-1-78952-102-3
Aimee Mann – Jez Rowden 978-1-78952-036-1
Joni Mitchell – Peter Kearns 978-1-78952-081-1
The Moody Blues – Geoffrey Feakes 978-1-78952-042-2
Mike Oldfield – Ryan Yard 978-1-78952-060-6
Tom Petty – Richard James 978-1-78952-128-3
Queen – Andrew Wild 978-1-78952-003-3
Renaissance – David Detmer 978-1-78952-062-0
The Rolling Stones 1963-80 – Steve Pilkington 978-1-78952-017-0
Steely Dan – Jez Rowden 978-1-78952-043-9
Steve Hackett – Geoffrey Feakes 978-1-78952-098-9
Thin Lizzy – Graeme Stroud 978-1-78952-064-4
Toto – Jacob Holm-Lupo 978-1-78952-019-4

U2 – Eoghan Lyng 978-1-78952-078-1
UFO – Richard James 978-1-78952-073-6
The Who – Geoffrey Feakes 978-1-78952-076-7
Roy Wood and the Move – James R Turner 978-1-78952-008-8
Van Der Graaf Generator – Dan Coffey 978-1-78952-031-6
Yes – Stephen Lambe 978-1-78952-001-9
Frank Zappa 1966 to 1979 – Eric Benac 978-1-78952-033-0
10CC – Peter Kearns 978-1-78952-054-5

Decades Series
Alice Cooper in the 1970s – Chris Sutton 978-1-78952-104-7
Curved Air in the 1970s – Laura Shenton 978-1-78952-069-9
Fleetwood Mac in the 1970s – Andrew Wild 978-1-78952-105-4
Focus in the 1970s – Stephen Lambe 978-1-78952-079-8
Marillion in the 1980s – Nathaniel Webb 978-1-78952-065-1
Pink Floyd In The 1970s – Georg Purvis 978-1-78952-072-9
The Sweet in the 1970s – Darren Johnson 978-1-78952-139-9
Uriah Heep in the 1970s – Steve Pilkington 978-1-78952-103-0

On Screen series
Carry On… – Stephen Lambe 978-1-78952-004-0
David Cronenberg – Patrick Chapman 978-1-78952-071-2
Doctor Who: The David Tennant Years – Jamie Hailstone 978-1-78952-066-8
Monty Python – Steve Pilkington 978-1-78952-047-7
Seinfeld Seasons 1 to 5 – Stephen Lambe 978-1-78952-012-5

Other Books
Babysitting A Band On The Rocks – G.D. Praetorius 978-1-78952-106-1
Derek Taylor: For Your Radioactive Children – Andrew Darlington 978-1-78952-038-5
Iggy and The Stooges On Stage 1967-1974 – Per Nilsen 978-1-78952-101-6
Jon Anderson and the Warriors – the road to Yes – David Watkinson 978-1-78952-059-0
Nu Metal: A Definitive Guide – Matt Karpe 978-1-78952-063-7
Tommy Bolin: In and Out of Deep Purple – Laura Shenton 978-1-78952-070-5
Maximum Darkness – Deke Leonard 978-1-78952-048-4
Maybe I Should've Stayed In Bed – Deke Leonard 978-1-78952-053-8
The Twang Dynasty – Deke Leonard 978-1-78952-049-1

and many more to come!

Would you like to write for Sonicbond Publishing?

We are mainly a music publisher, but we also occasionally publish in other genres including film and television. At Sonicbond Publishing we are always on the look-out for authors, particularly for our two main series, On Track and Decades.

Mixing fact with in depth analysis, the On Track series examines the entire recorded work of a particular musical artist or group. All genres are considered from easy listening and jazz to 60s soul to 90s pop, via rock and metal.

The Decades series singles out a particular decade in an artist or group's history and focuses on that decade in more detail than may be allowed in the On Track series.

While professional writing experience would, of course, be an advantage, the most important qualification is to have real enthusiasm and knowledge of your subject. First-time authors are welcomed, but the ability to write well in English is essential.

Sonicbond Publishing has distribution throughout Europe and North America, and all our books are also published in E-book form. Authors will be paid a royalty based on sales of their book. Further details about our books are available from www.sonicbondpublishing.com. To contact us, complete the contact form there or email info@sonicbondpublishing.co.uk